DIDEROT AND THE BODY

THE EUROPEAN HUMANITIES RESEARCH CENTRE

UNIVERSITY OF OXFORD

The European Humanities Research Centre of the University of Oxford organizes a range of academic activities, including conferences and workshops, and publishes scholarly works under its own imprint, LEGENDA. Within Oxford, the EHRC bridges, at the research level, the main humanities faculties: Modern Languages, English, Modern History, Literae Humaniores, Music and Theology. The Centre stimulates interdisciplinary research collaboration throughout these subject areas and provides an Oxford base for advanced researchers in the humanities.

The Centre's publications programme focuses on making available the results of advanced research in medieval and modern languages and related interdisciplinary areas. An Editorial Board, whose members are drawn from across the British university system, covers the principal European languages. Titles include works on French, German, Italian, Portuguese, Russian and Spanish literature. In addition, the EHRC co-publishes with the Society for French Studies, the British Comparative Literature Association and the Modern Humanities Research Association. The Centre also publishes *Oxford German Studies* and *Film Studies*, and has launched a Special Lecture Series under the LEGENDA imprint.

Enquiries about the Centre's publishing activities should be addressed to:
Professor Malcolm Bowie, Director

Further information:
Kareni Bannister, Senior Publications Officer
European Humanities Research Centre
University of Oxford
47 Wellington Square, Oxford OX1 2JF
enquiries@ehrc.ox.ac.uk
www.ehrc.ox.ac.uk

LEGENDA

European Humanities Research Centre

University of Oxford

Diderot and the Body

ANGELICA GOODDEN

LEGENDA

European Humanities Research Centre
University of Oxford
2001

Published by the
European Humanities Research Centre
of the University of Oxford
47 Wellington Square
Oxford OX1 2JF

LEGENDA is the publications imprint of the
European Humanities Research Centre

ISBN 1 900755 56 4

First published 2001

British Library Cataloguing in Publication Data
A CIP catalogue record for this book is available from the British Library

LEGENDA series designed by Cox Design Partnership, Witney, Oxon
Printed in Great Britain by
Information Press
Eynsham
Oxford OX8 1JJ

Chief Copy-Editor: Genevieve Hawkins

CONTENTS

Acknowledgements		ix
Abbreviations		x
Introduction		1
1	Bodies versus Minds	15
2	Making Up (and Dismantling) the Body	39
3	Propriety and Impropriety	65
4	Eloquent Bodies	89
5	Fleshly Indulgence, Bodily Torment	114
6	Sexing and Gendering	147
	Conclusion	177
	Select Bibliography	187
	Index	199

ACKNOWLEDGEMENTS

I am most grateful to St Hilda's College for granting me the term of sabbatical leave that enabled me to set about writing this book, and to the Faculty of Medieval and Modern Languages at the University of Oxford for generous help in funding my research.

ABBREVIATIONS

Corr. Correspondance de Diderot, ed. Georges Roth and Jean Varloot, 16 vols. (Paris: Minuit, 1955–70)

Corr. litt. Friedrich Melchior Grimm, Guillaume-Thomas-François Raynal, Jakob Heinrich Meister *et al.*, *Correspondance littéraire, philosophique et critique*, ed. Maurice Tourneux, 16 vols. (Paris: Garnier, 1877–82)

O.C. Œuvres complètes de Diderot, ed. Herbert Dieckmann *et al.*, 25 vols. (Paris: Herrmann, 1975–86)

O.Esth. Œuvres esthétiques de Diderot, ed. Paul Vernière (Paris: Garnier, 1968)

O.Phil. Œuvres philosophiques de Diderot, ed. Paul Vernière (Paris: Garnier, 1964)

O.Rom. Œuvres romanesques de Diderot, ed. Henri Bénac (Paris: Garnier, 1962)

INTRODUCTION

Diderot wrote constantly about the body, and its image permeates every literary genre he practised. His art criticism intently discusses the shape and structure of bodies even when it questions the academic hierarchy that gave the human form prime importance in painting; his philosophical works debate the mind–body problem with all the vigour of their post-Cartesian empiricist times, without conclusively settling the question of matter's predominance over spirit; his novels describe human relationships and actions in terms of physical make-up as well as mental properties; his dramatic theory stresses the importance of body-language as against verbal discourse in theatrical performance; and his correspondence dwells recurrently on medical matters and the hygienic treatment of the human 'machine'. If at times he writes about the body abstractly, at others he does so with a material emphasis that gives his work great immediacy and vividness.

Diderot saw the body as central to the science of man, announcing in the *Eléments de physiologie* that 'Je défie qu'on explique rien sans le corps'.[1] Here his remark is deliberately polemical, because he is discussing a range of human dispositions and indispositions and refusing to account for them in metaphysical terms. He thinks, in other words, that the concept of an immaterial animating soul is nonsensical, however firmly rooted in philosophical tradition it may be. The *Eléments* therefore attack Marat, the doctor and future Revolutionary, for asserting in his treatise *De l'homme* that man's spiritual self is distinct from his physical one as well as superior to it:

C'est sottise à ceux qui descendent de l'ame au corps. Il ne se fait rien ainsi dans l'homme. Marat ne sait ce qu'il dit, quand il parle de l'action de l'ame sur le corps, s'il y avoit regardé de plus près, il auroit vu que l'action de l'ame sur le corps est l'action d'une portion du corps sur l'autre. (p. 59)

In saying that the Cartesian *res extensa* and *res cogitans* cannot be dissociated from one other, Diderot is claiming that the philosophy of dualism is misguided. This may have become a common enough view

among eighteenth-century materialist philosophers, but he takes it
further than most; for he argues both that nothing can be explained
without the body *and* that the body explains almost everything about
man.

The *Eléments de physiologie* (begun in the 1760s and worked on for
the rest of Diderot's life) and the philosophical dialogue *Le Rêve de
d'Alembert* (1769) are the works of a 'hard' physicalist who will not
countenance 'soft', and possibly metaphysical, theories. Yet their
materialist interpretations of the organism are qualified elsewhere.
The *Réfutation d'Helvétius* (1773–4), for instance, wonders whether an
intangible life-force does inhabit the body, and suggests that
movement may actually be conferred on matter by some external
power. This is precisely the opposite of what *Le Rêve de d'Alembert*
argues when it allows 'Diderot' to remark: 'Otez l'obstacle qui
s'oppose au transport local du corps immobile et il sera transféré'[2]
(since all matter possesses a form of potential energy). Diderot was
able to entertain conflicting ideas, or ideas that were incompatible
with one another, because he mistrusted unwavering beliefs and rigid
philosophical systems. For all his flexibility, however, he was consistent
in wanting to demolish the type of ignorance that set supernatural
explanations above rational ones, seeing this as a particularly urgent
matter when the ignorance was manifested by educated people. For
superstitious country folk the case was altogether different. 'Le Païsan
qui voit une montre se mouvoir, et qui n'en pouvant connoitre le
mecanisme, place dans l'aiguille un esprit, n'est ni plus, ni moins sot
que nos spiritualistes' (*Eléments*, p. 60).

Yet Diderot's uncompromising statement about the need to invoke the
body in order to explain anything has more than a polemical and
materialist significance. If he was a confirmed epistemologist, he also
had more down-to-earth interests. His interest in sexual response and
gendered assumptions about 'proper' human behaviour, his keen
study of human biology and medicine and his alertness to physical
beauty and ways of depicting the human form in art are everywhere
in evidence. His focus on the body was sometimes a means of
silencing metaphysical debate, but it also allowed him to highlight
other issues that seemed crucially important. Discussing the body was
a prelude to considering the nature of pleasure, denouncing the
pointless mortification of the flesh (particularly by Christian ascetics),
recommending the practical and hygienic treatment of the human

machine, pinpointing the similarities and contrasts between male and female organisms, and so on.

As an imaginative writer Diderot naturally attended to the way bodies convey thoughts and feelings as well as the capacity for action. This is an abiding theme of his novels, short stories and dramas as well as of his art criticism and philosophical dialogues. Admittedly, the modern reader may find the way in which it expresses itself—in over-emphatic externalization—artistically regrettable: this is particularly true of *La Religieuse*, with its complaisant scenes of bodily torment, and some of the passages in the art criticism that deal with sentimental or melodramatic painting. Yet such overtness matched the mood of Diderot's 'sensible' times. He can appear histrionic, but his genuine dramatic gifts are more evident in his dialogues and prose fiction than in the overstated plays he expressly wrote for theatrical performance. These strengths are especially apparent in a dialogue such as *Le Neveu de Rameau* (1761), where his interest in facial expression, gesture and movement is constantly on display. But they are also clear in the *Entretiens sur 'Le Fils naturel'*, a theoretical work on acting that accompanied his drama *Le Fils naturel* of 1757.

Diderot's enthusiasm for the body is reflected in his fascination with medicine, and the number of medical collaborators he assembled for the *Encyclopédie* confirms it. He was a notably keen amateur pathologist who liked investigating the effects of disease and mechanical upset on body and mind, an obvious theme in *La Religieuse* (1760), *Le Neveu de Rameau* and short stories such as *Ceci n'est pas un conte* and *Mme de La Carlière*. Diderot's doctor acquaintances encouraged him, directly or indirectly, to examine the human organism with an empiricist's attentiveness and a psychologist's alertness to the meaning of pathogenic states. This is not to say that he was simply concerned with disease. Good health and the difficulty of maintaining it exercised him as much, both for personal reasons and because he worried acutely about the wellbeing of family and friends. Indeed, his correspondence reveals a preoccupation with bodily equilibrium that might seem obsessional were it not in tune with his enlightened times: the eighteenth century, which saw the birth of modern medicine, regarded medical issues as central to the science of man.

So it is unsurprising that Diderot should be engaged by such issues even in his art criticism, whether he is commenting on Greuze's depiction of a paralytic old man[3] or warning a character in a picture against consorting with diseased-looking prostitutes (*Salons*, ii. 12).

The end of *Le Rêve de d'Alembert* contains a rather flippant aside on venereal disease (p. 97), a subject also occasionally alluded to in Diderot's correspondence. Sometimes it is linked with cautions against masturbation, the seemingly harmless alternative to penetrative sex which the eighteenth century did not actually regard as safe (even if Diderot rarely describes the practice in the horrified tones of its greatest medical exponent, the contemporary physician Samuel Tissot).[4] Nor does he allow himself to speculate whether self-administered sexual release of this kind might persuade the little boy savage of *Le Neveu de Rameau* not to sleep with his mother, which is the 'natural' course of events imagined in the course of the dialoguists' conversation about educating the young.[5] The topic of incest, conversely, is equally discussed in the primitivist dialogue of 1772, the *Supplément au Voyage de Bougainville*.[6]

It hardly needs to be said that Diderot's referential boldness requires the fearless use of body language, in the sense of language about the body (as distinct from body-language, or the language *of* the body). Like many thinkers of his time he regretted the fact that French had lost its old expressiveness, but he was often hesitant about embracing a new, open form of corporeal discourse—a free discourse that contrasted with the restraint of seventeenth-century writers. Not that other authors of the period were necessarily any freer. Before 1750 the body's operations had been conventionally veiled in the coded language of worldly novelists like Crébillon *fils*, if they were not ignored altogether in *précieux* psychological musings *à la* Marivaux. The end of the century, where one might have expected greater verbal relaxation, would offer discretion mingled with indiscretion—discretion of word and indiscretion of deed. Laclos's *Les Liaisons dangereuses*, for example, symbolizes intercourse with the description of a lock being oiled to receive a key, and leaves unwritten the words of the 'catechism of debauchery' which the *roué* Valmont teaches the *ingénue* Cécile Volanges. Sade, on the other hand, is endlessly explicit.

In *Jacques le fataliste*, it is true, Diderot does convey an unabashed delight in corporeality, sounding like a disciple of Montaigne: 'Et que vous a fait l'action génitale, si naturelle, si nécessaire et si juste, pour en exclure le signe de vos entretiens, et pour imaginer que votre bouche, vos yeux et vos oreilles en seraient souillés?'[7] His article 'Jouissance' in the *Encyclopédie* is equally forthright: 'Pourquoi rougistu d'entendre prononcer le nom d'une volupté, dont tu ne rougis pas d'éprouver l'attrait dans l'ombre de la nuit? [...] Songe que c'est le plaisir qui t'a tiré du néant.' But not even *Jacques le fataliste* stands up for the referential principles it invokes. When it describes lovemaking, it does so by implication rather than direct statement: 'et tout alla fort bien—Et puis très bien encore.—Et puis encore très bien' (pp. 696–7). Suspension points regularly do duty for what cannot be decently expressed: 'je rêve... je rêve... je rêve...', Dame Marguerite exclaims as she reaches a climax (p. 706), her inarticulacy matching that of the peasant's wife who murmurs 'l'o...reil...le': 'Et à la suite de cette o...reil...le, je ne sais quoi, qui, joint au silence qui succéda, me fit imaginer que son mal d'oreille s'était apaisé d'une ou d'une autre façon; il n'importe: cela me fit plaisir' (p. 512). Indeed, the symptomology of orgasm is far more determinedly eluded here than in *La Religieuse*, where the heroine's word-shame indicates her half-willed naivety, a semi-conscious desire to preserve sexual ignorance in the face of the lesbian Superior's arousal. But where a character in an intendedly naturalistic drama displays the same kind of verbal embarrassment, the cause probably lies elsewhere. Dorval, the hero of *Le Fils naturel*, uses elaborate periphrasis to suggest that he possesses sexual feelings, and in so doing seems to be revealing Diderot's reluctant or unconscious submission to the polite canons of seventeenth-century drama he thought he was overthrowing. Dorval declares to a woman who desires him that 'Je ne suis point étranger à cette pente si générale et si douce qui entraîne tous les êtres et qui les porte à éterniser leur espèce' (iv. 3), a statement that effectively denies all validity to the referential principles invoked in *Jacques le fataliste*. Diderot's aesthetic liking for the sketch, about which there will be more to say, may partly explain this vagueness; but it seems mainly attributable to his moralistic taste for repression.

This tendency marches ill with a certain 'complaisance charnelle'[8] characteristic of Diderot's age, and which makes its literature as well as its visual art fertile territory for exploring the body's physical realities—though it can scarcely be argued that the eighteenth century was more preoccupied than other ages with human sexuality. Diderot's attention to the material fabric of the body is as often sexological as it is philosophical or scientific, and his lexicon naturally varies from one work to the next.[9] The investigation of human biology, particularly reproduction and sex differences, in *Le Rêve de d'Alembert* means that the organs of generation are frequently mentioned or implied. The title of the early novel *Les Bijoux indiscrets* (1748) makes clear that the female genitals are to be the main focus of interest, although the conventional organ of speech is implicated in the story too. The entire body of Suzanne Simonin and the physical excitement she both stimulates and undergoes are vividly presented in *La Religieuse*; and the subject of the *Supplément au Voyage de Bougainville*, a dialogue which debates the relative sexual freedom of Tahiti and the Christian West, involves some discussion of the anatomy and physiology of sex. But *Le Neveu de Rameau* is as much concerned with ingestion, digestion and excretion as with genital activity, while the *Lettre sur les aveugles* of 1747 deals with the organ of sight and the *Lettre sur les sourds et muets* (1751), at least intermittently, with those of speech and hearing. Finally, the *Paradoxe sur le comédien* (1769) and the essay 'Sur les femmes' (1772) highlight the bodily parts that allegedly defined sensibility and femaleness (or female pathology), the diaphragm and womb respectively.

The eighteenth century, which began to emphasize the biological and anatomical differences between males and females as well as confirming their similarities, also found separate terms for organs that had previously been assimilated under a single (male) name. The ovaries and testicles were finally distinguished linguistically, and anatomical parts that had lacked a label (such as the vagina) acquired one.[10] Made particular, woman's body took on a new meaning: its bones, reproductive organs and even nerves were gendered. This development led to an increased confidence in the use of body language, at least in specific contexts. When, in *Le Rêve de d'Alembert*, d'Alembert says accusingly to Dr Bordeu, 'Je crois que vous dites des ordures à mademoiselle de Lespinasse', he is told that 'Quand on parle science, il faut se servir des mots techniques'. The point is taken: 'Vous avez raison; alors ils perdent le cortège d'idées accessoires qui les rendraient malhonnêtes' (p. 58). The proliferation of sex talk that Michel Foucault associated with the eighteenth century[11] was the direct result of medical advance, scientific discovery and a climate of erotic realism, but it did not occur without hindrance.

Toussaint's *Les Mœurs* (1748) observes, not unexpectedly, that the social need for 'pudeur' has brought about the development of two wholly distinct languages:

L'une est celle des médecins, des matrones et des rustres: ses expressions sont crues, énergiques et choquantes. L'autre a des mots choisis, des périphrases mystérieuses, des tournures énigmatiques, des termes entortillés. Elle donne aux sujets un fard qui les embellit, ou qui du moins leur ôte ce qu'ils avaient de rebutant: elle les couvre d'une gaze légère qui, sans les cacher aux yeux, en rend la vue plus supportable. C'est cette langue que les gens bien nés parlent devant le beau sexe. Quoiqu'elle puisse sembler obscure, au fond elle ne l'est pas; on est convenu de s'entendre à demi-mot. Nos dames ont l'intelligence aisée et l'oreille délicate: ce serait leur faire injure que de s'exprimer devant elles avec trop de clarté; leur imagination, dit un écrivain moderne, aime à se promener à l'ombre.[12]

The same veiling of sexual reference is demanded by Mlle de Lespinasse in the final dialogue of *Le Rêve de d'Alembert*, when she asks Dr Bordeu for 'de la gaze, un peu de gaze' as they advance into a discussion of cross-breeding (p. 96). Nor will she allow him to continue his risky speculations on alternative sites of female sexual pleasure comparable to that of the clitoris: 'Je vous entends. Non. Celle-là est toute seule de son espèce; et c'est dommage' (p. 52). There is a point, at least in the company of women, at which the vocabulary of sexuality may not be freely employed. Buffon makes a related observation, though without resorting to female stereotypes, at the beginning of the section of *L'Histoire naturelle de l'homme* that deals with puberty: 'Pourrions-nous écrire l'histoire de cet âge avec assez de circonspection pour ne réveiller dans l'imagination que des idées philosophiques? [...] Nous tâcherons seulement d'entrer dans ces détails avec cette sage retenue qui fait la décence du style.'[13]

The alternative philosophy is the one proposed several years later by Mercier, who writes in *L'An 2440* that no form of language can be deemed inherently base and thus unfit for use as a referential instrument: if ideas need expression, then the expression itself is necessary.[14] Diderot's views on the matter vary. The *Lettre sur les sourds et muets* declares that any attempt to remove idiomatic verve for reasons of politeness is an act of wilful impoverishment, and contrasts the energy of ancient Greek and Latin with the false delicacy of French in this respect. 'Noble' language is the fearless language that calls things by their name; 'proper' language uses the sterilized discourse of circumlocution. 'Quelle perte pour ceux d'entre nos écrivains qui ont l'imagination forte, que celle de tant de mots que nous revoyons avec plaisir dans Amyot et dans Montaigne!'[15] But four years later his *Encyclopédie* article 'Encyclopédie' supports the practice of preferring a 'proper' word to a less polite one where the latter would, however expressively, have evoked 'des idées petites, basses, obscènes, ou rappel[é] des sensations désagréables'.

The problems of language were not the only ones facing a writer who wanted to approach the body as directly as possible. The question of perception raised even more basic issues. Condillac, Diderot's contemporary, criticized philosophers of his day for their 'misguided' desire to give everything bodily form, a prejudice which in his view condemned all their speculations to superficiality. The tendency he deplored arose from the growth of experimental science in the eighteenth century, and an accompanying phenomenological bias that was bound to discourage abstract reflection. Condillac was far from attacking the hegemony of the senses, however. He simply blamed the modern (and ancient) preoccupation with sight above all the other senses, because he himself believed touch to be primordial: it told man about the existence of a 'non-moi', as sight alone could not do, and so freed him from the prison of solipsism.[16]

Perhaps Condillac's strictures were partly aimed at Diderot, with whom he had particularly close relations in the late 1740s and early 1750s. Diderot, who was proud of his own visual percipience, followed Aristotle and others in rating sight as the best example of perception. He refers to his pictorial gifts in the *Salon* of 1767:

Mon imagination s'est assujettie de longue main aux véritables règles de l'art, à force d'en regarder les productions [...] j'ai pris l'habitude d'arranger mes figures dans ma tête comme si elles étaient sur la toile peut-être [que] je les y transporte, et que c'est sur un grand mur que je regarde, quand j'écris. (iii. 110)

It was Diderot who boldly *depicted* desire (as well as its consummation) in *La Religieuse*, as opposed to merely letting it *speak* (as the female pudenda do in *Les Bijoux indiscrets*). It was he who allegedly exclaimed 'Son' pittor' anch'io!' as he wrote La *Religieuse*, a book full of tableaux and chromatic contrasts, and who regularly suggested subjects for his artist friends to paint. And it was certainly he who, considering the non-pictorial nature of performed drama in his own day to be proof of decadence, developed the theory of the stage tableau.

But Diderot was also the philosopher who argued in the *Lettre sur les aveugles* that variations in sensory equipment (such as possessing or not possessing the power of sight) result in varying interpretations of the physical and moral world, and who asked whether the sense of touch might not be an adequate substitute for vision. The *Lettre* addresses the question Molyneux had asked of Locke, namely whether a man born blind who became sighted could distinguish on purely visual evidence between a globe and a cube. (Locke and Molyneux both answered in the negative.) Diderot had greatly wanted to be present when a girl operated on for cataract had the bandages removed from her eyes, so as to gain further information on this matter; and his preoccupation with the issue is underlined by an invented scene he inserted in the *Lettre* in which the blind Cambridge professor of mathematics Saunderson is heard exclaiming on his deathbed that to believe in God he would need to be able to touch him.[17] All this constitutes proof of a strong materialist concern with what might otherwise have seemed merely metaphysical matters. But there is much else to suggest that Diderot's intellectual interests were profound, not superficial in the way Condillac took much modern philosophy to be.

Throughout his writing Diderot is engaged by the nature of physical and moral sensibility, the organic operations of emotion and the material make-up of man. He attends to the body as a unit, seeing its outward activity as a function of its inner structure in the same way as its hidden impulses are a product of external stimuli. When he declared that anatomical dissection should be more widely practised,[18] it was primarily because he saw a need to open the body up both literally and figuratively in order to understand its workings better— a paradigm example of the Enlightenment preoccupation with visualizing the invisible,[19] and so a more serious urge than Condillac's dismissive words on modern philosophy had suggested. The physiological interests developed in the *Eléments de physiologie* reveal his determination to understand the ways in which bodies bring forth undefined properties through dynamic action, a preoccupation also apparent in his obsession with mutability.

Diderot was both a connoisseur and an *amateur* of the body. He enjoyed the paradox of trying to recreate its forms by non-plastic, non-visual means, while simultaneously finding language a frustratingly restrictive means of representation. But he saw the limitations of representational art as clearly as he did the difficulty of trying to write (about) the body. He rarely challenged the established hierarchy that assigned the highest status to depictions of the human body in action, yet he was clearly aware—as was Lessing, whose treatise *Laokoon* (1766) deals with the respective limitations of painting and literature—that pictorial art cannot depict movement. This makes it incapable, among other things, of capturing the physiology rather than the anatomy of bodies. Language, conversely, moves in time, and so can represent changing moral or physical states, though it may be inadequate to image and convey certain aspects of sensuous reality.

Diderot was strongly attracted to literary genres such as the novel that sought to maximize this dynamic potential, wanting to move beyond the static verbal portraiture practised by seventeenth-century writers and those, such as Marivaux, whom they influenced. If he shared Marivaux's belief that a principal use of literary language was to convey a person's moral characteristics,[20] he applied it in more emphatically pictorial ways. Because the province of literature is narrative or expository time, it is able to surmount the obstacle faced by visual art, whose medium is space. This is what makes Diderot's *Salon* commentary on Michel Van Loo's 1767 portrait of him so apt: it describes *in language* the changeability that characterized his person (and which he complains is absent from the portrait), something no visual depiction could possibly capture. Physical images may be better at depicting the substance of bodies, but words alone translate their constantly altering states as well as their unseen impulses. Rousseau, who had no taste for the visual arts, denied that a painted portrait could ever plumb its sitter's psychological depths, though he perversely chose to argue this view in connection with the picture painted of him by Allan Ramsay, the eighteenth century's quintessential portraitist of the soul.[21] Diderot's opinion was less extreme, but his criticism of the Van Loo portrait is based on a similar premiss: the fluid self has been frozen into a dumb and unrepresentative image that conveys nothing of his restless energy or philosophical profundity.

Diderot's material approach to the corporeal, then, never prevented him from paying attention to intangible values, but he generally expressed such values in terms of a new eighteenth-century secularism based on organic reality rather than on abstract perception. His 'concrete anthropology'[22] helped to inaugurate an age of body specialists rather than specialists on the soul, of professionals whose concerns were hygienic and eugenic rather than sacramental. His interest in social procreation[23] is illustrated by a range of texts—the play *Le Fils naturel*, some memoirs and letters describing how he prepared his daughter for marriage and childbirth, and the commentary on a sketch by Greuze which, according to Diderot, 'prêche la population' (*Salons*, ii. 155).

When Diderot wrote about imaginary Tahitian savages in the *Supplément au Voyage de Bougainville*, he dwelt on their efforts to improve the nation's stock by prudently breeding with 'superior'

Westerners. But he also stressed the Tahitian rejection of Western customs—mainly religious habits—that punished the body by forbidding its free sexual expression. Not that he presented the savage world as granting equal freedom to all bodies in this respect; but he showed the constraints it imposed to be rational (issuing from the utilitarian principle that beneficial population increase ought to be encouraged) rather than irrational (based on spiritual principles lacking all practical application). If the body is to be deprived, Diderot thinks, it must be for some evident purpose, and the purposes imagined by the Christian religion are indefensible. In certain cases he finds some justification for displaying and exalting the body's suffering, but it has nothing to do with religious mortification of the flesh. When in his letter to Landois of 9 June 1756 he recommends that criminals be publicly hanged, it is because the spectacle may caution onlookers against committing punishable offences rather than because it gratifies their morbid curiosity,[24] and when he calls for malefactors to be dissected alive it is so that useful anatomical knowledge may be gained, not in order to satisfy sadistic or prurient urges. He is even prepared to allow women to be present at such spectacles, despite being convinced that they are congenitally frail and liable to suffer serious organic upset.

Diderot's women are both weak and strong, twittering birds in aviaries (as the essay 'Sur les femmes' has it), visceral erotic beings (in Les Bijoux indiscrets) or mystic Delphic oracles ('Sur les femmes' again). He distinguishes between the discreet voice of 'le sexe' (the whole class of females, which may articulate no bodily desire) and the voice of sex, which speaks unambiguously. But he does not merely contrast two aspects of womanhood. He also compares women with men, most interestingly in the Mme de La Pommeraye episode of Jacques le fataliste, the Polly Baker story in the Supplément au Voyage de Bougainville, and one or two of his short stories. It is hardly surprising that he should be much more informative about the female body than about the male, and yet his treatment of women is often routine. On the whole he disappoints as a feminist, partly because the interest in gender categories pursued in the Eléments de physiologie, Le Rêve de d'Alembert and (to an extent) La Religieuse is too readily subsumed under a loose kind of erotic paternalism. In no sense, as was claimed fairly recently, does he study woman's body more as a doctor and sociologist than as a specialist in eroticism,[25] though both of the former roles interest him. The author of 'Sur les femmes' fails to represent the female body fully and responsibly by boldly breaking the taboos and codes imprisoning it,[26] and fails even in works that are free of the prejudices of 'Sur les femmes'. Only the Polly Baker episode, one or two of the *contes* and the occasional letter to his lover Sophie Volland tell a different story.

None the less, it is also clear that Diderot's writings reject many of the traditional limitations on bodily expression, however qualified the freedom he allows even the savage women of Tahiti in this respect. He had little time for the artfulness of corporeal dressage, which he regarded as the constricting relic of an earlier age, and took particular pride in looking shabby as well as behaving informally. This was because he saw the body as an untrammelled, vital, material entity, an expansive organism that delighted in its fleshly being. Curbing its instincts was, he thought, usually pointless, particularly when it was done to protect the intellect. Leibniz, a perfect example of *res cogitans* rather than *res extensa*, seemed to him less than half a man: he was simply an automaton, a 'machine à réflexion, comme le métier à bas est une machine à ourdissage'. His forfeiting of life-enhancing sensuous pleasure was an extreme version of the philosopher's asceticism in *Le Neveu de Rameau*, a futile self-denial that overrated the importance of commitment to abstractions: 'entrez chez lui, présentez-lui les plus belles femmes et qu'il en jouisse, à la condition de renoncer à la solution de ce problème [i.e., a problem of metaphysics or geometry], il ne le voudra pas'.[27] This remark may also recall works such as Tissot's *De la santé des gens de lettres* (1768), which issues a similar warning against excessive devotion to cerebral work. Diderot believed firmly enough in the claims of the body to see the force of the arguments Tissot advanced against too much sitting and writing: reducing the body to the brain and stomach implied the functional elimination of its third centre of gravity, the genital area. Indeed, Tissot took this effective atrophying of the sex organs to be one possible reason why great men rarely produced great sons.[28]

The material emphasis of Diderot's attitude to the body has determined my own approach in this book. Few topics in literary theory are more modish than that of the human body, but much of the work that has been published refers only fleetingly to the *stuff* bodies are made of.[29] For Diderot, in contrast, this stuff is of the essence. Accordingly, I have chosen to focus on the body as mass rather than on the body as text, which has entailed paying less attention to studies that take the body to be a form of code or symbol containing a transposed meaning (such as Anne Deneys-Tunney's *Ecritures du corps*) than to those (such as Anne C. Vila's *Enlightenment and Pathology*) that stress the links between the physical organism and psychic experience. Vila's work, which has greatly influenced mine, also represents a more catholic and down-to-earth approach than criticism based on Freud's and Lacan's insights, however fruitful these have undoubtedly been. Equally, although Michel Foucault's *Histoire de la folie à l'âge classique* brilliantly describes the physical manifestations of madness in works such as *Le Neveu de Rameau*, his overall preoccupation with bodies as illustrative of things outside themselves (penal codes, for instance) generally prevents him from attending to them as material entities in their own right.

Other works have more or less polemically realigned the debate on what bodies really represent. One is Dorinda Outram's *The Body and the French Revolution*, which argues that to see bodies as providers of direct experience for their owners is truer to the eighteenth-century conception of corporeality than any metaphoric interpretation could be. This suggests a fruitful avenue for present-day *dix-huitiémistes* to explore, and I have happily followed her lead.

Diderot's commitment to the notion that the body *presents*—directly and materially—rather than *represents* was abiding, however taken he was with the concept of the illustrative body in the 'physiognomical' *La Religieuse* and the 'gestural' *Le Neveu de Rameau*. In his *Plan d'une université* he remarked on the enormous significance of the body's physical presence as constitutive of the whole person, and recommmended 'l'étude du corps humain, la plus belle des machines, ainsi que la plus essentielle à connaître pour nous, *dont elle est une bonne portion*'.[30]

Notes to Introduction

1. *Eléments de physiologie*, ed. Jean Mayer (Paris: Didier, 1964), 58.
2. *Le Rêve de d'Alembert*, ed. Jean Varloot (Paris: Editions sociales, 1962), 4.
3. *Salons*, ed. Jean Seznec and Jean Adhémar, 4 vols. (Oxford: Clarendon Press, 1957–67), i. 233 ff.
4. See Tissot's *L'Onanisme* (Toulouse: Laporte, 1775).
5. *Le Neveu de Rameau*, ed. Jean Fabre (Geneva: Droz, 1963), 95.
6. *Supplément au Voyage de Bougainville*, in *Œuvres philosophiques de Diderot*, ed. Paul Vernière (Paris: Garnier, 1964), 497.
7. *Jacques le fataliste*, in *Œuvres romanesques de Diderot*, ed. Henri Bénac (Paris: Garnier, 1962), 715.

8. See Jean-Pierre Seguin, *Diderot, le discours et les choses* (Paris: Klincksieck, 1978), 71.

9. Seguin, *Diderot*, 72 ff.

10. See Thomas Laqueur, *Making Sex* (Cambridge, Mass., and London: Harvard University Press, 1990), 149 f.

11. See Michel Foucault's *Histoire de la sexualité*, i: *La Volonté de savoir* (Paris: Gallimard, 1976), 27.

12. François-Vincent Toussaint, *Les Mœurs* (Amsterdam, 1748), 164 f.

13. Georges-Louis Leclerc, comte de Buffon, *De l'homme*, ed. Michèle Duchet (Paris: Maspero, 1971), 76.

14. Louis-Sébastien Mercier, *L'An 2440*, quoted in Ferdinand Brunot, *Histoire de la langue française des origines à nos jours*, new edn., 13 vols. (Paris: A. Colin, 1966–72), 6/2, 1, 1206.

15. *Lettre sur les sourds et muets*, ed. Paul Hugo Meyer, *Diderot Studies* 7 (1965), 8.

16. See René Démoris, 'Condillac et la peinture', in *Condillac et les problèmes du langage*, ed. Jean Sgard (Geneva and Paris: Slatkine, 1982), 320 f. See also his *Chardin, la chair et l'objet* (Paris: Olbia, 1999), 187.

17. *Lettre sur les aveugles*, in *O.Phil.* 119.

18. See his addition to d'Alembert's *Encyclopédie* article 'Cadavre'.

19. See Barbara Maria Stafford, *Body Criticism* (Cambridge, Mass., and London: MIT Press, 1991), p. xvii and *passim*.

20. See Henri Coulet, *Marivaux romancier* (Paris: A. Colin, 1975), 320.

21. See Jean-Jacques Rousseau, *Œuvres complètes*, ed. Bernard Gagnebin and Marcel Raymond, 5 vols. (Paris: Gallimard, 1959–95), i. 1149. When, in the *Confessions*, Rousseau imagines himself facing God book in hand, he assumes that only the written word will be capable of revealing 'ce que j'ai fait, ce que j'ai pensé, ce que je fus' (i. 1121).

22. See Anne-Marie Jaton, 'Du corps paré au corps lavé', *Dix-huitième Siècle* 18 (1986), 217.

23. The phrase is Foucault's, *Sexualité*, 137.

24. See *Correspondance*, ed. Georges Roth and Jean Varloot, 16 vols. (Paris: Minuit, 1955–70), i. 209 ff.

25. See Huguette Cohen, 'La tradition gauloise et carnivalesque dans *Les Bijoux indiscrets* et *Jacques le fataliste*', in *Colloque international: Diderot*, ed. Anne-Marie Chouillet (Paris: Aux amateurs des livres, 1985), 230.

26. On this general point see Helena Michie, *The Flesh Made Word* (New York and London: Oxford University Press, 1987), 125.

27. See *Réfutation d'Helvétius*, in *O.Phil.* 568 and 569.

28. See Anne C. Vila, *Enlightenment and Pathology* (Baltimore: Johns Hopkins University Press, 1998), 99.

29. See Terry Eagleton, 'Edible Ecriture', in *Consuming Passions*, ed. Sian Griffiths and Jennifer Wallace (Manchester: Manchester University Press, 1998), 20.

30. *Plan d'une université*, in *Œuvres complètes de Diderot*, ed. Jules Assézat and Maurice Tourneux, 20 vols. (Paris: Garnier, 1875–7), iii. 463. See also *Mémoires pour Catherine II*, ed. Paul Vernière (Paris: Garnier, 1966), xvii, 'Sur la maison des jeunes filles': 'Le corps est pour tous les hommes une partie si importante d'eux-mêmes!' (p. 86).

CHAPTER 1

Bodies versus Minds

Sensory Knowledge

A commentary in the 1765 *Salon* on Fragonard's picture *Le Grand-Prêtre Corésus se sacrifie pour sauver Callirhoé* addresses in transposed literary form a question discussed in Plato's *Republic*. Are humans in thrall to mere images of the ultimate, believing copies to be unmediated truth, or are they capable of perceiving reality directly? Diderot pretends to have had a dream recalling *The Republic* after an evening spent reading some of Plato's dialogues, and bases his critique on the alleged dream. The *Salon* commentary discusses Fragonard's canvas as a version of Plato's allegory, in which prisoners in a cave take the shadows thrown by a fire to be substance. Diderot correspondingly describes Fragonard's vague and ambiguous figures as though they too swirled and flickered, conveying nothing definite and confusing the mind of the beholder. Is Corésus a man or a woman? Are his acolytes hermaphrodites? Why do the figures hint rather than straightforwardly represent? Is their shadowiness meant to suggest that every earthly body lacks the solidity of concrete fact, and that all the perceptual tools at man's disposal are inadequate to the task of informing him about reality?[1] 'Grimm', intruding into Diderot's dream, briskly tells him: 'Dans la caverne, vous n'avez vu que les simulacres des êtres, et Fragonard sur sa toile, ne vous en auroit montré non plus que des simulacres. C'est un beau rêve que vous avez fait; c'est un beau rêve qu'il a peint' (*Salons*, ii. 195).

According to the Platonic tradition the senses, whose objects are fleeting and unstable, cannot be the source of true knowledge: the intellect alone is capable of reaching the changeless world of the real. In other words, the reality that humans think they perceive is nothing but a sensory copy of the ultimate Idea. One may doubt, however, whether Diderot actually subscribed to this notion. As a man of his sensationalist times, he was inclined to think that the body's various perceptions did accurately inform the mind, even if he occasionally sided with Plato. The *Lettre sur les sourds et muets* describes an imaginary people that has been divided into five sects corresponding to the body's five senses, and relates what happens when they quarrel with one another. The sect associated with sight is condemned to the madhouse as visionary; that with smell, deemed imbecile; that with taste, adjudged intolerably capricious and over-delicate; that with hearing, denounced as detestable because of its curiosity and pride; and that with touch, berated as materialistic (p. 94). But for the most part Diderot enthusiastically and anti-Platonically supported the belief that the senses were the purveyors of true knowledge, and regarded the hypothetical pre-sensory body as a mere husk, like the statue of Condillac's *Traité des sensations* (1754) or Locke's blank slate on which the experiences procured by sense-impressions ideationally write.

Obviously, these are naïve images: they ignore the reality of a psychic life involving the faculties and organic tendencies that precede sensation. But the development of sensationalism in the eighteenth century was to some extent a polemical undertaking designed to undo the detached theorizing of the previous age and dismantle its over-intellectualized philosophical systems. Making loud claims about body's hegemony over mind, which involved celebrating the physical nature of man, did not necessarily imply an out-and-out rejection of dualism. As we shall see, *Le Neveu de Rameau* keeps mind and body in a kind of daring equipoise—something that strictly materialist convictions on the part of its author, of the kind he will later develop in *Le Rêve de d'Alembert*, ought to have precluded.

Determinism or Choice?

Diderot's expansive philosophy of the body made him reluctant to accept that it should be subjected to rigid prescriptions, whether religious or moral; but he was bound to reflect on the degree to which free will, and hence intention, govern human response. (This is a central theme of *Jacques le fataliste*.) Does mind control any of body, if indeed it is separate from body? Is any purpose served by wanting something to be the case, or has everything been foreordained? Do humans possess free will, or is the way we behave dictated by the laws of our organization and the chain of events? (This is a main subject of the letter to Landois and of *Le Rêve de d'Alembert*.) Such questions are particularly urgent ones where the operations of the passions are concerned, because the very concept of passion suggests that which is undergone rather than actively controlled.

On the one hand, it may seem that the relationships our minds and bodies form are designated ones. Diderot presents a humorous version of this idea in the chapter 'Des insulaires' of *Les Bijoux indiscrets*, where the islanders are shown as bonding on the basis of anatomical 'fit': 'Un bijou féminin en écrou est prédestiné à un bijou mâle fait en vis' *(O.Rom.*, p. 53). On the other hand, the reverse situation is presented in *Jacques le fataliste* with the story of the 'gaîne' and the 'coutelet', who attack each other for changing partners at random: 'Gaîne, ma mie, vous êtes une friponne, car tous les jours vous recevez de nouveaux Coutelets [...]. Mon ami Coutelet, vous êtes un fripon, car tous les jours vous changez de Gaîne'. Eventually an arbitrator tells them that God prescribed promiscuity (p. 605).

Yet even *Les Bijoux indiscrets* raises the question of determinism and choice in a more serious way than 'Des insulaires' suggests. It does this by postulating a distinction between irresistible mechanistic forces and the operation of free will in the women whose chattering 'bijoux' are activated by the magic ring Sultan Mangogul points at them. If the women cannot stop their indiscretions being broadcast when Mangogul decides to test them, they *can* apparently avoid committing indiscretions in the first place. In other words, the brain controls the actions of their bodies, as it controls the conventional organ of speech until supernatural powers are invoked. Women, Diderot seems to be arguing, have a higher and a lower voice at war with each other,[2] the higher voice claiming supremacy over the lower because it is connected with mind and detached from bodily constraints. When it speaks, it does so as a result of choice, not because an external instrument forces its confidence. But the novel scarcely supports this hierarchy. One chapter, 'L'Echo', describes how the voluntary voice of the hypocritical Ismène claims a virtue which is disproved as soon as the irrepressible voice of her genitals speaks, divulging the fact that they have countless sexual secrets to give away.

Diderot is not saying that women's bodies are governed by an affective automatic unconscious manifested in sexuality rather than a voluntary consciousness based on the brain, though he would hardly have denied the part that involuntary response plays in sexual arousal. The point, rather, is that he never shows the body's concession to be inevitable and unreflective. If physiology were determined in such a reductive sense, then all women would act like one another; but the novel reveals that they do not. (Mangogul's favourite Mirzoza, for example, is chaste.) All *Les Bijoux indiscrets* has really shown, in line with much libertine fiction of its own and later times, is that most females have sexual desires and frequently yield to them. This is not very different from the case of males, who cannot govern their erections: they may decide not to put them to any purpose, but given the opportunity probably will. Since men and women are both programmed to find sex pleasurable, they tend to indulge in it when circumstances permit.

All this suggests that if Diderot's purpose in *Les Bijoux indiscrets* was to rob female desire of dignity by reducing it to mechanical terms, it was unsuccessful. But perhaps, and contrary to traditional critical views on the novel, he intended to do something else. He may well have wanted to ridicule the common opinion that inserting a projection into a hole is a matter of deep moral concern: the flippancy of the chapter 'Des insulaires' suggests as much, and other writings of his do so too. But sometimes he is at pains to dignify sex by associating it with the characteristically conscious and voluntary component of human love. Removed from the realm of instinct, it stands above the desire of animals as civilization stands above barbarity: hardly a startling premiss to advance, but one that needed to be stressed in an age that emphasized the mechanical similarities between man and beast. Although Diderot allows a character in the short story *Ceci n'est pas un conte* (1773) to observe that 'on n'est le maitre ni d'arrêter une passion qui s'allume, ni d'en prolonger une qui s'éteint',[3] other works (*La Religieuse*, *Le Fils naturel* and *Jacques le fataliste*) distinguish between an involuntary consent of the body to sexual arousal and a voluntary concession by the will to its promptings. In his fictional writings at least, he was reluctant to embrace wholeheartedly the philosophy of bodily (or genetic) determinism argued by the dialoguist Lui in *Le Neveu de Rameau*, with respect either to emotion or to any corporeal drive.

For at least some of the time the Nephew, Lui, presents his entire disposition as moulded by the 'fibres' he was born with, saying that he lacks certain moral perceptions because he is without the physical receptors with which to apprehend them (pp. 76, 89). (The term 'fibre' initially belonged to the vocabulary of vegetable and animal anatomy, but the Nephew's psycho-physiology extends it into the composite area covered by sensibility.) When his interlocutor Moi appears unimpressed by this explanation, Lui swiftly abandons it in favour of an appeal to environmental influence. '[P]eut etre c'est que j'ai toujours vécu avec de bons musiciens et de mechantes gens; d'ou il est arrivé que mon oreille est devenue tres fine, et que mon cœur est devenu tres sourd' (pp. 89–90)—a statement which allows the sense of 'oreille' and 'cœur' to vacillate between the metaphorical and the material. Yet the degree of *symbolic* reference to the body's responses is not high, here or elsewhere in the dialogue. It suits Lui to make moral perception a physical matter, but the monism he upholds is evidently a matter of personal convenience.

Diderot's own resistance to the full implications of materialist determinism, which are enthusiastically argued in *Le Rêve de d'Alembert*, is nowhere so clear as in his personal relationships. He is unwilling to see human motivation solely in terms of Kant's abhorred empirical self, because that would mean interpreting it simply as a product of biological make-up or neurological structure. Instead, he declares that taking physical explanations to be the only valid explanations for human conduct can be impoverishing. Although he states in a letter to Mme de Maux, probably written at the end of September 1769 (the year when he first drafted the monist *Rêve de d'Alembert*), that 'Si je crois que je vous aime librement, je me trompe. Il n'en est rien', he goes on to declare: 'j'enrage d'être empêtré d'une diable de philosophie [i.e., materialist determinism] que mon esprit ne peut s'empêcher d'approuver, et mon cœur de démentir' (*Corr.* ix. 154). After all, he was a disciple of Spinoza, who distinguished between 'actions' and 'passions', and assigned love to the former category as the practice of a human power that could be effected only in freedom. In his relationship with Sophie Volland he emphasized the lover's role as an active party who controls feeling rather than being controlled by it. This may seem an unlikely position for Diderot to have adopted, since his own passions were notoriously combustible; but there can be little doubt that he, like Rousseau, saw love as following on judgement as preference follows on comparison. He wrote to Sophie on 2 September 1760:

Quand mon estime croît pour vous de jour en jour, dites, est-il possible que ma tendresse diminue? [...] Si j'avois à dire de ma Sophie, ce seroit ceci: Plus je vis avec elle, plus je lui vois de vertus; plus elle s'embellit à mes yeux, plus je l'aime; plus elle m'attache... (*Corr.* iii. 52)

Given that cognition is involved in emotional response, feelings which are based on experience and knowledge can always change.

The change may be a form of intensification, such as Diderot experienced with Sophie. But it may also lead to a diminution, something he describes in his short stories and the Mme de La Pommeraye episode of *Jacques le fataliste*. Gardeil, the faithless and ungrateful lover of *Ceci n'est pas un conte*, is not seen as blameworthy *in principle* for having fallen out of love with Mlle de La Chaux, merely guilty *in practice* for coldly deserting a woman he has exploited professionally. Mme de La Pommeraye cannot forgive the marquis des Arcis for his infidelity, but the fact that her revenge miscarries may indicate that the marquis is guilty of no more than rashly protesting undying love for a woman he eventually and 'naturally' tires of. If the sentimentally luxuriating literature of the eighteenth century often suggests to a more sober age that the expression of emotion is to a high degree under the individual's control, it seems equally clear that the expression of emotion is not equivalent to emotion itself. Gardeil is perhaps reprehensible in his refusal to maintain any semblance of a lover's discourse (whereas the more frivolous des Arcis manages to preserve some appearances), but the fact of the matter is that the intention to love, whether verbalized or not, is rarely converted into love itself. Jacques suggests this truth in the novel Diderot wrote under Spinoza's influence, but which seems to contradict Spinoza's conception of love as action: 'Est-ce qu'on est maître de devenir ou de ne pas devenir amoureux? Et quand on l'est, est-on maître d'agir comme si on ne l'était pas?' (p. 498).

Bodily Detachment

Trying to exalt the power of mind over emotion, whether or not the latter finds definite bodily expression, may seem a futile enterprise. But is it equally misguided to elevate body above spirit, always supposing that they are separable? Perhaps Diderot's view is that the two may be kept in equipoise. On the one hand, 'il y a un peu de testicule au fond de nos sentiments les plus sublimes et de notre tendresse la plus épurée', as he wrote to his friend Damilaville on 3 November 1760 (*Corr.* iii. 216)—a sentiment he elsewhere attributes to Baron d'Holbach's mother-in-law Mme d'Aine. It was necessary to emphasize testicles, whether or not one followed the common eighteenth-century practice of conferring them on women as well as men, in order to give human energy its full worth and underline the Enlightenment rejection of barren *politesse*. But as the *Réfutation d'Helvétius* makes clear, Diderot had no desire to equate the fact of loving with the act of love. 'N'y a-t-il que du plaisir physique à posséder une belle femme? N'y a-t-il que de la peine physique à la perdre ou par la mort ou par l'inconstance?' (p. 567).

As a psycho-physiological complex, love is not to be reduced to the routine physical process described in *Les Bijoux indiscrets*. This is why Diderot can turn metaphysician in a famous letter to Sophie Volland of October 1759:

Ceux qui se sont aimés pendant leur vie et qui se font inhumer l'un à côté l'autre ne sont peut-être pas si fous qu'on pense. Peut-être leurs cendres se pressent, se mêlent et s'unissent [...] il me resteroit donc un espoir de [...] m'unir, de me confondre avec vous, quand nous ne serons plus. S'il y avoit dans nos principes une loi d'affinité, s'il nous étoit réservé de composer un être commun, si je devois dans la suite des siècles refaire un tout avec vous, si les molécules de votre amant dissous venoient à s'agiter, à se mouvoir, à rechercher les vôtres éparses dans la nature! (*Corr.* ii. 283-4)

This may sound like the purely material conception of the human organism later to be developed in *Le Rêve de d'Alembert*, but in fact Diderot's emphasis transcends the physical. The process he describes is only one way, admittedly, of entering another's body and becoming merged with it. But very often we feel our bodies as irredeemably particular, and cannot imagine experiencing them in the way someone outside ourselves might do. As Sartre remarks in *L'Etre et le néant*, I cannot consider my body externally, take up a visual perspective on my seeing, touch myself touching.[4] Merleau-Ponty observes that the body is incapable of becoming a mere object because it is that by means of which there *are* bodies: it is neither tangible nor visible, being what touches and sees. But Diderot seems to dispute the notion that one cannot view oneself detachedly. Suzanne Simonin, in *La Religieuse*, has a remarkable ability to look upon her own body as though severed from it, a duality Diderot posits because he needs both internal and external focalization[5] in order to maximize the pathetic force of her narrative. When, to take a familiar example, Suzanne describes how she appears when unconscious, she is allowing Diderot to compound the intimacy of first-person discourse with the empirical clarity of the third person (p. 261). The blending of voices is highlighted in the dramatic account of the night before she takes her vows:

Je ne me couchai point; j'étais assise sur mon lit; j'appelai Dieu à mon secours; j'élevais mes mains au ciel, je le prenais à témoin de la violence qu'on me faisait; je me représentais mon rôle au pied des autels, une jeune fille protestant à haute voix contre une action à laquelle elle paraît avoir consenti... (p. 245)

She then, as though from outside herself, gives a detailed account of her faint, the feverish seizure that makes her knees knock and her teeth chatter, and the half-delirium that follows. Perhaps she could have been a witness to at least part of this, as she could of her actions at a later stage—undressing, wandering from her cell, lying in her shift outside the Mother Superior's door. But she is also at pains to stress the distance at which she stood from such events, separated as much from their physical reality as from their psychological implications: 'je n'avais aucune connaissance de ce qui s'était passé' (p. 245).

More oddly still, particularly in the sexually charged scenes that unfold subsequently, Suzanne's distance enables her to depict states of 'sensible' stimulation, including her own, without any corresponding skill at diagnosing their causes. This state persists even when she is possessed of the facts that clarify them, and means that her narrative preserves a de-eroticized and even clinical tone throughout.[6] So at the point when she might have been able to fashion experience into a new perspective, 'writing' her body in all its pathos and suffering, she still appears strangely apart from it; and this despite her double narrative vision, internal and external. One interpretation of her condition, which does not exclude others, is that she has too much painful knowledge to handle, and shuts down as a result—a manifestation of trauma that Diderot depicts with devastating acuity. Rather than retrospectively mastering those who abused and tormented her, which the gift of narrative should have enabled her to do, she is taken over by something like the force of alienation we shall later notice in Rameau's nephew (see Chapter 5 below). And because she is disempowered in this way, the detailing of experiences that might otherwise have appeared almost masochistically complaisant—the whippings, beatings, slashings, tramplings underfoot—gains added meaning. It shows the extent to which she has been made into an unresisting, will-less body for those around her, an object to inflict physical or emotional torment on, a thing for others to manipulate or degrade.[7]

There are various ways of interpreting the masochism of Suzanne-Diderot's account. Our readiness to accept Leo Spitzer's celebrated argument that a sexual rhythm pervades Diderot's writing, making its energy appear the translation of a powerful libido,[8] depends in large part on our understanding of his complex 'sensibilité' and that of the eighteenth century in general. We may with good reason see sensibility itself as a more or less sublimated sexual phenomenon, in which case its presence in Diderot is no more remarkable than in, say, Rousseau or Bernardin de Saint-Pierre. Whatever the case, it cannot be doubted that his enthusiastic embracing of a psycho-physiological explanation of human conduct encouraged him to discuss widely diverging areas of human life in corporeal (if not necessarily sexualized) terms.

The Bodily Continuum

It is of course true that Diderot's own adherence to a physicalist view of man and the world is often 'metaphysically' tempered, as in the 1759 letter about spiritual union to Sophie Volland; it may even be undercut by a more extended argument for mind's supremacy over matter, however unexpected this would be in the apparently impenitent anti-dualist of *Le Rêve de d'Alembert* (which accounts for heredity, growth and all the simpler forms of animal behaviour in terms of the interior motions of bodies). And though he is often trenchant in attacking the bloodless *cogito*, he might have reflected that Descartes's scepticism about the existence of the body did not at all prevent him from attending to it philosophically. Rather, in demoting the corporeal Descartes associated it intimately with the mental by making it the junior partner in a potent binary structure, as resonantly formulaic as heart and reason, nature and culture and even male and female (all oppositions of particular interest to the eighteenth century and Diderot). In fact, such an association often seemed philosophically correct to Diderot too, but he emphasized the relative weight of its components differently. In the same spirit *Jacques le fataliste* declares the distinction between a physical and a moral world to be meaningless. If Diderot's mature philosophy, as worked out in *Le Rêve de d'Alembert*, is an extreme form of materialism which takes the real world as consisting in material things varying in their states and relations, elsewhere he simply accords matter primacy and mind (or spirit) a secondary rather than non-existent position.

His objection to the Cartesian notion that, while extension is the essence or essential property of bodies, thought is the essence or essential property of mind rested on his conviction that persons were complete biological mechanisms with a variety of properties, of

which thought was one. (An ambitious example of this new holistic
approach was Buffon's *Histoire naturelle*, which aimed to give a total
picture of man's development as a material and biological entity.)
Diderot's unsystematic writings unquestionably took a progressively
more materialist turn, though the Encyclopédie article 'Spinoziste'
describes Spinozist philosophy in terms that he would later adopt
himself: 'Le principe général de ceux-ci est que la matière est sensible
[...]. De là ils concluent qu'il n'y a que la matière et qu'elle suffit pour
tout expliquer'. The distinction of the two substances is ridiculed
in the first dialogue of *Le Rêve de d'Alembert* with the argument that
metaphysical dualism poses more problems than it resolves (an
argument also made in the *Eléments de physiologie*) and also because
sentience, which according to the Lockeian doctrine is the pre-
requisite of thought, is a universal property of bodies. This is a view
that the *Réfutation d'Helvétius* will later call into question on the
grounds that its persuasiveness derives merely from the number of
difficulties it settles ('ce qui ne suffit pas en bonne philosophie',
p. 566). But *Le Rêve de d'Alembert*'s introductory dialogue proposes it
more than half-seriously, using the example of the shattered marble
bust by Falconet to demonstrate how the inert may be made active,
or in modern terminology how potential energy (the 'force morte' or
nisus, which is actually a virtual power rather than a dead force)
becomes a 'force vive', or kinetic:

DIDEROT.—Je prens la statue que vous voyez; je la mets dans un mortier [...].
Lorsque le bloc de marbre est réduit en poudre impalpable, je mêle cette
poudre à de l'humus ou terre végétale [...]. Lorsque le tout s'est transformé
en une matière à peu près homogène [...] j'y sème des pois, des fèves, des
choux et je me nourris des plantes. (pp. 6–7)

Despite his hostility towards the concept of an animating soul,
Diderot's late acknowledgement that universal sentience was more a
philosophical convenience than a demonstrable fact meant that he was
perforce drawn to the vitalist doctrine of the Montpellier medical
school, whose members included his friend Théophile Bordeu.
Vitalism is the scientific doctrine which denies that living processes
are fully explicable in terms of the activities of their material parts.
Although Bordeu posited no supernatural energizing power, but a
vague vital principle distinct from matter, its non-specific nature
predictably alarmed 'hard' materialists like d'Holbach and La Mettrie,
who assumed that the hypothesis was simply an excuse for smuggling

spiritualizing religious concepts back into science. Diderot grew less sure of that with time, dissociating himself from extreme mechanistic interpretations of the body because they seemed to preclude active consciousness:

La différence de l'animal ou de la machine de chair, et de la machine de fer ou de bois, de l'homme ou du chien et de la pendule: c'est que dans celle-ci tous les mouvemens necessaires ne sont accompagnés ni de conscience ni de volonté, et que dans celle-là egalement necessaires, ils sont accompagnés de conscience et de volonté. (*Eléments de physiologie*, p. 35)

The advantages of making the body's workings mechanical were obvious to a medically trained man like La Mettrie: they meant that medical science could assert an exclusive claim on its territory, leaving no room for theologians or moralists. But Diderot thought differently.

His ambivalence emerges clearly from the section of the *Eléments de physiologie* dealing with 'phénomènes du cerveau', under the sub-heading of 'maladies'. Diderot argues, not unexpectedly, that all sensations and affections are corporeal, which means that there is a physical medicine equally applicable to the body and the so-called soul.[9] This view derived support from the Enlightenment's habit of using the sensible or reactive body both as a somatic metaphor and as a concrete hygienic compendium, an organism whose nervous structure led as easily to mental as to physical breakdown. But practising such a 'medecine phisique' was virtually impossible, according to Diderot, because of the complex interrelationships the physician had to master (which appears essentially to mean that its non-material components were provokingly elusive). The *Eléments de physiologie* also fail to adumbrate another difficulty relating to the meaning of 'corporeal' medicine and psychology. Diderot seems to be arguing that phenomena like memory and emotion, along with sensation, are in fact material, as well as being caused by matter; but he does not explain what 'material' (or 'corporeal') really signifies. Does he simply, and rather disappointingly, mean that psychic reactions are necessarily embodied because their essence is translated into overt behaviour? One might deny this more confidently were it not for the fact of Diderot's periodic attraction to the simplistic behaviourism of his age—behaviourism not according to the Hobbesian theory (all mental states being interpretable in terms of matter in motion), but in the cruder sense of 'externalized emotion' evidenced in works like the play *Le Fils naturel* and the novel *La*

Religieuse. Or is he distinguishing a phenomenon like bodily memory, as a brain event, from corpuscular occurrences like the contraction of muscle tissue or the motion of the nerves? There is clearly a confusion between mechanical and/or biological causes and the feelings and thoughts they generate: we can now see, for example, as many in the eighteenth century could not, that anger and sadness are not identical with particular bodily events. This confusion, however, is not peculiar to Diderot's time: the problem is one familiar to most proponents of materialism, eighteenth-century and later.[10]

Involuntary Motions and Human Liberty

Perhaps this is one reason why the monist philosophy advanced in *Le Rêve de d'Alembert* could not be confidently elaborated earlier, even though Diderot's materialism already seems settled in the letter to Landois of 1756. It is less surprising, therefore, that an early novel like *Les Bijoux indiscrets* should promote a version of dualism—the individual's consciousness of being split between and conditioned by two mutually exclusive principles, one of which is regarded as 'higher', spiritual and anti-mechanistic—than that a subsequent dialogue like *Le Neveu de Rameau* should do so, albeit in different terms. But Diderot's dialogical turn of mind made the positing of oppositions irresistible, even if he gave one of them stronger support than the other. Most of his works, with the exception of *La Religieuse* and, to a degree, *Le Rêve de d'Alembert*, maintain this principle of ideological contrast—*Le Fils naturel*, the *Supplément au Voyage de Bougainville*, *Ceci n'est pas un conte*, *Jacques le fataliste* and others.

Had Diderot really intended *Les Bijoux indiscrets* to deal seriously with the question of mind's impotence over matter, he might have dwelt longer on a crucial sexual distinction between men and women. The 'indocility of the organ', a recurrent theme in his writings, works in two directions: the organ may state its desires at unsuitable times, or fail to state them when such a declaration would be useful. Women, crudely speaking, are always 'disponible' (whether desirously or not); men are at the mercy of an involuntary physiological process. Chapter 53 of *Les Bijoux indiscrets* tells the story of an impotent youth who was cured of his affliction only when he found a partner who loved him for other than erotic reasons. Otherwise the novel focuses on woman's ever-readiness and tireless sexual appetite, seeing the apparently chaste merely as exceptions that prove the rule.

The male dilemma is nicely captured in the 1767 *Salon*, where Diderot remarks on the time when he sat for his portrait to the Prussian artist Anna Therbusch, stripping naked and appearing before her 'en modèle d'académie':

Comme depuis le péché d'Adam on ne commande pas à toutes les parties de son corps comme à son bras, et qu'il y en a qui veulent quand le fils d'Adam ne veut pas, et qui ne veulent pas quand le fils d'Adam le voudrait bien: dans le cas de cet accident, je me serais rappelé le mot de Diogène au jeune lutteur: *Mon fils, ne crains rien, je ne suis pas si méchant que celui-là.* (*Salons*, iii. 252–3)

(The same reference occurs in the 'Suite de l'entretien précédent' of *Le Rêve de d'Alembert*.) The austere diet of Diogenes, Rameau's nephew comments, surely tamed the indocility of his member, though the philosopher Moi disagrees: 'Vous vous trompez. L'Habit du Cynique etoit autrefois, notre habit monastique avec la même vertu. Les cyniques etoient les Carmes et les Cordeliers d'Athenes' (p. 107). A reading-note of Diderot's inserted in the 1771 *Correspondance littéraire* pours scorn on the claim made in Augustine's *City of God* that, as Diderot puts it, 'la partie de nous–même qui sert à nous reproduire, si indocile, si capricieuse aujourd'hui, se disposant ou se refusant au plaisir également à contre-temps, obéissait à l'homme innocent, comme son bras et ses autres membres.'[11] The *Eléments de physiologie* return to this subject as Diderot asks his reader to reflect on the impotence of the will to govern bodily response:

ce n'est jamais vous qui voulez manger ou vomir, c'est l'estomac; pisser, c'est la vessie; et ainsi des autres fonctions. Veuillez tant qu'il vous plaira, il ne s'opérera rien, si l'organe ne le veut aussi. Vous voulez jouir de la femme que vous aimez, mais quand jouirez-vous? Quand l'organe le voudra. (p. 287)

This statement may recall the theories associated with the real-life Bordeu, who believed in the relative autonomy of the organs. It also echoes the letter to Landois in its absolute denial of human liberty, and of the supervening mind's ability to control human action. In a section of the *Eléments* on voluntary and involuntary movement Diderot remarks on how 'Le mouvement de l'organe de la génération est sollicité quelquefois inutilement': the motion of *solicitation* may be voluntary (which means no more than 'prompted by some determining motive'), but the ensuing response, or otherwise, of the organ is not.

A letter to Sophie Volland of December 1765 claims that there is almost no man whose virility is equal to the unexpected challenge to prove it, once he has reached a certain age:

Un homme pressoit très vivement une femme, et cette femme soupçonnait que cet homme n'avoit pas la raison qu'il faut avoir pour être pressant. Et elle lui disoit: 'Monsieur, prenez y garde; je m'en vais me rendre'. Passé cinquante ans, il n'y en a presque aucun de nous que cette franchise n'embarrassât. Faites en l'essai dans l'occasion, et vous verrez. (*Corr.* v. 228)

This casts a different light on the indulgence of the male organ alluded to in very specific terms in the essay 'Sur les femmes', though Diderot's reference there is to the reliability of male orgasm once the penis has become erect. Although the fact that it cannot be coerced into doing what it does not want to do may seem an advantage, the phenomenon of impotence was obviously a utilitarian ill where begetting children mattered (as it did in the *Supplément*'s Tahiti as well as in Diderot's France, which feared depopulation). Frigidity, on the other hand, meant nothing more serious than the loss of female pleasure, and this, as we shall see below (p. 140), was thought to be positively conducive to procreation.

Diderot's interest in involuntary physiological movements and their implications for human liberty had been fuelled by his study of Robert Whytt's *Essay on the Vital and Other Involuntary Motions of Animals*: the book dates from 1751, but Diderot read it in the annotated 1763 edition. The notes and additions recall Whytt's quarrel with the physiologist Albrecht von Haller about irritability (or contractility—the shortening of part of the body when something touches it) and sensibility (or the transmission of a contact to the *sensorium commune*). Diderot himself conflated the two properties, seeing irritability as a motive reaction of sensibility.[12] The history of the reflex had in fact begun with Descartes's separation of involuntary motions from the activity of the soul.[13] Whytt's observation that 'A frog lives, and moves its members for half an hour after its head cut off [*sic*]' implied that there might be a multiplicity of organizing centres or 'brains' in the body, each serving a particular organ[14]—a notion facetiously translated in *Les Bijoux indiscrets* into Mirzoza's hypothesis that the debauchee's soul resides in the instrument of his pleasures. The *Eléments de physiologie* further explore the implications of irritability in organs that have been severed from the body:

Piquez le coeur d'un animal vivant, il a son mouvement: amputez ce coeur, piquez-le, mouvement: coupez le en morceaux, piquez ces morceaux, même phênomene. Sur le champ de bataille les membres séparés s'agitent comme autant d'animaux: Preuve que la sensibilité appartient à la matiere animale:

ce sont toutes parties souffrantes, l'animal vivant; toutes parties vivantes, l'animal mort. (p. 22)

Whytt's essay provided him with some related information on the persistent irritability of the heart and the intestines after death (p. 25), to which Diderot added the ghoulish observation that 'La tête même séparée du corps voit, regarde et vit' (p. 28). All this led him to the conclusion that there were two, if not three, distinct forms of life:

> La vie de l'animal entier
> La vie de chacun de ses organes
> La vie de la molécule (p. 27)

'Organisation', Determinism and Puppetry

It was his reading of Whytt that led Diderot to suggest the organicist interpretation of the body we have already encountered, but where the vitality of the component parts coexists with the concept of a unified whole governed by the *sensorium commune*. He may also have been aware of Alexander Stuart's theory that nerve-endings were the 'brains' of the organs in which they were found. But his insistence on the involuntary type of sensibility exhibited, *inter alia*, by the sex organs is sufficiently marked to qualify any notion that intellectual life and its impulses took precedence over material urges in his science of man. Indeed, the emphasis on instinct in various of his writings makes Diderot appear an evident 'homme de la nature'—not in a loose Rousseauist sense, but in the catholic sense that he considered man's nature to be at least as unschoolable (or determined) as susceptible to training (and hence modifiable). Put slightly differently, education can do nothing (*pace* Helvétius) where the organization is lacking. Organization (according to Furetière's 1727 dictionary definition a 'terme d'anatomie qui signifie la structure, la conformation, la figure d'un membre, d'une partie') is a 'given' that cannot be bypassed.

This is another theme of the letter to Landois. In it Diderot states that effect follows inexorably from cause in the actions of humans, such that 'le mot *liberté* [i.e., free will] est un mot vide de sens' (i. 213). This means, he says, that 'il n'y a point d'action qui mérite la louange ou le blâme. Il n'y a ni vice, ni vertu, rien dont il faille récompenser ou châtier' (i. 214). In that case there is clearly no point in punishing the wrongdoer; he must simply be destroyed as one who cannot help being a threat to society. Yet Diderot does not regard men in general as unmodifiable beings; indeed, it is precisely because they *are* modifiable that criminals must be publicly executed. Readers who still find it hard to reconcile the utter determinism that makes Diderot's malefactor simply 'unluckily born' (in the words of *Le Rêve de d'Alembert*, 'On est irrésistiblement entraîné par le torrent général qui conduit l'un à la gloire, l'autre à l'ignominie', p. 86) with the notion that reward and punishment are just and logical methods of correcting wrongdoing and encouraging good may be reassured to find that the *Encyclopédie* article 'Liberté', by de Jaucourt, puts the case slightly differently: 'Il faut bannir ces mots ["récompense" and "châtiment"] de la morale. On ne récompense point, mais on encourage à bien faire; on ne châtie point, mais on étouffe, on effraye.' Jacques the fatalist shares this opinion, 'ne connaissant ni le nom de vice ni le nom de vertu':

Il prétendait qu'on était heureusement ou malheureusement né. Quand il entendait prononcer les mots récompenses ou châtiments, il haussait les épaules. Selon lui la récompense était l'encouragement des bons; le châtiment, l'effroi des méchants. (p. 670)

De Jaucourt's article qualifies the idea that 'L'homme n'est [...] pas différent de l'automate' with the rider that he is 'nullement différent d'un automate qui *sent*; c'est une machine plus composée'.

This view of man as an automaton deserves fuller discussion. Given the eighteenth century's enthusiasm for mannikins, puppets and mechanical instruments, it was not necessarily the insult it appears to those who are convinced of human autonomy. Diderot was as intrigued as anyone by the complex clockwork figures (particularly the flautist and the duck) made by the engineer Jacques Vaucanson,[15] partly for the reason he was fascinated by the life-size human dummies made by the wax modeller Mlle Biheron: manufactured bodies were the only wholly biddable ones, and could be useful tools for opening up the organism to closer scrutiny. According to d'Alembert's *Encyclopédie* article 'Automate', Vaucanson's articulated duck was anatomically instructive as well as mechanically impressive: 'toute la méchanique du canard artificiel a été vûe à découvert, le dessein de l'auteur étant plutôt de démontrer, que de montrer simplement une machine'. Of course, when in the *Paradoxe sur le comédien* Diderot describes the actor as a 'pantin merveilleux' he is not implying that his bodily activities are really controlled by an external agent (the playwright), though in the 'vile pantomime' of human existence referred to in *Le Neveu de Rameau* all bodies are seen as bending to the will of a higher power. The hand-memory of the musician mentioned in *Le Neveu de Rameau* illustrates another kind of corporeal control, an enforced obedience that goes against what is flippantly called the real inclination of the 'lower' parts:

> Et puis vous voyez bien ce poignet; il etoit roide comme un diable. Ces dix doigts, c'etoient autant de batons fichés dans une metacarpe de bois; et ces tendons, c'etoient de vieilles cordes de boyaux plus seches, plus roides, plus inflexibles que celles qui ont servi a la roue d'un tourneur. Mais je vous les ai tant tourmentées, tant brisées, tant rompues. Tu ne veux pas aller; et moi, mordieu, je dis que tu iras; et cela sera... Ils y sont faits; depuis dix ans, je leur en ai donné bien d'une autre façon. Malgré qu'ils en eussent, il a bien fallu que les bougres s'y accoutumassent, et qu'ils apprissent a se placer sur les touches et a voltiger sur les cordes. (p. 26)[16]

Elsewhere in the dialogue we witness the same reduction of the human body to the status of object, as the starving man's gut is likened to the gut of a violin string.

Perhaps the hand's dressage in some way resembles that of the entire recalcitrant body as described by the marquise de Merteuil in letter 81 of Laclos's *Les Liaisons dangereuses*: willy-nilly, it must obey the purposes of mind. It is in this sense that the human being may be called his or her own work, which is what Merteuil calls herself. The Nephew's words, in the same spirit, bring to mind the image of the body politic, where the subjects attempting rebellion are forced to bow to the governing will of the head. The eighteenth century was fascinated by the concept of controlling the body, if in a different way from the dressage-obsessed seventeenth (see Chapter 3 below). The kind of physical self-mastery boasted of by Merteuil—a suppression of spontaneous bodily response that makes her appear impassive when she is undergoing pain or experiencing pleasure—is no doubt an extreme case. But it illustrates a new philosophy of human autonomy which two aspects of contemporary culture might have seemed to call into question, one the philosophy of determinism and the other discoveries about the nervous system.

The so-called animal propensities alluded to in works such as *Le Neveu de Rameau*, with its references to the menagerie of social outcasts and their concern with satisfying physical needs, are sharply distinct from the 'higher' ones apparently governed by acts of conscious will, and it is partly in this contrast that the divergence between the philosopher Moi and the nephew Lui consists. True, *La Religieuse* seems a more obvious source for reflections on the conflict between spirit and flesh, mind and body, because they are essentially bound up with the religious life. But the resolutely secular *Neveu de Rameau* depicts the tensions equally forcefully. Diderot's monistic conviction that mind is a part of body does not prevent him from occasionally seeing them as antagonists, and in the person of the Nephew body inevitably has the upper hand. To be forced to do as Moi advises and abandon the life of pleasure for the sake of abstract values would be, Lui says, to be 'tiré comme par deux forces contraires' and made to '[marcher] de guingois dans le chemin de la vie' (p. 90). As a believer in the primacy of organic sensation and the paramount claims of hedonism he cannot accept the need to subordinate them to a vague imperative that would set his very body against itself. Body, in this dialogue, is far from being the metaphor it had been since antiquity, something to be translated into the abstractions of religious or philosophical thought; it is a raging actuality whose needs are far more pressing than those of the spirit. Lui's debate with Moi about this and other issues is inconclusive precisely because it raises questions about the dualist interpretation of man that Diderot did not care to resolve. It is, then, a crucial text in his exploration of links between the human body and the ethical and psychological faculties of mankind.

The areas of behaviour that most preoccupy Lui, all basic bodily processes, show the extent to which he is ruled by primitive reflexes. The Philosopher likes to regard his own conduct as more complex, and in some respects it undoubtedly is. It is he, not Lui, who emphasizes the function of *choice* as a fundamental principle in human life, and so makes a case for the relevance of morality—precisely what is denied in the letter to Landois and by the Bordeu of *Le Rêve de d'Alembert*. Although his case is contested by Lui, the Nephew's denial of free will seems more a matter of personal convenience than one of general conviction. One of Moi's roles in the dialogue, as the hierarchically 'higher' force, is to suppress or inhibit the operations of Lui's 'lower' levels of response; but his success is limited. The simple language of stimulus and response is all that Lui understands, or affects to grasp, and it enables him to maintain the viability of his stereotyped reflex behaviour. Moi is proud of his more elevated mental and psychological functions because he sees them as separate from automatic bodily responses. But one of Lui's achievements in the course of their conversation is to show that their respective actions differ in degree rather than kind.

Moi feels indignant at Lui's disregard for the finer forms of sensibility and the polite social requirements that, in the Philosopher's view, properly govern life. If he admires in Lui a 'tact [si] fin' and a 'si grande sensibilité pour les beautés de l'art musical' (p. 84), he is repelled as well as amused by his lack of bodily inhibition, and by a 'biological' philosophy which seems to preclude all reference either to the psychic domain or to that of higher intentionality. The Nephew's repertoire of *physical* actions and mannerisms indicates a rejection of Moi's opinion that the stimulus to conduct should come from within rather than simply be provoked by events in the outer world, but that in coming from within it should not be basely visceral. Moi too has spontaneous drives and propensities, but he manages to control them in the interests of his superior internalized values:

J'ai un coeur et des yeux; et j'aime a voir une jolie femme. J'aime a sentir sous ma main la fermeté et la rondeur de sa gorge; a presser ses levres des miennes; a puiser la volupté dans ses regards, et a en expirer entre ses bras. Quelquefois avec mes amis, une partie de debauche, meme un peu tumultueuse, ne me deplait pas. Mais je ne vous dissimulerai pas, il m'est infiniment plus doux encor d'avoir secouru le malheureux, d'avoir terminé une affaire epineuse, donné un conseil salutaire [...], rempli les devoirs de mon etat. (p. 42)

Lui, however, is obliged to place more emphasis than Moi on 'lower' instinctual forms of behaviour: as an often starving parasite, he has a much greater preoccupation with simply staying alive.

The superiority Moi feels towards Lui is essentially the superiority of mind over matter, but it is not allowed to stand uncontested. The Philosopher regards the Nephew as both mechanical in his actions and the prisoner of social constraints that he himself has allegedly avoided. He takes a certain pleasure—inconsistently, as we shall see—in detailing Lui's base submission to the desires of his masters: 'Il s'etoit introduit, je ne sais comment, dans quelques maisons honnétes, ou il avoit son couvert, mais a la condition qu'il ne parleroit pas, sans en avoir obtenu la permission. Il se taisoit, et mangeoit de rage. Il etoit excellent a voir dans cette contrainte' (p. 6). But, apart from the ambivalent Philosopher, can others really claim to be autonomous? Lui's patron Bertin is reduced to the same instrumental level as Lui the

parasite and jester, simply a tool in the service of someone's pleasure—
the 'petit marteau' whose whim it is to place himself underneath the
'lourde enclume' of his mistress's body as she thuds rhythmically down
upon him (p. 71). Mme de Merteuil will later dismiss women as
'machines à plaisir', mere constructions for sexual commerce, but
Bertin appears more like the man Merteuil's former lover Valmont
describes himself as—a 'simple commissionnaire du plaisir'. To the
extent that human activity is programmed, the bodies that engage in
it are indeed mechanical. But perhaps the analogy should not be
pushed too far. Bertin may look like a puppet, a 'pagode immobile a
laquelle on auroit attaché un fil au menton, d'ou il descendroit jusque
sous son fauteuil' (p. 47), but he undoubtedly pulls the strings.
Equally, the Nephew is more fully in possession of himself than any
machine could possibly be. His 'concert', after all, *embodies* the
imagined instrument he performs on: he can play himself without any
props, though admittedly he cannot produce any musical sound. He
is like the 'instrument philosophe' mentioned by 'Diderot' in the first
dialogue of *Le Rêve de d'Alembert*, who is 'en même temps le musicien
et l'instrument': 'Supposez au clavecin de la sensibilité et de la
mémoire, et dites-moi s'il ne saura pas, s'il ne se répétera pas de lui-
même, les airs que vous aurez exécutés sur ses touches' (p. 14).

Diderot was intrigued by the possibility of giving life to the
nerveless man-made body, and this note from the *Eléments de
physiologie* is a token of his interest:

Que serait-ce qu'un metier de la manufacture de Lion si l'ouvrier et la
tireuse faisaient un tout sensible avec la trame, la chaine, et le simple [i.e.,
the 'simple' or set of weighted lines in a draw-loom]? Ce serait un animal
semblable à l'araignée qui pense, qui veut, qui se nourrit, se réproduit et
ourdit sa toile. (p. 22)[17]

Automata like Vaucanson's are incapable of functioning without the
activity of an operator, but Lui, whose body *is* his instrument, puts it
and himself into operation at the same time. This makes him a more
considerable figure than Moi is inclined to allow (since he believes
whatever originality Lui possesses to be compromised by the social
pantomime he has become caught up in).

In any case, one might want to question the Philosopher's right to
regard himself as free spirit in comparison with the Nephew's base
body: in earlier life, as Lui points out, he had been as guilty of dancing
the vile dance as any of the reprobates and time-servers he despises.

It is true, however, that now he barely appears corporeal: no physical description of him is given,[18] and if he pursues 'catins' they are merely his wayward thoughts. Yet Lui is no more willing than Moi to be reduced to the level of mere bodily substance, despite the dialogue's dwelling on his constant preoccupation with food: he certainly has a mind, if not the conscience whose absence in him so shocks the Philosopher. But this mind is rarely separated from his viscera, whose urgent demands fuel most of his purposive activity. 'Son premier soin, le matin, quand il est levé, est de sçavoir ou il dinera; après diner, il pense ou il ira souper' (p. 5). Perhaps, though, his innards do not dictate everything: his artistic sensibility cannot simply be reduced to the promptings of a hungry gut, and his frustration at being an artistic failure rather than a genius conveys a real anguish.

Diderot is careful to suggest that his exuberant 'performances', in which he mimics all the instruments of the orchestra without actually having any of them to play, are governed by the adjacent organ of the diaphragm, the alleged seat of sensibility whose uncontrolled spasms are described in other works of Diderot's as ruining art. The *Paradoxe sur le comédien* argues that to be at the mercy of one's diaphragm, as women in general and artists seized by the frenzied impetus of creativity habitually are, is to be condemned to a condition of inferiority. True and lasting achievement in art and life belongs to the man—and it seems necessarily to be a man (see Chapter 6 below)—who controls his sensibility through the operations of intellect. If Lui's performances are art at all, then they are deemed second-rate both because of their impermanence and because of their essential emptiness.

It is a familiar critical observation that there is no victor in the debate between Moi and Lui, which might be taken to mean that, for all the materialist emphasis of this imaginative work, body does not assert final authority over mind. Yet if the Philosopher's intellect wins some victories, so do the Nephew's vitality and the sheer strength of his organs. Moi's world, for all its seeming order and sense of stable values, is pale and complacent; Lui's is colourful and energetic, despite its precariousness and moral barrenness. And as body trips off to the opera at the end of the dialogue, it somehow seems to have scored the more dazzling points. Diderot is still convinced of *cogito*'s bloodlessness, preferring to present dualities rather than argue for philosophical dualism.

Sensibility and Perception

As Diderot emphasizes elsewhere, body and mind are anyway at bottom physiological issues.[19] By focusing on sensibility as a property of the nervous system as well as an emotional and moral disposition, eighteenth-century thinkers succeeded in bringing together medicine and philosophy, physicalism and ethics. This in turn made possible a discussion of the way bodily conditions affect one's perception of the world—the kind of discussion Diderot had so dangerously engaged in in the *Lettre sur les aveugles,* whose boldness led to his imprisonment at Vincennes. If all knowledge comes from the senses, then the possession or lack of organs must crucially shape the ideas one conceives: as the *Lettre* puts it, 'je n'ai jamais douté que l'état de nos organes et de nos sens n'ait beaucoup d'influence sur notre métaphysique et sur notre morale, et que nos idées les plus purement intellectuelles [...] ne tiennent de fort près à la conformation de notre corps' (p. 92). Depending on the perceptual means at one's disposal, one cognates the world in a particular way, which means that there is never a fixed 'version' of it to be apprehended—precisely the view of perpetual flux that Diderot shared with Montaigne. When Lui affirms in *Le Neveu de Rameau* that he lacks certain moral perceptions because he does not have the 'fibre' that would have enabled him to apprehend them, he is arguing in this tradition. On the other hand, as is well known, sensory deprivation may sharpen perception. The *Lettre sur les aveugles* observes that Sophie Volland's blind niece Mélanie de Salignac had been trained to perfect the senses she did possess, and that 'il est incroyable jusqu'où l'on y avait réussi. Le tact lui avait appris, sur les formes des corps, des singularités souvent ignorées de ceux qui avaient les meilleurs yeux' (p. 158). This sensibility, of course, is the purely physical kind alluded to in Fouquet's *Encyclopédie* article of the same name. Its links with the moral variety described in de Jaucourt's article 'Sensibilité (morale)' are not made clear, though body–mind links so signally preoccupied Diderot. Elsewhere he goes to some lengths to caution against the uncritical conflation of the two types, without wanting to deny their common physiological origin. In *La Religieuse* Suzanne Simonin's credulous association of the lesbian Mother Superior's physical sensibility—her proneness to weep and display other signs of organic emotion—and her presumed moral goodness is shown to be a dangerous mistake, though a contemporary story by Marmontel about a woman choosing as son-in-law the suitor who weeps most at a moving play shows how the climate of the times encouraged it.[20] The body's motions and emotions may be subject to more conscious control, in other words, than the naïve observer assumes, however powerful the sway of an individual's given 'organisation'.

From all this it seems unclear that possession of either the 'higher' or the 'lower' powers of sensibility is a good, at least where the mental power to contain bodily impulses is lacking. In *Le Rêve de d'Alembert* Bordeu seems to set the power of mind above the impulses of body when he tells his listener about a priest who overcame the pain of an operation by clutching a crucifix and thinking of God (pp. 75–6). This does not, however, mean a victory for 'hard' dualism over monistic materialism, since Bordeu emphasizes that the mind performing the act of will remains in intimate contact with the body experiencing pain. Elsewhere Diderot shows the reverse process: the organism may so insistently announce its subjection to overpowering sensation, like the toothache or gout he himself was a martyr to, that the sufferer altogether loses the power of thought. These opposing currents neatly underline the fluidity of Diderot's beliefs about perception and the mind–body problem. Bodily perceptions, and the emotions and thoughts engendered by the experience of perception, are conditional on the state of the organs and the corresponding disposition of mind. It follows that Diderot's focus on body is itself necessarily conditional, dependent on a mind already stocked with concepts that the body's various parts have furnished. In that sense, it is indeed true that nothing can be explained without the body.

Notes to Chapter 1

1. Stafford, *Body Criticism*, also detects the influence of Berkeley's philosophy of subjective idealism in this passage (pp. 384 f.).
2. See Aram Vartanian, 'Diderot the Dualist in Spite of Himself', in *Diderot: Digression and Dispersion*, ed. Jack Undank and Herbert Josephs (Lexington, KY: French Forum, 1984), 251. Much of my argument in this chapter is indebted to Vartanian's essay.
3. *Ceci n'est pas un conte*, in *Quatre Contes*, ed. Jacques Proust (Geneva: Droz, 1964), 100.
4. See Richard M. Zaner, *The Problem of Embodiment* (The Hague: Nijhoff, 1964), 164 f.
5. On this concept see Gérard Genette, 'Discours du récit', *Figures III* (Paris: Seuil, 1972), and William F. Edmiston, *Hindsight and Insight: Focalization in Four*

Eighteenth-Century French Novels (Pennsylvania: Pennsylvania State University Press, 1991).

6. See Vila, *Enlightenment*, 154, 170 ff, and Anne Deneys-Tunney, *Ecritures du corps de Descartes à Laclos* (Paris: Presses Universitaires de France, 1992), 148, 151 ff.

7. See Deneys-Tunney, *Ecritures*, 150.

8. Leo Spitzer, 'The Style of Diderot', *Linguistics and Literary History* (Princeton: Princeton University Press, 1948); also Aram Vartanian, 'Erotisme et philosophie chez Diderot', *CAIEF* 13 (1961), 367–90.

9. See also John Yolton, *Locke and French Materialism* (Oxford: Oxford University Press, 1991), 193.

10. Yolton, *Locke*, 194.

11. *Œuvres complètes*, ed. Assézat and Tourneux, iv. 38. The reference is to *City of God* bk. XIV, ch. 15.

12. See Bernd Baertschi, *Les Rapports de l'âme et du corps* (Paris: Vrin, 1992), 37 f.

13. See R. K. French, *Robert Whytt, the Soul and Medicine* (London: Wellcome Institute, 1969), 83.

14. French (*Robert Whytt*, 90) contests Georges Canguilhem's assertion in *La Formation du concept de réflexe au XVIIIᵉ siècle* (Paris: Presses Universitaires de France, 1955) that Whytt failed to consider the possibility of such organizing centres.

15. See André Doyon and Lucien Liaigre, *Jacques Vaucanson* (Paris: Presses Universitaires de France, 1966).

16. See also Jacques Proust, 'De l'*Encyclopédie* au *Neveu de Rameau*: l'objet et le texte', *L'Objet et le texte* (Geneva: Droz, 1980), 184.

17. See also Proust, 'De l'*Encyclopédie*', 190.

18. See Vartanian, 'Dualist', 260 f.

19. See Vila, *Enlightenment*, 13, 154.

20. Jean-François Marmontel, *La Bonne Mère*, in *Œuvres complètes*, 11 vols. (Liège: Bassompierre, 1777), i.

CHAPTER 2

Making Up
(and Dismantling) the Body

Anatomy and Dissection

Mme de Vandeul's biographical essay on her father contains the following note: 'Mon père croyait qu'il était sage d'ouvrir ceux qui n'étaient plus; il croyait cette opération utile aux vivants; il me l'avait plus d'une fois demandé; il l'a donc été.'[1] Diderot thought that he had trained her not to be squeamish by making her attend anatomy classes as a young unmarried woman. But she remarks that she had never been able to read the 'horrible' transcript of his dissection, which allegedly revealed that

La tête était aussi parfaite, aussi bien conservée que celle d'un homme de vingt ans. Un des poumons était plein d'eau; son cœur était les deux tiers plus gros que celui des autres personnes. Il avait la vésicule du fiel entièrement sèche, il n'y avait plus de matière bilieuse; mais elle contenait vingt-une pierres dont la moindre était grosse comme une noisette.

In fact, this is not quite what Diderot's autopsy report says. The document, signed by doctors Dupuy, Bacher and Lesne, reveals that Diderot's heart was at least one-third bigger than normal, and makes no mention of either lung containing water. Indeed, they were 'tressains, de la couleur naturelle a l'age du sujet, mais d'un tiers moins grands qu'ils n'auroient du etre'.[2]

No doubt Angélique de Vandeul would have been less repelled had she been reading about someone else's dissection: there was, after all, a long-standing tradition of treating such occasions as a social amusement,[3] and Molière's Thomas Diafoirus is being less eccentric than modern audiences may assume when he invites his fiancée to watch a body being opened up.[4] Diderot himself, who much regretted the inadequacy of his own education in anatomy and physiology,[5] considered that dissection was far too little practised. It had much to teach both lay and medical observers,[6] according to his addition to d'Alembert's *Encyclopédie* article 'Cadavre', but was not for the faint-hearted: 'Il ne faudroit pas se contenter d'un examen superficiel; il faudroit fouiller les visceres, et remarquer attentivement les accidens produits dans chacun et dans toute l'économie animale.' Yet, he continued,

La conservation des hommes et les progrès de l'art de les guérir, sont des objets si importans, que dans une société bien policée les prêtres ne devroient recevoir les *cadavres* que des mains de l'anatomiste, et qu'il devroit y avoir une loi qui défendît l'inhumation d'un corps avant son ouverture. Quelle foule de connoissances n'acquerroit-on pas par ce moyen! Combien de phénomènes qu'on ne soupçonne pas et qu'on ignorera toujours, parce qu'il n'y a que la dissection fréquente des *cadavres* qui puisse les faire appercevoir! La conservation de la vie est un objet dont les particuliers s'occupent assez, mais qui me semble trop négligé par la société.

Bordeu, who is heard to remark in *Le Rêve de d'Alembert* that 'on ne dissèque pas assez' (pp. 53–4), supported these views.

But obtaining cadavers was easier said than done. It was claimed of Mlle Biheron, Angélique Diderot's anatomy teacher, that she was forced to pay 'des personnes peu scrupuleuses' to steal dead bodies for her to dissect and model her wax dummies from,[7] because only the public schools of medicine were entitled to ask the Paris hospitals for corpses. In any case, they themselves received no more than one-thirtieth of their need.[8] (The Dean of the Faculty of Medicine had jurisdiction over the distribution of the remains of recently executed criminals, but the hospitals were often unwilling to release them to surgeons.) Until the Collège de chirurgie was granted permission in 1770 to obtain cadavers from the Hôpital général 'de la même manière que l'on est dans l'usage de faire pour les professeurs d'anatomie du Jardin du Roi et de Saint Cosme', the professor of anatomy at the Collège, Antoine Portal, had to pay for bodies to dissect out of his own pocket.[9] Private schools were in an even worse position. They resorted to paying grave-robbers to steal corpses for them from cemeteries, as Mlle Biheron allegedly did, bribing hospital attendants, colluding with hospital surgeons and even having murders expressly committed. As late as the end of the eighteenth century, the great physician Bichat was making night-time forays to churchyards.[10]

In 1771 Diderot told Dr Antoine Petit, one of his many medical friends and at that time the 'maître d'anatomie' at the Jardin du Roi, that his knowledge of anatomy was confined to what he had learnt at college, from attending the courses of the surgeon César Verdier (who had published an *Abrégé de l'anatomie du corps humain* in 1734) and from visiting the *cabinet* of Mlle Biheron (*Corr.* xi. 72). Verdier's lectures actually left no trace on his work, and much of his technical knowledge in fact came from reading Haller's *Primae lineae physiologiae*. Yet it does seem possible, as we shall see, that Verdier's particular areas of expertise—the bones and the muscles—informed some of Diderot's writings, such as those sections of the *Salons* that discuss the anatomy and osteology of figures in historical and mythological painting.

Mlle Biheron, a one-time neighbour of Diderot's in the place de l'Estrapade, became his teacher as well as his protégée. He introduced friends and visitors to her *cabinet*, which she opened every Wednesday to the public for the modest sum of three *livres*. 'Il n'a guère passé d'étrangers à Paris qui n'aient visité cette fille singulière et qui n'aient vu ses ouvrages', he wrote in the *Mémoires pour Catherine II* (p. 88), trying to interest the Empress in her work. Grimm, like d'Alembert, did Biheron's week-long course in anatomy, and promised to recommend her to Catherine. This effort came to nothing, though the Czarina did eventually buy some of Biheron's wax models for the Hermitage. The British physician Sir John Pringle praised her, saying that her figures were indistinguishable from real cadavers except for the fact that they did not smell,[11] and she was also supported by the surgeon Sauveur Morand, who eulogized her work at the Académie des sciences on 23 June 1759.[12] Even the politician John Wilkes seems, at Diderot's behest, to have welcomed her in London, where the jealousy of the Paris medical profession caused her twice to take refuge, and where she may have taught in 1771.[13] (On 10 July 1772 Diderot would tell Wilkes that 'Mlle Biheron se loue infiniment de vous', *Corr.* xii. 84.)

In his *Mémoires secrets* Bachaumont, who was commenting on Biheron's work as early as 1763, remarked that her models were apparently constructed from a variety of materials,[14] though Diderot believed that they were simply made of wax.[15] Mercier would later observe that they did not melt in the heat,[16] while Grimm admitted that he had no idea what their basic substance was.[17] In Bachaumont's view, the models 'pourraient être fort utiles pour plusieurs opérations', and Biheron deserved encouragement from the government. She remained poor, however, lacking wealthy patrons (perhaps, as Grimm suggested, because she had never been pretty), and had to rely on opening her *cabinet* and giving anatomical demonstrations to subsist.

Diderot's own support for this gifted but unfortunate artist recalls his similarly disinterested patronage a few years earlier of the equally ill-endowed and struggling Anna Therbusch.[18] It was only slightly more successful. Like Grimm, he failed to 'sell' Biheron to Catherine II, though he pressed the empress to employ her as a teacher at Smolnyi Monastir, her school for girls in St Petersburg. He emphasized the moral benefits which such a devout woman's instruction would bring in a letter to Betzki of 15 June 1774,[19] and remarked in the *Mémoires pour Catherine II* that

Une fille devient mère, et une teinture légère d'anatomie lui convient si fort, et avant de le devenir, et quand elle le devient, et après qu'elle l'est devenue!

C'est ainsi que j'ai coupé racine à la curiosité dans ma fille. Quand elle a tout su, elle n'a plus rien cherché à savoir. Son imagination s'est assoupie et ses mœurs n'en sont restées que plus pures. (p. 86)

But Diderot's pedagogical boldness was not quite what it appeared. The *Mémoires* reveal that Angélique, who did the anatomy course with twenty other girls of decent birth and a hundred society ladies a year or two before her marriage, was not allowed to see 'les parties de la génération de l'un et de l'autre sexe', a privilege granted only to married women (p. 88). The result was to make her 'smattering' of anatomy deficient in an area that must have seemed of particular importance to a future wife, and the one most likely to provoke both her curiosity and her imagination. Given all of this, it hardly seems surprising that Mme de Vandeul had no stomach for her father's real dissection. After all, she had been brought up on a sanitized copy, something that was to prepare its beholder for life (or, as Diderot puts it in the *Mémoires pour Catherine II*, 'le péril et les suites de l'approche de l'homme' and 'la valeur de tous les propos séducteurs qu'on a pu lui tenir', p. 87) only by being *other* than life. Mlle Biheron's models, secret constructions of unknown substances, were as much 'tissus de fausseté' as the works of art described in the *Salons*.

Other sources of anatomical enlightenment available to Angélique Diderot, on the other hand, were more informative. Some of the *Encyclopédie*'s plates are highly explicit, and an intelligent woman with an inquiring spirit would have found much of interest in them (and not merely in the many obstetric engravings). One set, for example, shows the genitals of hermaphrodites in a highly naturalistic manner, and among the complete figures depicted are subjects gazing intently at their sex organs. This clarity reflects a general trend in medical texts of the eighteenth century, which contained increasingly graphic illustrations of the female genitals (normally covered up in earlier publications).[20] Even when not hidden away, the organs of reproduction had often been presented as mere disembodied parts, and so had barely appeared erotic. Some of Biheron's models take this form; but the new fashion suggests a mood of greater voyeurism as well as a move towards more intense scientific scrutiny. Or is the voyeuristic strain in the mind rather than in the depiction? Diderot, at least, emphasized the unsuggestive pedagogic usefulness of the complete and life-size models made by Biheron, which Angélique and other future wives studied.

Obviously, the fact that Diderot, Grimm, d'Alembert and other men claimed to have profited greatly from her courses implied that Biheron was more than an expert in obstetrics: d'Alembert, according to the *Mémoires pour Catherine II*, said that he had learnt more anatomy from her than from six months listening to the physician Ferrein. But in the *Mémoires* Diderot particularly stresses her expertise in obstetric matters, presumably because he imagines that this will be of most relevance to Catherine's schoolgirls. One of Biheron's most famous productions was an articulated model of a woman whose hinged belly opened up to reveal a foetus in her womb, as well as other internal organs which could be removed and examined at leisure: this was the work for which she was highly commended at the Académie des sciences in 1770. (Her success, incidentally, may explain the professional hostility that forced her to flee to England.) Angélique's training, Diderot remarks in the *Mémoires*, gave her 'une fermeté qu'on n'a peut-être jamais vue à aucune femme ignorante'. Of course he is exaggerating for effect. Although he seems genuinely to have believed that woman's lack of learning conduced to her enslavement, he does not always sound as distressed by the fact as he might: the highly ambiguous 'Sur les femmes', for instance, sometimes implies that keeping the female sex unenlightened is society's proper way of subjugating them. And if Diderot took his daughter's education seriously, his moralistic and bourgeois self was clearly happy to see her remain in a state of crucial anatomical ignorance.

Biheron had begun making her models only after spending years observing real dissections, and her passion for anatomy saved her from what the *Correspondance littéraire* calls the 'dégoût souvent invincible de voir opérer et démontrer sur des cadavres' (ix. 276–7). According to Delacoux, she worked on putrefying cadavers that often remained in her *cabinet* for days before she began dissecting (p. 34); yet Mme de Genlis reports that she still called this garden annexe her 'petit boudoir', and that it 'faisait ses délices'.[21] She was an empiricist after Diderot's heart, probing as deeply as he required any dissecter of the human form—artist, writer or philosopher—to do. As he remarked to Catherine II, she showed both the hidden body ('le cerveau, le cervelet et toutes ses parties [...], les poumons, le cœur, l'estomac, la rate, les intestins, la vessie, la matrice, les muscles, les veines, les artères etc.') and the outwardly revealed parts of eye, ear, chest and, to selected observers, the genitals (p. 86).

The anatomical model belonged to a tradition well established by the mid-eighteenth century,[22] but Biheron's were much more realistic than most of their predecessors. Yet Boileau had earlier remarked that there should be limitations to the lifelikeness of any wax model, because

L'imitation parfaite d'un cadavre, représenté en cire avec toutes les couleurs sans aucune différence sensible, cette imitation ne serait pas supportable; de même d'un crapaud, d'une couleuvre etc. Et c'est pourquoi les portraits que Benoît [a famous seventeenth-century wax modeller] faisait en cire, n'ont pas réussi; parce qu'ils étaient trop ressemblants.[23]

But if the same model were done in marble or as a painting, the imitations would please, because however perfect they were the eye and mind would perceive the difference between art and nature that Benoît's work allegedly obscured. Biheron's work may also have seemed superficially related to later, more popular offerings in Paris, like the waxwork shows of the Swiss Curtius (the uncle of the future Mme Tussaud), who drew in crowds with his displays at the Palais-Royal and on the boulevards. But Biheron's models differed essentially from Curtius's. For one thing, they were not portraits of known people, and for another they were instruments of teaching rather than entertainment. Above all, they were concerned with far more than the depiction of externals. Commentators naturally saw the mimetic fidelity of her creations as an essential part of the Enlightenment project of demonstrating how the human organism functioned in all its mechanical detail.

Since Biheron was, as Grimm remarked, 'infiniment dévote',[24] she had no interest in attempting to reduce the human body to a simple physical system of causes and effects. Her lessons in corporeal intelligence stopped short of discussing the unknown and unverifiable life-forces that Diderot fearlessly debates in *Le Rêve de d'Alembert*. The fact, too, that she was an anatomist rather than a physiologist—that is, she was concerned with the structure of the organism rather than its dynamic functioning—meant that she could legitimately withhold comment on what vital principle might lurk inside the human frame.

Depicting the Body

Sometimes, though not in the case of Biheron's models, Diderot's enthusiasm for grasping the structure of the body became over-demanding. Having begun to worry whether modern artists attended dissections as conscientiously as Leonardo and Michelangelo had done, he asked Dr Petit how deeply they needed to have studied anatomy in order to depict the human figure with authority. Petit gave a cautious answer: 'Il suffit, à mon avis, pour remplir cet objet [of perfecting "les arts plastiques"], de voir et d'observer avec attention'.[25] Diderot himself regarded anatomical accuracy as particularly important in sculpture, where 'un membre, même faiblement estropié, ôte à une statue presque tout son prix';[26] he writes in the 1765 *Salon* that sculptors need to observe the model even longer than painters, whose use of colour can easily seduce the otherwise critical eye. He alleges, however, that both types of artist actually ignore it after the age of 50 (*Salons*, ii. 212). Yet Diderot's conviction that anatomical precision mattered in sculpture is contradicted by his comments in the same *Salon* on the Laocoon group. Asking why Laocoon's foreshortened leg is longer than the other one, he answers in terms of aesthetic values rather than the demands of representational accuracy: 'C'est que, sans cette incorrection hardie de dessin, la figure eût été déplaisante à l'œil; c'est qu'il y a des effets de nature qu'il faut pallier ou négliger' (ii. 211). Furthermore, the concreteness of sculpture entails other kinds of adaptation in which the claims of artistic propriety supervene over those of exact mimesis. When the artist sculpts a naked seated woman, Diderot writes, he cannot simply re-present the spreading fat of her buttocks; he has to lie, converting flesh into a substance as hard and resilient as stone, in order to prevent it from looking unappetizing. Alternatively, he has to throw drapery over the offending part to conceal its bulge.

This kind of expedient is like others Diderot presents in the *Salons*, tricks of the trade employed to overcome difficulties that are beyond the resources of art. They show how often it is obliged to bend the mimetic rule that Diderot himself only intermittently upholds. For he shared Boileau's view that art has to be seen as *not* the thing itself in order to persuade and please the beholder: the *Salons* call the direct reproduction of phenomena as they appear to the artist unworthy. It is not merely a matter of avoiding the 'puanteur' and moral indelicacy of real life—what Addison described as the 'dunghill' that art transforms into something sublime—and so betraying the fabricated nature of the artefact. The painting or sculpture must announce that it is a transposition of nature if it is to seem admirable;[27] trompe-l'œil, Diderot says elsewhere, is not artistically impressive, because it is taken for reality. True art, by contrast, advertises the way it diverges from the real, and so transcends nature.

Whether Biheron intended her models to be works of art rather than simple pedagogical tools must be a matter of conjecture. According to Boileau, the kind of truth to life they manifested should have robbed them of artistic status, but Angélique Diderot was certainly aware of their fabricated nature.

Diderot's uncertainty about the merits of exact resemblance was generally resolved into an acceptance of art's falsehood. The successful painting or sculpture, he thought, heightened reality rather than hopelessly trying to re-present it. He objected to artists reshaping the world they imitated out of ignorance or incompetence, but also thought that knowing too much about the human form could adversely affect the way they rendered it. 'L'étude profonde de l'anatomie a plus gâté d'artistes qu'elle n'en a perfectionné. En peinture comme en morale, il est bien dangereux de voir sous la peau.'[28] On the face of it, this is a puzzling statement: it seems to fly in the face of the mimetic principles Diderot has been enunciating. What he seems to mean is that certain forms of knowledge can inflate the pride of the knower and so make him eager to display his learning at all costs. A painter who has studied the *écorché* in the academy, for example, is inclined to emphasize musculature 'en dépit de la peau et des graisses' even when he is depicting the female form; and yet 'On sait bien que les contours sont doux dans les femmes, qu'on y discerne à peine les muscles, et que toutes leurs formes s'arrondissent'. Artists trained from the model rather than real life, he concludes, are rarely able to strike the balance between capturing a woman's characteristic plumpness and conveying the hint of her concealed strength.

Whatever his reservations, and despite the cautions Dr Petit had voiced, Diderot still insisted that artists needed to understand anatomical principles. Anatomy had been an official subject of study at the Académie royale de peinture et de sculpture since its foundation, but it was inadequately taught in the eighteenth century: by the 1750s courses had become optional, and were given outside the confines of the institution. In 1764 the Académie appealed to the Crown for funds to pay for 'une belle figure anatomique en cire colorée' with movable muscles, for pupils to work from; but until 1772 Jean Suë, formerly the chief surgeon at the Hôpital de la Charité and an 'adjoint à professeur' at the Académie, was still demonstrating exclusively from the skeleton and cadaver. Although living models were available thereafter, the prize in anatomy founded by La Tour in 1776 was never awarded.[29]

One reason for this may have been that artists were encouraged to concentrate on prestigious large-scale history paintings: Diderot thought that the 'grande machine' foresook precise delineation because it depended on sweeping overall effect.

L'immensité du travail rend le peintre d'histoire négligent dans les détails. Où est celui de nos peintres qui se soucie de faire des pieds et des mains? Il vise, dit-il, à l'effet général; et ces misères-là n'y font rien. Ce n'était pas l'avis de Paul Véronèse; mais c'est le sien. Presque toutes les grandes compositions sont croquées. (*Essais sur la peinture*, p. 712)

The fact that life drawing at the Académie was done from the male model, and so effectively discouraged close observation of the female frame, may explain another conventional weakness in figurative painting. The male shape was taken to be normative, and not until roughly mid-century was the specific aspect of the woman's skeleton definitively represented.[30] The habit of enveloping women in a blanket of fat, which survived so long and seems to epitomize the sensuousness of ancien régime art, may partly derive from ignorance of their underlying shape: it meant that the most straightforward way of depicting sexual difference was simply via the flesh.

It might be thought that the dissemination of more accurate information about the female anatomy would have contributed to a general clarifying of woman's position relative to man in the social, cultural and political life of the Enlightenment, but it scarcely seems to have done so. If some now saw her as *other* rather than *lesser*, the fact that the female skull was smaller than the male was still standardly used as evidence that women must continue to be excluded from areas of public life where the intellectual superiority associated with big (male) heads was required.[31] The publication of more scientific anatomical *drawings* in the course of the eighteenth century ought similarly to have had a positive effect on the teaching and practice of life drawing in the Académie, but to judge by some of Diderot's Salon critiques this was not always the case. His commentary in the 1767 *Salon* on the flaccid body of an imploring mother in Doyen's *Le Miracle des ardents* implies that the artist simply took the easy way out of a testing situation: an undefined mass shrouded in a billowing costume is simpler to paint than an anatomically precise form. Doyen, an artist much influenced by Rubens, was above all a colourist, and often grew impatient with the difficult requirements of exact draughtmanship. The rococo softness of the upper part of the *Miracle des ardents* gives way to a passionate pre-Romantic emotionalism lower down, but Diderot still finds the melodrama of the scene compromised by a blowsy impressionism of style. The unfocused airiness of the angels surrounding St Genevieve, for instance, makes their bodies look boneless, turning them into

des espèces de cupidons soufflés et transparens; tant qu'il sera de convention que ces natures idéales sont de chair et d'os, il faudra les faire de chair et d'os. C'était la même faute dans votre ancien tableau de *Diomède et Vénus*, la déesse ressemblait à une grande vessie sur laquelle on n'aurait pu s'appliquer avec un peu d'action sans l'exposer à crever avec explosion. (*Salons*, iii. 181)

Diderot frequently castigates this kind of ineptitude in the *Salons*. In the same year as Doyen exhibited the *Miracle des ardents*, Fragonard submitted a 'belle et grande omelette d'enfans' painted in a 'cotoneux' manner: 'Ce mot n'a peut-être encore été dit, mais il rend bien et si bien, qu'on prendrait cette composition pour un lambeau d'une belle toison de brebis [...] dont les poils entremêlés ont formé par hasard des guirlandes d'enfans' (iii. 279–80). As Diderot remarks in the *Essais sur la peinture*, children may be a 'masse informe et fluide qui cherche à se développer' (p. 668), but that does not excuse a complete neglect of osteology. In 1765 he registers his displeasure at Vien's depiction of a supposedly starving child in another plague scene: the infant's belly sags, he holds his mother with his chubby arms, and 'il est si mou, qu'on le prendroit pour une belle peau rembourrée de coton; il n'y a point d'os là-dessous. J'ai beau chercher quelques traces effrayantes des horreurs de la famine et de la peste, quelques incidens horribles qui caractérisent ces fléaux, il n'y en a point' (*Salons*, ii. 88).

Every time Diderot refers to the portrayal of human figures in such terms—sacks of wool, mounds of whipped cream, banks of snow, bits of fleece, fluffy omelettes—he is attacking the aversion to recti-linearity which he associates with Boucher's school.[32] Yet even the supposedly severe and classicizing work of Vien is infused with a perfumed prettiness that constitutes the charm of the eighteenth century's 'aimable antiquité'. The label of regenerator Vien is occasionally given goes against the evidence of his paintings, which reveal a clear affinity with an earlier idiom. Though Diderot's diatribes against Boucher are sharpened by the distaste he allegedly feels for a man who used colour in the service of a meretricious frivolity, the semblance of restraint Vien derives from his easy classicism actually masks a sensuality that is no less real. Indeed, Diderot half-acknowledges it in his commentary on Vien's 1763 *Marchande d'amours*:

C'est une petite ode tout à fait anacréontique. C'est dommage que cette composition soit un peu déparée par un geste indécent de ce petit Amour-papillon que l'esclave tient par les ailes; il a la main droite appuyée au pli de son bras gauche qui, en se relevant, indique d'une manière très-significative la mesure du plaisir qu'il promet. (*Salons*, i. 210)

If the robust fleshiness of Boucher has been bypassed, the attempt at seduction remains.

Diderot had nothing against fleshiness *per se*; it was the various implications fat carried that he took issue with. When he poured scorn on flabby women and plump cherubs in the *Salons*, it was not just because they offended against some severe and moralizing anti-rococo principle; they might also betray the artist's lack of anatomical knowledge, or his lazy inattention.[33] Nor do the moral objections to voluptuousness always seem very sincere. The generous curves of Boucher's women promise a pleasure that the hedonist in Diderot cannot gainsay, but which the bourgeois *père de famille* must deny. Is this why he ignores the meretriciousness of Greuze's women? In general he only half-denies the appeal of breasts and buttocks, as this quotation from the *Pensées détachées sur la peinture* makes clear:

Je ne suis pas un capucin; j'avoue cependant que je sacrifierais volontiers le plaisir de voir de belles nudités, si je pouvais hâter le moment où la peinture et la sculpture, plus décentes et plus morales, songeront à concourir, avec les autres beaux-arts, à inspirer la vertu et à épurer les mœurs. Il me semble que j'ai assez vu de tétons et de fesses; ces objets séduisants contrarient l'émotion de l'âme, par le trouble qu'ils jettent dans les sens. (p. 767)

One might have expected that women artists would offend less regularly against the model when painting their own sex, but Diderot finds them just as guilty of promoting fleshiness as men. Perhaps he is being unfair. After all, the female body is physically and physiologically an 'adiabatic system' or storehouse of energy not usually intended for violent motor activity, which according to some recent authorities explains why its muscles are generally flabby and underdeveloped.[34] It might seem natural, therefore, for the artistic representation of women to emphasize the subcutaneous fat that accentuates their contours. If Diderot professes intolerance of this, he also protests against the general anatomical deficiencies he perceives in women's work. The fact that these might stem from a lack of training perhaps suggests that he should have been less critical. Female artists, who were debarred from attending classes and lectures at the Académie royale de peinture et de sculpture, had to study the nude privately, and naturally used such models as they could find. Diderot, however, is often dissatisfied with them for doing so. He takes Anna Therbusch to task for painting in her *Jupiter métamorphosé surprend Antiope* a nymph '[dont les] bras, les cuisses, les jambes sont de chairs, de chairs si molles, si flasques, mais si flasques, mais si molles, qu'à la place de Jupiter j'aurais regretté les frais de la métamorphose' (*Salons*, iii. 250–1). Antiope, in other words, has been based on a chambermaid, 'à son col, à ses doigts courts, à ses jambes grêles, à ses pieds, dont les orteils [sont] difformes, à son caractère ignoble'. But male artists are lampooned for resorting to the same class of (female) model, without Diderot's bothering to reflect that no other sitter may have been available to them either. In the *Salon* of 1763 he attacks Carle Van Loo for having chosen to depict in *Les Grâces enchaînées par l'Amour* women with 'le gros embonpoint d'une servante d'hôtellerie' (i. 196), and in 1767 he remarks that La Grenée's *La Poésie et la Philosophie* has given the figure of Philosophy the arm of a servant (iii. 104), though he does not explain what defines it as such. Two years later he finds the same artist guilty of painting the Virgin Mary with the head and arms of a peasant woman (iv. 79–80).

Sometimes his sexualized perceptions are expressed in a different way. The commentary on Carle Van Loo's *Les Grâces enchaînées par l'Amour* expertly notes that one of the Graces has 'les traces des muscles du corps de l'homme' (i. 197), but then unconvincingly disclaims expertise in another anatomical area—'Sans s'entendre beaucoup en proportions, on est choqué du peu de distance de la hanche au-dessous du bras'. Is Diderot really ignorant of female proportions, or is it rather that he still lacks critical confidence? By the end of the decade he has become more assured, openly correcting the draughtmanship of the same La Grenée whose accuracy he had praised at its beginning. The *male* figures in a picture exhibited in 1769 are described as distorted and crippled, the *females* as suffering from dislocation of the limbs. Perhaps La Grenée's models were at fault: the creatures depicted 'from life' might actually have been corpses obtained from the hangman or surgeon, or malefactors broken on the wheel.[35] But Diderot has also found a critical voice, and deepened his acquaintance with the human body by starting to assemble material for the *Eléments de physiologie*.[36]

Although a note he wrote himself between 1778 and 1780 recommended the reading of 'la phisiologie de haller' (that is, the *Primae lineae physiologiae*) as though it were new to him (*Eléments*, p. xiv), he had in fact studied the work much earlier: he refers to it negatively in the *Pensées sur l'interprétation de la nature* of 1753, but rates it much more highly when he resumes his studies in the 1760s. Haller's *magnum opus*, the *Elementa physiologiae corporis humani*, was published in 1766. Neither this work nor the *Primae lineae* would necessarily have taught Diderot about canonical proportions, and in any case, as we shall see, he had become at least as interested in deviations from the anatomical and physiological norm since the middle of the century. But the dissemination of works like Haller's focused his attention on bodily forms and functions in ways that paralleled his lifelong interest in body-language, and lent increased authority to his discussions.

This emerges clearly in his critique of Greuze's *Septime Sévère reprochant à Caracalla son fils d'avoir attenté à sa vie dans les défilés d'Ecosse*. Some of his confidence, it is true, must derive from his sharing the opinion of the Académie royale de peinture et de sculpture, which in 1769 refused Greuze the title of history painter on the strength of this work, and of La Grenée, who answered Greuze's petulant response to the Académie's verdict by silently marking the examples of incorrect draughtmanship on the canvas itself (*Salons*, iv. 104). Diderot's own commentary is pitilessly direct:

Le Septime Sévère est ignoble de caractère [...]. Il est mal dessiné, il a le poignet cassé. La distance du cou au sternum est démesurée, on ne sait où va ni à quoi appartient le genou de la cuisse droite qui fait relever la couverture

[...]. Greuze est sorti de son genre: imitateur scrupuleux de la nature, il n'a pas su s'élever à la sorte d'exagération qu'exige la peinture historique. (iv. 105–6)

Diderot's use of the word 'exagération' is less pregnant with meaning than at first appears. The inference is simply that Greuze's main characters are petty, with Caracalla appearing even baser than his father—'c'est un vil et bas coquin [qui] irait à merveille dans une scène champêtre et domestique' (iv. 106). The *anatomical* exaggeration Diderot notes in the figure of Sévère is a straightforward breach of the proportional norm, and reprehensible on that account. Only when the artistic imperative is sufficiently compelling, in other words, may the canon of regularity be ignored, as in the Laocoon group. Ironically, though, one of the main faults of Greuze's picture may simply have been that it was ahead of its time. Its bas-relief composition and the uncompromising spirit of antiquity it evoked anticipated a style that would be perfectly acceptable a few years later, but could not be countenanced in 1769. The reasons given for Greuze's rejection, after all, were hardly compelling: as Diderot's dismissive commentaries repeatedly reveal, other paintings that flouted anatomical and physiological conventions were unblinkingly accepted by the Académie.

Indeed, had Greuze not severed all links with the institution in a fit of pique, he might have derived some pleasure from administering the same sort of correction to La Grenée's work as La Grenée had done to his. In 1771 La Grenée's *Mars et Vénus* prompted in Diderot a reflection that was probably fuelled by the research he had done for the *Eléments de physiologie*, and perhaps by his anatomical studies with Mlle Biheron:

Je ne puis m'empêcher de faire remarquer à M. La Grenée ce qu'il sait cependant mieux que moi, que les intestins mobiles et contenus dans le bas-ventre suivent ordinairement la pente que le corps leur donne; qu'ainsi Vénus couchée du côté gauche, la partie droite de son ventre doit paraître applatie, puis que la gauche est sensée remplie. Un plâtre peut présenter ce mauvais effet, mais la nature bien observée dit et montre le contraire. (*Salons*, iv. 170)[37]

The advice Dr Petit gave to Diderot at about this time, that the painter should *see* and *observe* attentively, may come to mind.

Bodily Unity

The paramount principle of bodily unity leads Diderot to brand as flawed whatever creates incoherence, like the dislocated shoulders and legs painted by La Grenée and the disproportionate outstretched arm of Greuze's emperor, rather than to criticize irregularity *per se*. *Natural* irregularity is entirely acceptable, as the *Essais sur la peinture* argue:

Malgré l'ignorance des effets et des causes, et les règles de convention qui en ont été les suites [i.e., normative rules unsupported by actual observation], j'ai peine à douter qu'un artiste qui oserait négliger ces règles, pour s'assujettir à une imitation rigoureuse de la nature, ne fût souvent justifié de ses pieds trop gros, de ses jambes courtes, de ses genoux gonflés, de ses têtes lourdes et pesantes, par ce tact fin que nous tenons de l'observation continue des phénomènes, et qui nous ferait sentir une liaison secrète, un enchaînement nécessaire entre ces difformités.

Un nez tors, en nature, n'offense point, parce que tout tient; on est conduit à cette difformité par de petites altérations adjacentes qui l'amènent et la sauvent. Tordez le nez à l'Antinoüs, en laissant le reste tel qu'il est, ce nez sera mal.

Nous disons d'un homme qui passe dans la rue, qu'il est mal fait. Oui, selon nos pauvres règles; mais selon la nature, c'est autre chose. Nous disons d'une statue, qu'elle est dans les proportions les plus belles. Oui, d'après nos pauvres règles; mais selon la nature? [...] Si j'étais initié dans les mystères de l'art, je saurais peut-être jusqu'où l'artiste doit s'assujettir aux proportions reçues, et je vous le dirais. Mais ce que je sais, c'est qu'elles ne tiennent point contre le despotisme de la nature, et que l'âge et la condition en entraînent le sacrifice en cent manières diverses. (pp. 666–7)

The apparent deference to the 'mysteries of art' and 'received proportions' is again disingenuous. Diderot's hostility towards academic ideals and the doctrine of canonical proportions was absolute. He was remarkable even for his time in his promotion of nature and the 'beau désordre' that, he believed, expressed truth more fully than any 'esprit de système' could ever do. To harden experiment and hypothesis into rule is to run counter to the principle of movement that presides over his writing.

This attitude is most straightforwardly expressed when Diderot is discussing the integral coherence of the human figure in art. In 1765 La Grenée is again found wanting:

Il m'a paru que dans une de [ses] compositions la Sainte Anne n'étoit pas aussi vieille du bas du visage que du front et des mains. Quand on a le front plissé de rides et les jointures des mains nouées, le cou est couvert de longues peaux lâches et flasques. (*Salons*, ii. 94)

The famous commentary the same year on Greuze's *La Jeune Fille qui pleure son oiseau mort* is lyrically effusive on the 'truth' of the composition, but finds it false in another way:

Sa tête est de quinze à seize ans, et son bras et sa main, de dix-huit à dix-neuf. C'est un défaut de cette composition qui devient d'autant plus sensible, que la tête appuyée contre la main, une des parties donne tout contre la mesure de l'autre [...]. C'est, mon ami, que la tête a été prise d'après un modèle, et la main d'après un autre. (*Salons*, ii. 147)

The notion that the requirements of unity justify what normative rules decree to be excessive or exaggerated[38] is found in other writings of Diderot's. The short story *Les Deux Amis de Bourbonne* ends with a discussion of three kinds of *conte*, one of them the *conte merveilleux* whose very essence is to enlarge experience beyond the everyday.

La nature y est exagérée; la vérité y est hypothétique; et si le conteur a bien gardé le module qu'il a choisi, si tout répond à ce module et dans les actions, et dans les discours, il a obtenu le degré de perfection que le genre de son ouvrage comportoit, et vous n'avez rien de plus à lui demander. En entrant dans son poëme, vous mettez le pied dans une terre inconnue, où rien ne se passe comme dans celle que vous habitez, mais où tout se fait en grand, comme les choses se font autour de vous en petit. (*Quatre Contes*, pp. 65 f.)

The same principle applies, *mutatis mutandis*, in the visual arts. Diderot illustrates it in the 1765 *Salon* with a discussion of anatomical exaggeration that is naturalized in terms of fitness for a given purpose. The body of Hercules, he writes, breaches the normative proportions of academic art, whose ideal representative is Antinous. Hercules is not simply an enlarged Antinous, but a warrior whose activity has developed parts of his body more fully than others. Whereas Antinous represents 'l'extrême de l'homme oisif [qui] est né grand comme il est', Hercules embodies a 'système exagéré dans certaines parties désignées par la condition de l'homme' (*Salons*, ii. 115–16).

Diderot's interest in the concept of conditions had been announced earlier, in his theoretical writings on the *drame*. The *Entretiens sur 'Le Fils naturel'* of 1757 declare the need for this new genre to portray social types rather than individuals:

ce ne sont pas, à proprement parler, les caractères qu'il faut mettre sur la scène, mais les conditions [...]. C'est la condition, ses devoirs, ses avantages, ses embarras, qui doivent servir de base à l'ouvrage [...]. Les conditions! Combien de détails importants, d'actions publiques et domestiques, de vérités inconnues, de situations nouvelles à tirer de ce fonds! Et les conditions n'ont-elles pas entre elles les mêmes contrastes que les caractères?[39]

Hercules' condition is that of 'l'homme laborieux'. Given his occupation of warrior and slayer of monsters, Diderot asks, where will his bodily development be most apparent? Not in the head or feet, but

Sur le cou [...]. C'est l'origine des muscles et des nerfs, et le cou sera exagéré de grosseur un peu au-delà de la proportion colossale [i.e., the proportions Hercules would exhibit if he were simply an enlarged version of Antinous]. J'en dis autant des épaules, de la poitrine, de tous les muscles propres à ces parties, mais surtout des muscles. Ce sont les bras qui portent la massue, et qui frappent. C'est là que doit être vigoureux un tueur d'hommes, un écraseur de bêtes. (*Salons*, ii. 116)

Gauging the rightness of a form like Hercules' by comparing it with the ideal body of Antinous is as wrong-headed as judging the wide-hipped, generous bodies of Tahitian women described in the *Supplément au Voyage de Bougainville* by the refined and over-delicate ones of their Parisian counterparts. Functional adaptiveness is the proper criterion for assessing anatomical and physiological norms by. Diderot had said something similar in a letter to Sophie Volland of 2 September 1762, remarking that the concept of beauty should be redefined in terms of suitability for performing a particular task. The body of a porter, a dancer or a smith may be called beautiful, whatever its proportions, if it is right for the requirements of his job.

Le bel homme est celui que la nature a formé pour remplir le plus aisément qu'il est possible ces deux grandes fonctions: la conservation de l'individu, qui s'étend à beaucoup de choses, et la propagation de l'espèce, qui s'étend à une. (*Corr.* iv. 129).

'Nature' does not imply anything fixed, since usage and habit can alter the proportions of a body. According to this logic, a hunched back could be called beautiful if it had developed as a result of a porter's daily activities, like his broadened shoulders and bandy legs.

Diderot's interest in the question of the body's adaptability became almost obsessive. The letter to Dr Petit which protests his ignorance of anatomy returns to the subject of the Antinous-type and the Hercules-type, asking for information about the bodily changes that would occur if the former became the latter. (Diderot claimed to want the information for an academic speech to be delivered in St Petersburg, but there is no evidence that he was then planning a visit to Russia, or

ever made such an address.) He asked Petit to imagine not just the
model of the Farnese Hercules 'assommeur de grands chemins', but
also its degeneration into an overweight apoplectic villain, a jealous
lover and finally a lame hunchback. 'En conséquence, j'aurai par degrés
successifs les effets d'une condition, d'une maladie, d'une passion et
d'une difformité, sur les organes extérieures d'une figure originellement
de la plus parfaite régularité' (Corr. xi. 71). Petit's reply, which mingles
common sense and old-fashioned humoral metaphysics, concludes that
the perfect regularity of an idler like Antinous is chimerical, particularly
in the modern world where swaddling-bands, corsets and the artificial
striking of 'society' attitudes all corrupt the ideal. Real-life activities
result in workmen developing big hands and arms, bent backs, small
stomachs and skinny legs, dancers and walkers sturdy buttocks and legs,
and horse-riders protuberant stomachs. Diderot echoes this observation
in the Essais sur la peinture: 'Parmi les artisans, il y a des habitudes de
corps, des physionomies de boutiques et d'ateliers' (p. 699). The Pensées
détachées sur la peinture of 1776–7 onward take up the theme with
reference to the wrestler, who 'n'a pas le bras droit aussi arrondi, aussi
coulant que le bras gauche. Si vous peignez un lutteur, conservez-vous
ce défaut?' (p. 814)—a question one is surprised to find Diderot asking,
given his professed liking for truth rather than idealization.

Elsewhere, though, he makes clear that the new ideal owes little to
the classical demand for regularity. Whatever perfection is, Diderot
asserts, it cannot be understood by reference to existing ideal models.
As the letter to Sophie Volland of 2 September 1762 had argued, the
ideal may precisely be one that flouts accepted canons in the interests
of fresh aesthetic perceptions. It is almost like saying that the useful
work of art necessarily outshines the useless one—a tendentious
claim, but one typical of the Enlightenment.

Deviation

The attack on norms, a constant in Diderot's thought, helps to explain
why the subject of monstrosity interested him so greatly:[40] monsters
may be seen simply as deviations from the standard pattern. As
d'Alembert remarks in Le Rêve de d'Alembert, 'L'homme n'est qu'un
effet commun—le monstre qu'un effet rare; tous les deux également
naturels, également nécessaires' (p. 43). Where, Diderot asks, does one
draw the dividing-line between a malformed man and a freak? At
what point does the active man's bodily development—the porter's

hunched back, Hercules' bulging muscles—become monstrosity? Some anatomical features are such sharp deviations from the standard pattern that they cause dysfunction and even death, which suggests that viability is an important defining criterion. The *Eléments de physiologie* announce that nature exterminates beings—'êtres contra-dictoires'—whose organism does not accord with that of the rest of the universe. 'Elle ne laisse subsister que ceux qui peuvent coéxister supportablement avec l'ordre général' (p. 5). Buffon's *Histoire naturelle de l'homme* provided Diderot with the story of Siamese twins who lived for twenty years joined at the head, shoulders, back, buttocks and thighs, and then died within minutes of each other (*Eléments*, pp. 32, 65, 212). The *Eléments* describe the case of a homosexual Prussian soldier born with a womb, who conceived a child through anal intercourse but died before it could be born: although he was in most respects an anatomically normal male, his 'monstrosity' proved fatal (pp. 189–91). The same work refers to one woman with two wombs and two vaginas (p. 173), another who lacked a womb, a vagina, a clitoris and a vulva, and a third who in the absence of a vagina could conceive and give birth only via the anus (pp. 188–9).

These examples suggest that one possible criterion of monstrosity is the lack (or superabundance) of organs. In the *Lettre sur les aveugles* Saunderson argues that the existence of 'productions monstrueuses' like himself indicates the imperfect order of the universe, and hence the absence of a benevolent and omnipotent creator. 'Qu'avions–nous fait à Dieu, vous et moi, l'un pour avoir cet organe [of sight], l'autre pour en être privé?' (p. 122). The fact that bodily habits actually develop organs, one of the themes of Diderot's correspondence with Petit, might not seem far from the assumption that bodily *needs* would do the same—the view expressed by Bordeu in *Le Rêve de d'Alembert*: 'Les organes produisent les besoins, et réciproquement les besoins produisent les organes' (p. 42). The first half of the statement summarizes an argument advanced in Lucretius' *De rerum natura*, and is uncontroversial: man looks because he possesses eyes.[41] This in turn anticipates the thought of Lamarck, who later observed that 'ce sont [...] ses [the animal's] habitudes [...] qui ont, avec le temps, constitué la forme de son corps, le nombre et l'état de ses organes'.[42] But no declaration of personal need will ever cause Saunderson to become sighted. He is an individual aberration in terms of the general rule, and *ex nihilo* organic generation can occur only over the species as a whole. As Bordeu remarks in *Le Rêve de d'Alembert*,

Supposez une longue suite de générations manchotes,—supposez des efforts
continus,—et vous verrez les deux côtés [d'une] pincette s'étendre, s'étendre
de plus en plus, se croiser sur le dos, revenir par devant, peut-être se digiter
à leurs extrémités, et refaire des bras et des mains. La conformation originelle
s'altère ou se perfectionne par la nécessité et les fonctions habituelles.
(pp. 42–3)

As a freak of nature, Saunderson illustrates the phenomenon discussed
in *Le Rêve de d'Alembert* by Bordeu and Mlle de Lespinasse apropos of
the bundle of filaments that is said to constitute the elementary life-
form, with each filament developing into a separate organ (p. 50). (In
modern terms, Diderot is constructing a theory of embryogenesis on
the basis of the nervous system.) Suppressing a thread, according to
Bordeu, leads to the suppression of an organ: the creature who lacks
an optic nerve fails to develop an eye. Bordeu offers the example of a
latter-day Cyclops who was revealed on dissection to have only one
optic nerve; Biheron made a model of such a creature, a child who
lived only a matter of hours. Similarly, Bordeu reasons, an anatomist
dissecting an earless or noseless body would notice the absence of the
auditory and olfactory threads (p. 55). Doubling the filaments results
in a doubling of the organs (as with the monster-woman who had
two wombs and two vaginas); muddling the filaments leads to a
rearrangement of the anatomical parts—the head may appear in the
middle of the chest, or the lungs to the left. Bordeu suggests that the
malformation of the Siamese twins may have been caused by threads
being stuck together: 'Collez ensemble deux brins, et les organes se
confondront; les bras s'attacheront au corps; les cuisses, les jambes et
les pieds se réuniront, et vous aurez toutes les sortes de monstres
imaginables' (p. 55).

Adapting Bodies

The real and the fictive Bordeu's enthusiasm for dissection introduces
the theme of manipulating the body for a particular purpose (here the
advancement of medical science), a theme to which Diderot often
returns. In *Le Rêve de d'Alembert* the subject of eugenics is broached
in a discussion between Bordeu and Lespinasse about developing a
breed of man-goats to act as lackeys and so end the 'scandalous
tyranny' whereby humans are forced into degrading domestic service
(p. 102). Other reflections of Diderot's on organic manipulation seem
more frivolous. In *Les Bijoux indiscrets* Mirzoza speculates on reducing

humans to their most-used and apparently most vital part—dancers to their feet and legs, singers to their throat, most women to their 'bijou', gluttons to their jaws, coquettes to their two eyes and debauchees to the instrument of their pleasure. In the same vein Bordeu remarks to Mlle de Lespinasse that 'Nous marchons si peu, nous travaillons si peu, et nous pensons tant que je ne désespère pas que l'homme ne finisse par n'être qu'une tête'—to which Mlle de Lespinasse replies in the spirit of Mirzoza, 'j'espère que la galanterie effrénée...' (p. 43).

In real life Bordeu's view was that the over-stimulation or autonomous activity of one component part led to a disruption of the 'organological federation' sufficient to upset the harmony of the whole body.[43] For many doctors of the time, as we shall see, this was a familiar consequence of hysteria, though few eighteenth-century physicians any longer accepted the old link between this archetypal female complaint and the womb. Diderot broadly accepted such a conception of physiological unity, arguing in *Le Rêve de d'Alembert* that the distinctness of the organs did not preclude their forming a society—a continuous whole rather than the contiguous structure that the image of the swarm of bees represents in the same dialogue. 'Tous nos organes [...] ne sont que des animaux distincts que la loi de continuité tient dans une sympathie, une unité générale' (p. 30; see also p. 33).

Le Rêve de d'Alembert addresses the crucial question of the origin and function of the body and its alteration over time. Diderot's view remains unchanged from the one he attributed to Saunderson in the *Lettre sur les aveugles*: life is created spontaneously, as Lucretius had declared in *De rerum natura*,[44] and living forms are the product of chance agglomerations of molecules. He dissents from the theory of preformation, which he had first called into question in the *Pensées sur l'interprétation de la nature* and which he dismisses emphatically in the introductory dialogue of *Le Rêve de d'Alembert*:

DIDEROT.—Vous supposez que les animaux ont été originairement ce qu'ils sont à présent. Quelle folie! On ne sait non plus ce qu'ils ont été, qu'on ne sait ce qu'ils deviendront. Le vermisseau imperceptible qui s'agite dans la fange, s'achemine peut-être à l'état de grand animal; l'animal énorme qui nous épouvante par sa grandeur, s'achemine peut-être à l'état de vermisseau. (pp. 9–10)

Similarly, in the main dialogue Bordeu corrects Mlle de Lespinasse's misapprehension that 'vous avez toujours été une femme, sous la forme que vous avez', merely growing larger over time (p. 50). On the contrary, he tells her, she was originally an imperceptible point, then a thread, then a bundle of threads (nerve fibres) which developed to give organs, appendages and finally an entire body: the theory of epigenesis.[45]

Diderot's views on evolution across the different species have confused critics, but the evidence suggests that he was not a consistent believer in transformism. The pre-Lamarckian allusion to needs producing organs may seem to suggest otherwise, as does the reference in the *Eléments de physiologie* to an 'homme–singe': 'J'ai vu un homme–singe: Il ne pensait pas plus que le singe, il ne parlait point, mais il jettait des cris comme le singe; il s'agitait sans cesse comme le singe; il était décousu dans ses idées comme le singe; il se fachait, il s'appaisait, il était sans pudeur comme le singe' (p. 48). But it is clear that for Diderot 'imperfect' creatures are simply monsters that appear and disappear alongside more perfect forms rather than representing a lower stage of evolution to be improved upon. Viable beings are the successful product of the same chance agglomeration of molecules as gave rise to monsters, not the more evolved versions of earlier failures. They had no need to evolve from simpler forms, having always been organically viable. *Le Rêve de d'Alembert*, like the *Pensées sur l'interprétation de la nature*, regards each species as completing the cycle of its personal evolution and then vanishing; which is not what transformism implies.[46] 'Peut-être la longue suppression d'un bras amenerait-elle une race manchotte', the *Eléments de physiologie* surmise; but the organic change will remain *within* the human race. Lucretius' theory of spontaneous generation was for Diderot, as it was for Buffon, a major obstacle to the conception of a transformist theory.[47]

Diderot echoes the view of Buffon on generation, namely that the embryo is formed from a combination of molecules supplied by the testicles of both (*sic*) parents. The observation in the *Pensées sur l'interprétation de la nature* that 'on a découvert qu'il y a dans un sexe le même fluide séminal que dans l'autre sexe' (*O.Phil.*, p. 188) simply repeats what Buffon had written in *De l'homme*, and underlines Buffon's revival of the old analogy between the ovaries and the testicles. La Mettrie, on the other hand, had expressed scepticism about this matter in *L'Homme-machine* (1747), declaring that 'Je serais tenté de croire que la semence de la femme est inutile à la génération'.[48] But once conception has occurred, by whatever process, the embryo's development may be less straightforward than Diderot suggests in *Le Rêve de d'Alembert*. The *Eléments de physiologie*, for example, relay the imaginationist belief that emotional experiences undergone by the woman during pregnancy may be physically imprinted on her offspring, and Diderot utters a note of warning: 'Je ne voudrais pas qu'une mère fût exposée à voir pendant toute sa grossesse un visage grimacier. La grimace est contagieuse, nous la prenons; pourquoi la mere la prenant, l'enfant ne la prendrait-il pas?' (p. 208). But it is some way from this to the production of the anatomical monstrosities which the *Eléments* discuss elsewhere.

The *Encyclopédie* article 'Homme', which draws heavily on Buffon, sums up the doctrine to which Diderot would adhere throughout his life. It is an anthropological doctrine, in the sense which the eighteenth century gave to the word 'anthropology' (the study of the human body): 'Dans l'état de nature, l'*homme* qui exécuterait avec le plus d'aisance toutes les fonctions animales serait sans contredit le mieux fait; et réciproquement le mieux fait exécuterait le plus aisément toutes les fonctions animales.' The *Eléments de physiologie* and *Le Rêve de d'Alembert* in particular—the former more clinically than the latter—detail the types of operation that suitably adapted organs engage in, as well as describing the body's occasional failure to perform as a result of physical deficiency. The focus, unsurprisingly for Diderot, is often sexological. D'Alembert's impotence, for example, is hinted at in *Le Rêve de d'Alembert*, where despite his preference for the conventional means of procreation over the creation of 'hommes atomiques' by subdivision of one organic whole he regrets that humans cannot beget offspring as fish do: 'où le frai de l'homme pressé sur le frai d'une femme...' (pp. 34, 36).

For all that, Diderot repeatedly emphasizes the adaptability of bodies. The article 'Homme' claims, rather unexpectedly, that physical adaptability is more often required in society than in the state of nature, which perhaps simply means that social man has forfeited the harmony, the perfect integration of component parts, that characterizes him in his chimerical natural condition. On such an interpretation, civilized dressage results in the creation of a man-model whose body is unfit for the old 'fonctions animales', or refuses to perform them—the natural motions whose absence from Western society is regretted in the *Supplément au Voyage de Bougainville*. But according to a theory of civility that still retained some influence in the Enlightenment, he might thereby gain another kind of perfection, one defined by the norms and expectations of 'politesse'. This sort of bodily education, and Diderot's robust response to the premisses on which it is based, must now be examined.

Notes to Chapter 2

1. Mme de Vandeul, *Mémoires pour servir à l'histoire de la vie et des ouvrages de Diderot*, in *Œuvres complètes de Diderot*, ed. Assézat and Tourneux, i, p. viii.

2. See Herbert Dieckmann, 'The Autopsy Report on Diderot', *Isis* 61 (1950), 290.

3. See Kathleen F. Lander, 'The Study of Anatomy by Women before the Nineteenth Century', *Proceedings of the Third International Congress of the History of Medicine, London 1922* (Antwerp: De Vlijt, 1923), 130.

4. *Le Malade imaginaire* ii. 5; see also David Lebreton, *La Chair à vif* (Paris: Métailié, 1993), 179, and Philippe Ariès, *L'Homme devant la mort* (Paris: Seuil, 1977), 359.

5. See *Corr.* xi. 72, to Dr Antoine Petit (mid-July 1771).

6. See also Yves Laissus, 'Le Jardin du Roi', in *Enseignement et diffusion des sciences au XVIIIe siècle*, ed. René Taton (Paris: Herrmann, 1964), 315.

7. See A. Delacoux, *Biographie des sages-femmes célèbres, anciennes, modernes et contemporaines* (Paris: Trinquart, 1834), 34.

8. See Toby Gelfand, 'The "Paris" Manner of Dissection', *Bulletin of the History of Medicine* 46 (1972), 116 f.; Jean Mayer, *Diderot homme de science* (Rennes: Imprimerie bretonne, 1959), 383.

9. Bibliothèque nationale, Collection Joly de Fleury, 269 ff. 98–103; see also Gelfand, 'The "Paris" Manner', 104.

10. See Gelfand, 'The "Paris" Manner', 117.

11. See *Correspondance littéraire, philosophique et critique par Grimm, Raynal, Meister etc.*, ed. Maurice Tourneux, 16 vols. (Paris: Garnier, 1877–82), ix. 276 (1 Apr. 1771); *Mémoires pour Catherine II*, 88.

12. See P. Dorveaux, 'Les Femmes médecins', in *La Médecine anecdotique, historique, littéraire* (Paris: Rousset, 1901), 166 f.

13. See Diderot's letter to Wilkes of 19 Oct. 1771 (British Library, Add. Ms. 30 877 fol. 81, printed with slight errors in *Corr.* xi. 210–11).

14. Louis Petis de Bachaumont, *Mémoires secrets*, 36 vols. (London: John Adamson, 1780–9), i. 291 (29 Oct. 1763).

15. *Mémoires pour Catherine II*, 86.

16. Louis-Sébastien Mercier, *Le Tableau de Paris*, 12 vols. (Amsterdam, 1783), viii. 108; see also Dorveaux's report on Sauveur Morand's Académie eulogy, 167.

17. *Corr. litt.* ix. 276.

18. See *Salons*, iii. 251–2.

19. See *Corr.* xiv. 46, and Diderot's letter to Catherine II of 13 Sept. 1774 (*Corr.* xiv. 83).

20. See Ludmilla Jordanova, *Sexual Visions* (New York and London: Harvester Wheatsheaf, 1989), 68.

21. Mme la comtesse de Genlis, *Mémoires inédits*, 8 vols. (Paris and London: Coburn, 1825–6), i. 254.

22. See, *inter alia*, K. B. Roberts and J. D. W. Tomlinson, *The Fabric of the Body* (Oxford: Clarendon Press, 1992); J. Guiffrey, 'Le Cabinet anatomique du chirurgien Desnoues',· *Nouvelles Archives de l'art français* 6 (1890); M. Lemire, *Artistes et mortels*. *Les Cires anatomiques* (Paris: Chabaud, 1990); L. Premnia, 'The Waxwork in Medicine', *Images* 48 (1972); C. J. S. Thompson, 'Anatomical Mannikins', *Journal of Anatomy* 59 (1925); J. N. Haviland and L. C. Parish, 'A Brief Account of the Use of Wax Models in the Study of Medicine', *Journal of the History of Medicine* 25 (1970); E. J. Pyke, *A Biographical Dictionary of Wax Modellers* (Oxford: Clarendon Press, 1973, Supplement London, 1981).

23. See Auguste-Nicolas Laverdet, *Correspondance entre Boileau-Despréaux et Brossette* (Paris, 1858), 22 Oct. 1702.

24. *Corr. litt.* ix. 276.

25. *Corr.* xi. 74 (22 July 1771).

26. *Pensées détachées sur la peinture*, in *Œuvres esthétiques*, ed. Paul Vernière (Paris: Garnier, 1968), 804.

27. See Michel Delon, 'Violences peintes', *Recherches sur Diderot et l'Encyclopédie* 18–19 (1995), 75–6.

28. *Essais sur la peinture*, in *O.Esth*. 668.

29. See Jean Locquin, *La Peinture d'histoire en France de 1747 à 1785* (Paris: Laurens, 1912), 82, 83 f.

30. See Londa Schiebinger, *The Mind Has No Sex?* (Cambridge, Mass.: Harvard University Press, 1989), 191 ff.; Laqueur, *Making Sex*, 10.

31. See Schiebinger, 'Skeletons in the Closet: The First Illustrations of the Female Skeleton in Eighteenth-Century Anatomy', *Representations* 14 (1986), 71.

32. See *Salons*, iii. 71.

33. See, e.g., *Salons*, ii. 77.

34. See F. A. Garrison and E. C. Streeter, 'Sculpture and Painting as Modes of Anatomical Illustration', in Ludwig Choulant, *History and Bibliography of Anatomical Illustration*, trans. Mortimer Frank (New York and London: Hafner, 1945), 397 f.

35. See Delon, 'Violences peintes', 75 f.

36. Jean Mayer (*Diderot homme de siècle*, p. xi) dates the beginning of work on the *Eléments de physiologie* to 1765.

37. See *Eléments de physiologie*, 153 ff., on the intestines.

38. See Elsa Marie Bukdahl, 'Les symboles visuels et "la force de l'unité": classicisme et baroque dans le *Salon de 1767*', in *Le Regard et l'objet*, ed. Michel Delon and Wolfgang Drost (Heidelberg: Winter, 1989), 10 ff.

39. *Entretiens sur 'Le Fils naturel'*, in *O.Esth*. 153.

40. See G. N. Laidlaw, 'Diderot's Teratology', *Diderot Studies* 4 (1963); Emita B. Hill, 'Materialism and Monsters in *Le Rêve de d'Alembert*', *Diderot Studies* 10 (1968); Jean Mayer, 'Les Etres et les monstres dans la philosophie de Diderot', in *Colloque international: Diderot*, ed. Chouillet (q.v.); Marie-Hélène Huet, *Monstrous Imagination* (Cambridge, Mass.: Harvard University Press, 1993).

41. See Jacques Roger, *Les Sciences de la vie dans la pensée française du XVIIIe siècle*, 2nd edn. (Paris: A. Colin, 1971), 668.

42. Quoted in *Le Rêve de d'Alembert*, in *O.Phil*. 309 n. 1; also Roger, *Sciences de la vie*, 669.

43. See Vila, *Enlightenment*, 71.

44. See Roger, *Sciences de la vie*, 598.

45. See Daniel Brewer, *The Discourse of Enlightenment in Eighteenth-Century France* (Cambridge: Cambridge University Press, 1993), 196.

46. See, e.g., Ivan Kapitanovich Luppol, *Diderot, ses idées philosophiques* (Paris: Editions sociales, 1936), 92 ff.; Robert Niklaus (ed.), *Lettre sur les aveugles* (Geneva: Droz, 1951), pp. xliv and lx. For the opposing view see Lester Crocker, 'Diderot and Eighteenth-Century Transformism', in *Forerunners to Darwin*, ed. B. Glass *et al.* (Baltimore: Johns Hopkins University Press, 1959), 122 f.

47. See Roger, *Sciences de la vie*, 666.

48. Julien de La Mettrie, *L'Homme-machine*, ed. Maurice Solovine (Paris: Boissard, 1921), 137.

CHAPTER 3

Propriety and Impropriety

Sensibility and Control

Eighteenth-century sensibility was a double-edged phenomenon. In a positive sense, it was capable of nurturing feelings that conduced to the individual and collective good—sympathy, tolerance, pity and the virtuous 'amour de soi' that Rousseau saw as a precondition of compassion. It could shape perceptions in a way that promoted artistic as well as moral excellence, although, as *Le Neveu de Rameau* pointed out, the two currents often diverged. But the yielding to emotion which it encouraged could also be a dangerous indulgence, and if left unchecked might bring about the body's complete breakdown. The pathology of sensibility therefore became a cause of concern to moralists, since it threatened the humanitarian and curative goals the Enlightenment set itself. A unifying concept tying psychology and ethics to organic reality, in other words, was more worryingly complex than it superficially appeared.[1]

Of the articles which the *Encyclopédie* devoted to sensibility, Fouquet's (on the medical phenomenon) described its physiological and pathological manifestations and de Jaucourt's (on moral sensibility) its central role in the life of the spirit. But the attempt to divide the concept into two distinct areas was bound to fail, particularly in the light of a monist philosophy that saw mental conditions (including emotional ones) as a function of bodily events (see Chapter 1 above). Sensibility seemed to demand control both as a mood and as an organic response because it so readily tended towards extremism, but harnessing it in the interests of health, social good and artistic excellence was no easy matter.

Diderot investigated the problem of containing and shaping sensibility in a number of works. He depicts its physical dangers most starkly in *La Religieuse*, a novel that concludes with the failure to tame wayward emotion. The fact that it does so might seem to indicate the limitations of a 'hygienic' approach to rampant feeling, but it also sheds a troubling light on a matter Diderot raises in the *Pensées philosophiques* of 1746. There the beneficial consequences of allowing the passions free rein are stated:

On déclame sans fin contre les passions; on leur impute toutes les peines de l'homme, et l'on oublie qu'elles sont aussi la source de tous ses plaisirs. C'est dans sa constitution un élément dont on ne peut dire ni trop de bien ni trop de mal. Mais ce qui me donne de l'humeur, c'est qu'on ne les regarde jamais que du mauvais côté. On croirait faire injure à la raison, si l'on disait un mot en faveur de ses rivales. (*O.Phil.*, p. 9)

It is customary to emphasize the support Diderot gives to passion in this statement rather than his cautioning about its deadly effects. But however eager he was to rehabilitate strong feeling by reacting against the fear of its destructive potential that had been expressed by neo-classical writers, he could not deny its elemental and unruly force. So he was bound to pay attention to ways of trying to control emotion, however convinced he might remain of their ultimate futility.

Michel Foucault's argument that the bodily surveillance inaugurated in the seventeenth century resulted in a 'great confinement' of social misfits, embarrassments and outcasts might suggest that the following age was one of corresponding 'invisibility':[2] the institutional arrangements set up under Louis XIV were still in place, and the kind of social disdain for freakish oddity that Moi expresses in the case of Rameau's nephew was presumably commonplace. 'Je n'estime pas ces originaux la [...],' Moi announces, 'Ils m'arretent une fois l'an' (p. 5)—which implies that for the rest of the time they are kept out of his sight. But whatever his moralist's dislike for the impulses they manifest, the age of Diderot greatly relaxed the seventeenth century's emphasis on bodily suppression: its new ethos actually exalted corporeal expressiveness despite, or even because of, its irregularity. Diderot's happy support of real bodies that broke the rules of beauty and propriety, discussed in Chapter 2 above, made it inherently unlikely that he would sanction their confinement or exclusion. The asylum—the 'Petites-Maisons' which Moi calls Lui's rightful home after witnessing one of his frenzied pantomimic displays—hardly seems the best place for what is simply eccentric and mould-breaking behaviour. Embracing untrammelled feeling with all the enthusiasm of his 'sensible' age, Diderot was disinclined to quash expressiveness without good reason.

In his influential *Réflexions critiques sur la poésie et sur la peinture* (1719) the abbé Dubos had argued the case for a 'persuasion passionnelle' based on a feeling response to art,[3] claiming that since men suffer more from living without passions than from experiencing them they constantly search for the means to gratify their emotional desires. Art provides them with the release they seek, because it counterfeits human experience harmlessly. According to Dubos, literature and painting imitate events in the real world that provoke emotion in the beholder, but their distance from reality means that the imitations have no unpleasant consequences. Whereas in life undergoing emotion usually stimulates a physical response that may be expressed in action, in art it simply results in conviction.[4]

Social constraints may lead to the manipulation or suppression of the physical reaction, but in certain milieus these controls are ignored. Diderot's fiction examines some of the consequences that can ensue, showing them in particularly dramatic form in *La Religieuse*. Sometimes, it is true, breaches of bodily 'bienséance' can hardly be helped: they are spontaneous responses that seem to carry a threat out of all proportion to their actual manifestation. One striking example from *La Religieuse*, as melodramatically presented in its way as the scenes of the lesbian Superior's arousal, is the episode describing Suzanne's nosebleed.[5] Its occurrence as she pleads with her mother for mercy is both shocking and ludicrous: shocking in the contrast between the coursing red blood and the monochrome of the convent's costume, its unbidden violence a silent expression of Suzanne's raw desolation, its stain a reminder of what she, in her illegitimacy, exemplifies to the seemingly impassive Mme Simonin; and ludicrous in the way that many undignified and messy physical reactions are, particularly when they involve bodily secretions. We may think ahead to the description of the Superior foaming at the mouth as she reaches sexual climax (p. 344), and Suzanne's uncomprehending alarm at this new evidence of bodily transgression—transgression in the sense that, like other involuntary responses, it seems *impolite*. Not knowing what an orgasm looks like, she cannot determine specifically what kind of impropriety it represents: the 'wrong' reaction in the wrong place (a supposedly chaste convent).

The code of civility is something the Superior had seemed to flout in less emphatic ways from the time of Suzanne's first meeting with her, though initially her propensities simply appeared the result of disorganization:

quand elle marche, elle jette les bras en avant et en arrière. Veut-elle parler? elle ouvre la bouche avant que d'avoir arrangé ses idées; aussi bégaye-t-elle un peu. Est-elle assise? elle s'agite sur son fauteuil, comme si quelque chose l'incommodait: elle oublie toute bienséance. (p. 329)[6]

This code provided various strategies for covering up spontaneous physical manifestations the subject might wish to conceal, or which the world might wish him or her to hide. Not that the age of Diderot shared the kinds of concern with organized civility that previous centuries had shown, and which Renaissance works such as Castiglione's *Il Cortegiano* or Erasmus's *De civilitate morum puerilium* and their seventeenth-century progeny illustrate. The rehabilitation of passion, the widespread enthusiasm for a 'beau désordre' and the disaffection with system led the Enlightenment to spurn the mannerly obsessions of an earlier era. But not all the eighteenth century was enlightened, and learning how to be unnatural still counted for much in some quarters.

Renaissance conduct-books had been based on an ethics of refusal or suppression that was paradoxically meant to sharpen the pleasures of urbanity.[7] In foregoing the temptations of selfish aggression, it was assumed, the civilized man or woman experienced a gratification of purified intercourse that was by definition superior to the indulgence of instinct. Peasants, Furetière's dictionary of 1690 comments, lack 'civilité', which the *Dictionnaire de l'Académie* locates unambiguously in the 'monde'.[8] The form of control it presupposed might be entirely superficial, it is true: the recurrent theme of 'le paraître' in seventeenth-century imaginative and moralist writing suggests as much, implicitly acknowledging that normative codes of behaviour do less to change the 'être' of the individual than their proponents might hope. By the eighteenth century this awareness had hardened into radical estrangement, at least in intellectual circles.

De Jaucourt's *Encyclopédie* article 'Civilité, politesse, affabilité' attacks these concepts on the grounds that 'Sans émaner nécessaire-ment du cœur, elles en donnent les apparences, et font paraître l'homme au-dehors comme il devrait être intérieurement'. They are a hypocritical social convenience whose moral inferiority is evident in the fact that they promote 'savoir-vivre' rather than 'savoir-être'. (The latter was the concern of religious manuals directed at curing the sinful nature of man.) It is hardly surprising that *philosophes* such as Diderot and his friend Naigeon had little time for the polished world of salon society, although they were eager and even zealous members of d'Holbach's coterie in the rue Royale;[9] nor is it strange that the moody, uncouth d'Alembert felt uneasy about frequenting Mme du Deffand's salon, the most refined in Paris. (He later defected to the drawing-room of her one-time protégée, Julie de Lespinasse.) The chapter on civility in Mercier's *Le Tableau de Paris*, on the other hand, describes the deceptive appearance that civility allows its practitioners to preserve as distinctly advantageous in social terms: 'Une robe légère, jetée sur le moral, est donc aussi nécessaire peut-être qu'un vêtement l'est au physique de l'homme'.[10]

This is a nice analogy, making the aspect of 'paraître' a tangible bodily matter. But nothing could reconcile the supporters of natural values with the cover-up it implied. If spontaneous expression was a good thing, as the *Pensées philosophiques* suggest, then it was right to mistrust the strategies for masking it that polite society had invented. This is the implication of de Jaucourt's *Encyclopédie* article 'Passion (peint.)':

Mais comment faire des observations sur l'expression des *passions* dans une capitale, par exemple, où tous les hommes conviennent de paroître n'en ressentir aucune? Où trouver parmi nous aujourd'hui, non pas des hommes coleres, mais des hommes qui permettent à la colere de se peindre d'une façon absolument libre dans leurs attitudes, dans leurs gestes, dans leurs mouvemens, et dans leurs traits?

Il est bien prouvé que ce n'est point dans une nation maniérée et civilisée, qu'on voit la nature parée de la franchise qui a le droit d'intéresser l'ame, et d'occuper les sens; d'où il suit que l'artiste n'a point de moyens dans nos pays, d'exprimer les *passions* avec la vérité et la variété qui les caractérisent.

The civility taught by such seventeenth-century works as Nicolas Faret's *L'Honnête Homme* (1630) was the sort appropriate to a man destined for court life. The only professional activity for which 'polite' instructions were given was soldiering, and Faret accordingly supplied detailed information on the kind of bodily build best suited to military life. Although he described the corporeal training most likely to produce effective performance,[11] it is obvious that the ill-favoured had little to hope from it if their anatomical structure was defective: Faret remarks that 'la composition du corps même doit être d'une structure bien formée et bien proportionnée, ou du moins qui n'ait rien qui d'abord rebute les yeux de ceux qui le regardent' (pp. 228–9). Christian manuals on civility such as La Salle's *Règles de la bienséance et de la civilité chrétienne*, *à l'usage des écoles chrétiennes des garçons* (1736) usually justify their somewhat surprising concern with worldly dressage with the remark that proper bodily attitudes are always observed by God, and so must not offend him. Although it is not revealed how 'proper' attitudes have been determined, La Salle criticizes poor carriage in entirely worldly terms: it makes a person 'guindée dans son extérieur' in a way that is 'tout à fait contre la bienséance et les règles de la modestie'.[12] Men (or in this case boys) should never attract attention to themselves, but instead learn to 'ne pas remuer un seul membre de leur corps sans réflexion, et de ne le faire qu'avec beaucoup de retenue' (p. 2).

Il faut qu'il y ait toujours dans le port d'une personne quelque chose de grave et de majestueux, mais elle doit bien prendre garde qu'il n'y ait rien qui ressente l'orgueil et la hauteur d'esprit: car cela déplaît extrêmement à tout le monde.

This kind of 'politesse' was too inhibiting as well as too religiously coloured to appeal to Enlightenment writers on bodily hygiene, who deprecated any check on legitimate self-expression based on ascetic principles or on the uncritical assumption that secular civility was offended by it. Diderot has no patience with the mortification of the body associated with the Christian religion, as both *La Religieuse* and the *Supplément au Voyage de Bougainville* make clear. His *Encyclopédie* article 'Haire' observes that 'il y a quelquefois plus à perdre pour la bonté à un moment d'humeur déplacé, qu'à gagner par dix ans de *haire*, de discipline et de cilice'. Both Diderot and Rousseau dismissed the routines of corporeal dressage perpetuated by an over-refined and sophisticated society, Rousseau declaring in *Emile* that

au lieu d'occuper éternellement mon élève à des gambades, je le ménerois au pied d'un rocher; là, je lui montrerois quelle attitude il faut prendre, comment il faut porter le corps et la tête, quel mouvement il faut faire, de quelle maniére il faut poser tantôt le pied tantôt la main pour suivre légérement les sentiers escarpés, raboteux et rudes, et s'élancer de pointe en pointe tant en montant qu'en descendant. J'en ferois l'émule d'un chevreuil plustôt qu'un danseur de l'Opéra. (*Œuvres complètes*, iv. 391)

One of Diderot's letters to Sophie Volland attacks the way her sister is bringing up a son because it runs counter to the rule of nature. This vague observation has a familiar ring, and writing as he does three years after the publication of *Emile* Diderot can hardly be called original in formulating it; but however great the influence of Rousseau's book not everyone had been converted to its doctrine.

J'eus le courage de dire hier à Mad^e Le Gendre qu'elle se donnoit bien de la peine pour ne faire de son fils qu'une jolie poupée. *Pas trop élever* est une maxime qui convient surtout aux garçons. Il faut un peu les abandonner à l'énergie de la nature. J'aime qu'ils soient violents, étourdis, capricieux. Une tête ébouriffée me plaît plus qu'une tête bien peignée. Laissons leur prendre une physionomie qui leur appartienne. Si j'aperçois à travers leurs sottises un trait d'originalité, je suis content. Nos petits ours mal léchés de province me plaisent cent fois plus que tous vos petits épagneuls si curieusement dressés. Quand je vois un enfant qui s'écoute, qui va la tête bien droite, la démarche bien composée, qui craint de déranger un cheveu de sa frisure, un pli de son habit, le père et la mère s'extasient et disent: Le joli enfant que nous avons là! Et moi je dis: Il ne sera jamais qu'un sot! (25 July 1765; *Corr.* v. 65)

The impetus behind such observations, like the point of departure for Diderot's critique of manneredness in his aesthetic writings, is the conviction that artifice removes man from contact with the central truth that is vested in his body. This was not a new preoccupation, of course: the Renaissance, which produced conduct-books, also produced books that argued the body's right to be improper. Hence the carnivalesque and scatological elements in Rabelais's work, and Montaigne's 'naturalistic' theories on the upbringing of children. Their influence can be felt in the writings of Locke, Rousseau and Diderot.

Manneredness and the 'Truth of Nature'

Falsifying routine is as reprehensible in the artroom as in the schoolroom, and Diderot is no less withering about artists who become 'maniéré' than about over-tended children. Painters' models can teach only schematized untruths, he believes, because like one of the Graces lampooned in the 1765 *Salon* they have been 'arranged' by the likes of Marcel. Marcel was one of the eighteenth century's designers of 'bon ton', a minuet-master who inculcated the kind of simpering graces Diderot found deplorable. Rousseau attacked him too: the allusion in *Emile* to 'toutes les singeries de Marcel' as being 'bonnes pour le pays où il les fait' (p. 391) is a Swiss critique of a whole nation that sets show above substance. Marcel, on this interpretation, is the overseer of a pantomime whose participants feign superiority to the spectacle in which they participate, but are actually its dupes. Indeed, a note of Rousseau's claims that

Connoissant bien son monde [il] faisoit l'extravagant par ruse, et donnoit à son art une importance qu'on feignoit de trouver ridicule, mais pour laquelle on lui portoit au fond le plus grand respect [...]. Cette methode est toujours sure en France. Le vrai talent, plus simple et moins charlatan, n'y fait point fortune. La modestie y est la vertu des sots. (p. 391)

Suzanne Simonin, so often incapable of interpreting what she sees, is yet astute enough to perceive that the lesson in monastic graces she is given in the convent of Sainte-Marie after she has taken the veil is an indictment of the institution's 'mondanité', a useless form of dressage for an estate that is not of the world:

'ça, voyons un peu, marchez. Vous ne vous tenez pas assez droite; il ne faut pas être courbée comme cela...' Elle me composa la tête, les pieds, la taille, les bras; ce fut presque une leçon de Marcel sur les grâces monastiques: car chaque état a les siennes. (*La Religieuse*, p. 239)

But as the *Essais sur la peinture* declare, real bodily grace knows nothing of such contrivance.

La grâce de l'action et celle de Marcel se contredisent exactement. Si Marcel rencontrait un homme placé comme l'Antinoüs, lui portant une main sous le menton et l'autre sur les épaules: 'Allons donc, grand dadais, lui dirait-il, est-ce qu'on se tient comme cela?' Puis, lui repoussant les genoux avec les siens, et le relevant par-dessous le bras, il ajouterait: 'On dirait que vous êtes de cire, et que vous allez fondre. Allons, nigaud, tendez-moi ce jarret; déployez-moi cette figure; ce nez un peu au vent.' Et quand il en aurait fait le plus insipide petit-maître, il commencerait à lui sourire, et à s'applaudir de son ouvrage. (p. 702)

The influence of Hogarth's *Analysis of Beauty* may be felt here, as it may in Diderot's comment apropos of a portrait by Perronneau in the 1767 *Salon* that 'Le maître de grâces, le maître à danser détruisent le mouvement réel, cet enchaînement si précieux des parties qui se commandent et s'obéissent réciproquement les unes aux autres' (*Salons*, iii. 171). True expressiveness is certain to be compromised, if not actually excluded, when corporeal depictions are mannered:

Une autre chose qui ne choque pas moins, ce sont les petits usages des peuples civilisés. La politesse, cette qualité si aimable, si douce, si estimable dans le monde, est maussade dans les arts d'imitation. Une femme ne peut plier les genoux, un homme ne peut déployer son bras, prendre son chapeau sur sa tête, et tirer un pied en arrière, que sur un écran [i.e., a fire-screen of the kind typically decorated with motifs taken from Gillot, Watteau or Boucher]. (*Essais sur la peinture*, p. 714)

The same criticism of formulaic postures could of course also be levelled at neo-classical painting,[13] though Diderot does not voice it in the case of Vien's *Marchande d'amours*.

In the *Réfutation d'Helvétius* he remarks that physical grace is an aptitude, not a technique that can be taught (p. 581). In a different context—a discussion of the actress Mme Riccoboni's skills as a performer—the *Réfutation* again implies the limitations inherent in any attempt to train recalcitrant bodies: 'C'est que l'aptitude naturelle à la déclamation lui manquait' (p. 579; see also Chapter 1 above).[14] Helvétius's views on the universal possibility of modifying humans through habit and education, which seemed to Diderot to reduce them to the state of automata, are answered with an impassioned argument for individuality. Not that Diderot altogether denies the importance of habit, if not dressage—it all depends on circumstance— but he refuses to see man as a totally malleable organic mass (p. 559). 'Tout individu n'est donc pas propre à tout, pas même à être bon acteur, si la nature s'y oppose' (p. 580). He underlines this opinion with the story of his own attempts to learn dancing as a young man:

Je vais clandestinement, de la rue de la Harpe jusqu'au bout de la rue Montmartre, prendre leçon; je garde le maître fort longtemps. Je le quitte de dépit de ne rien apprendre; je le reprends une seconde, une troisième fois, et le quitte avec autant de douleur et aussi peu de succès. Que me manquait-il pour être un grand danseur? L'oreille? Je l'avais excellente. La légèreté? Je n'étais pas lourd, il s'en fallait bien. L'intérêt? On ne pouvait être animé d'un plus violent. Ce qui me manquait? La mollesse, la flexibilité, la grâce qui ne se donnent point. (p. 581)

The rigid bodily postures beloved of academic artists—not just Carle Van Loo, but La Grenée and Hallé as well—seem to him ridiculous because they wantonly reject the ease of natural form. Writing about the 1765 Salon, he calls Van Loo's Auguste a squat actress who lacks all sense of flowing movement, La Grenée's soldiers dead bodies watching a human sacrifice without moving a muscle, and the wife and daughters of Sciluras, in a painting by Hallé, flaccid sausages wrapped in drapery (*Salons*, ii. 92). Given the contempt he feels for such work, it is a little surprising to find him equally intolerant of pictures that show a kind of bustling life, and attacking them on the grounds that none of their figures could be converted into a classicizing bas-relief or a sculpture. But it is less surprising when the offending artist is Boucher. He is 'le plus mortel ennemi du silence que je connaisse', and his work conveys a mechanical busyness that puts Diderot in mind of fairground puppets ('il en est aux plus jolies marionnettes du monde', *Salons*, ii. 92).

The proper response to this teeming 'tapage' is the same, predictably enough, as to the wooden attitudinizing Diderot dismisses in other paintings: a recommendation that the artist return to the observation of nature. But he conveys no very clear sense of what this might mean. Although the *Lettre sur les sourds et muets* criticizes Charles Batteux for failing in his *Les Beaux-arts réduits à un même principe* to define the 'belle nature' allegedly imitated by all art, Diderot himself has a generously vague notion of the concept's reference.[15] A principle antithetically opposed to the artificial constructions of civility, it may appear as the unfettered immensity of the vegetable and mineral world, as the essence of the 'énorme', 'barbare' and 'sauvage' (principles that Diderot regarded as the sine qua non of poetic writing), as the unchecked energy of human appetite, and as various phenomena having everything to do with the life of instinct and nothing with the mannered constructions of human ingenuity. Imposed rules and regulations are abhorrent to nature, which functions according to its own rhythms.

Diderot's dislike of rules was the product both of his own taste for bohemian untidiness and of his intermittent conviction that regulation hampers the man of genius and compromises his unique powers of expression. The informality he championed is evident in his rejection of everything that smacked of etiquette, which he thought was spoiling Sophie Volland's nephew. His antipathy towards the polite conventions of social intercourse is captured in a story told about his trip to Russia in his old age, when, it is said, his daughter worried about the impression his unbuttoned exuberance and inexperience in courtly ways might make on the empress. Grimm wrote in November 1778 that 'il lui prend la main, il lui saisit le bras, il tape sur la table, tout comme s'il était au milieu de la synagogue de la rue Royale' (that is, among the habitués of d'Holbach's salon).[16] D'Escherny, a compatriot and disciple of Rousseau's, quotes from a letter which Catherine II allegedly sent to Mme Geoffrin, but whose original has never been traced:

'Votre Diderot est un homme extraordinaire; je ne me tire pas de mes entretiens avec lui sans avoir les cuisses meurtries et toutes noires; j'ai été obligée de mettre une table entre lui et moi pour me mettre, moi et mes membres, à l'abri de sa gesticulation.'[17]

This gesticulation was famous: according to d'Escherny, Diderot was regularly accused of excitedly seizing his companions' arms at table, while still managing to eat with an excellent appetite himself. This is the man whom the *Encyclopédie* article 'Génie' (attributed to Saint-Lambert, but Diderot is usually supposed to have had a hand in writing it) seems to be depicting in its picture of the genius governed by passions stronger than those of ordinary mortals, and dominated by 'enthousiasme'. The second *Entretien sur 'Le Fils naturel'* describes such a person as disdaining the pettiness and constriction of civilized urban life, seeking the 'horreur secrète' of caves and forests, the magnificence of raging torrents, the noble shores of lakes and the fertile lands of the plain. They are the only proper background to his solitary musings: '"O Nature, tout ce qui est bien est renfermé dans ton sein! [...] L'enthousiasme naît d'un objet de la nature"' (p. 98).

The bodily manifestations of seizure by this divine madness are spasms so uncontrollable that, according to Diderot's psycho-physiological theory, they acquire special significance, far greater than the controlled gestures of consciousness could ever possess. At least, this seems to be his view in 1757; but by the time of the *Paradoxe sur le comédien* (1769 onward) he has changed his mind. The anecdote related there about his encounter with the playwright Sedaine in 1765 shows how sharp the contrast between the 'old' and the 'new' Diderot actually was. In 1765 he had been an impenitent (though, he implies, artistically inferior) 'homme sensible':

Le Philosophe sans le savoir chancelle à la première, à la seconde représentation, et j'en suis affligé; à la troisième il va aux nues, et j'en suis transporté de joie. Le lendemain matin je me jette dans un fiacre, je cours après Sedaine; c'était en hiver, il faisait le froid le plus rigoureux; je vais partout où j'espère le trouver. J'apprends qu'il est au fond du faubourg Saint-Antoine, je m'y fais conduire. Je l'aborde, je jette mes bras autour de son cou; la voix me manque, et les larmes me coulent le long des joues. Voilà l'homme sensible et médiocre. Sedaine, immobile et froid, me regarde et me dit: '*Ah! Monsieur Diderot, que vous êtes beau!*' Voilà l'observateur et l'homme de génie. (p. 330)

Diderot now assigns ultimate value to activity that is the fruit of penetrating reflection, and so is both governable and sustainable by the will. This, according to the *Salons*, is what characterizes the art of a painter such as La Tour, though in 1767 Diderot refers to his controlled composure with disparagement:

J'ai vu peindre La Tour, il est tranquille et froid; il ne se tourmente point; il ne souffre point, il ne halète point, il ne fait aucune de ces contorsions du modeleur enthousiaste, sur le visage duquel on voit se succéder les images qu'il se propose de rendre, et qui semblent passer de son âme sur son front et de son front sur la terre ou sur sa toile. Il n'imite point les gestes du furieux; il n'a point le sourcil relevé de l'homme qui dédaigne le regard de sa femme qui s'attendrit; il ne s'extasie point, il ne sourit point à son travail, il reste froid, et cependant son imitation est chaude. Obtiendrait-on d'une étude opiniâtre et longue le mérite de La Tour? Ce peintre n'a jamais rien produit de verve, il a le génie du technique, c'est un machiniste merveilleux. Quand je dis de La Tour qu'il est machiniste, c'est comme je le dis de Vaucanson, et non comme je le dirais de Rubens. (iii. 168–9)

True genius no longer has any connection with sensibility, but is based on an art which, like the civility learnt from conduct-manuals, 'consiste [...] à rendre si scrupuleusement les signes extérieurs [...] que vous vous y trompiez' (p. 312; also pp. 372–3).

Modesty

Clearly, such an art of control differs absolutely from the spontaneous, energetic motions Diderot associates with nature (see also Chapter 5, pp. 133, 136–7 below). Like other *philosophes*, he regarded nature (particularly in the form of natural appetites, though his sexology is not without its ambiguities) as the touchstone of what is good and desirable—good and desirable, tautologously enough, because untouched by social interference. So why the periodic invasion into its preserves of the archetypal socialized phenomenon of 'pudeur'? Diderot thinks of shame as being one of the areas of moral life that define human sensibility. It does not have to involve the body—Moi regards Lui's most shameful self-exposure as being his enjoyment of the morally obscene story of the Renegade of Avignon—but it is hardly surprising that it should often do so. Not that this is always a rational response, as suggested in Chapter 1 above; for if humans are mixtures of instinct and will, they ought logically to feel no shame about actions and circumstances they are powerless to govern. Yet their attitude is complex,[18] even in Tahiti.

   Given that the savage sexual code discussed in the *Supplément au Voyage de Bougainville* is one based on pleasurable usefulness, it seems natural that the dialoguist B should present the natives' concern with 'pudeur' simply in terms of personal comfort and practicality. Orou's wife and daughters feel no embarrassment at witnessing his physical arousal, no doubt seeing sex as simply the 'frottement voluptueux de deux intestins' (an opinion Diderot approvingly quotes from Marcus Aurelius, p. 510) which gratifyingly results in conception. The reason why lovemaking is done in private is simply that 'L'homme ne veut être ni troublé ni distrait dans ses jouissances', and 'Celles de l'amour sont suivies d'une faiblesse qui l'abandonnerait à la merci de son ennemi' (p. 507). This is prudence, not 'pudeur'. In the civilized West, on the other hand, sexual activity is often illicit, which means that its manifestations must be concealed, or is seen as morally degrading rather than socially desirable.

But Diderot had argued the unnaturalness of 'pudeur' well before he wrote the *Supplément au Voyage de Bougainville*. According to the *Lettre sur les aveugles*, shame is merely a consequence of organic endowment, such that if certain organs are lacking the 'modest' response will not normally occur. Because shame is closely connected with sight, the blind cannot understand why one part of the body has to be covered up rather than another (p. 92). Orou cannot comprehend it either, because in Tahiti 'pudeur' and the body are associated in the Western sense only when sterile or infertile women take sexual pleasure, or when the ship's chaplain is shown to torment himself for making love with the women in Orou's family despite the edicts of his church. In the free imaginings of the *Lettre sur les aveugles*, the blind are unencumbered in roughly the same way as the Tahitians: they are far more concerned with utility than their sighted fellows, and their blindness frees them to act in essentially purposive ways. They concentrate on getting things done as expediently as possible, whereas humans possessing all their senses dissipate their energies on superfluities. Diderot seems to contradict a part of this thesis when he reveals that Mélanie de Salignac, Sophie Volland's blind niece, had 'le sentiment le plus délicat de la pudeur' (p. 158); but it emerges that this modesty was profoundly unnatural in her. She had learnt it from her mother's instruction, and consequently 'elle m'a répété [beaucoup] de fois que la vue de certaines parties du corps invitait au vice'. This view of decorum is essentially the same as the one promoted by writers on civility: decency is defined by what particular cultures happen to consider proper, but has no universal applicability. Indeed, ethnographers regard it as certain that the act of covering up the sex organs and the adoption of clothing in general were originally quite unconnected with shame. On the contrary, they served the need for ornamentation and the closely related intention of exercising sexual attraction by means of concealment.[19] The opinion that 'bienséance', if not more natural to woman than to man, is at least more strongly incumbent on her has a long history, and was bound to be explored afresh in a century in which, as the Goncourts noted, her body was constantly on show. Diderot's writings offer a fairly full account of the gradations in conduct—the advance and retreat, the concession and withdrawal, the flaunting and hiding—that constitute the female's code in social and especially sexual relationships. The tokens of her bodily response may be all the more remote, allusive and symbolic as her personality is refined and cultivated, though the erotic body-language of lovers like the lesbian Superior of *La Religieuse* is far more overt. Rather implausibly, this woman's fondness for undressing and admiring her acolytes' bodies does not initially strike Suzanne as a breach of propriety, though she comments that there is no true distance or sense of measure in her kind (p. 330). It is highly significant that the Superior comes to her cell on the first night at Sainte-Eutrope and undresses her too, going much further than the mere baring of neck and bosom she confines herself to in the case of the other nuns; and 'elle me fit mille caresses qui m'embarrassèrent un peu, je ne sais pas pourquoi' (p. 333). Suzanne is no more enlightened about the way the woman hides her head on her knees when she is most violently moved by the tale of her calvary (p. 347), though with the benefit of hindsight perhaps she should be.

A woman's decency is not necessarily compromised when she abandons the usual polite conventions, however, even where the clothing of specific erogenous zones is concerned. Diderot's commentary on La Grenée's *La Charité romaine* in the 1765 *Salon* shows the glory of maternity even as it appears to be compromised, but enhances it through a form of recomposition that underlines the pathos and dignity of the scene. The woman's charity in offering her breast to a starving prisoner, in this modified version, is cheapened neither by the intrusive gaze of a third party nor by the physical attractiveness of the old man she is feeding; instead her motherly gesture is exalted by a deliberate diminution of her sexual appeal.

Je ne veux point que ce soit une jeune femme; il me faut une femme au moins de trente ans, d'un caractère grand, sévère et honnête; que son expression soit celle de la tendresse et de la pitié [...]; qu'elle n'ait pas de beaux tétons bien ronds, mais de bonnes grosses et larges mamelles pleines de lait; qu'elle soit grande et robuste. (*Salons*, ii. 95)

Two versions of another picture which Diderot writes about in the same *Salon* drive home the notion that decency lies as much in the intention behind a body's presentation as in the presentation itself. Greuze's portrait of his wife has as its complement the sketch for *La Mère bien-aimée*, a picture which 'prêche la population, et peint très pathétiquement le bonheur et le prix inestimables de la paix domestique' (ii. 155). It is thus, Diderot remarks, 'excellent [...] pour les mœurs'. The mother is stretched out on a chaise-longue with a brood of children about her, contentment radiating from her tired but beautiful face. Diderot remarks that her half-open mouth and her attitude suggest nothing but the mingled exhaustion and pleasure of successful maternity, though as we shall see this is not entirely true. The near-identical portrait of Mme Greuze shows the same mixed expression, but together with other details—the backward thrust of the head, the knocking sideways of the bonnet—it actually evokes 'un paroxisme plus doux à éprouver qu'honnête à peindre'.

Cette bouche entr'ouverte, ces yeux nageans, cette attitude renversée, ce cou gonflé, ce mélange voluptueux de peine et de plaisir, font baisser les yeux et rougir toutes les honnêtes femmes dans cet endroit. Tout à côté, c'est la même attitude, les mêmes yeux, le même cou, le même mélange de passions, et aucune d'elles ne s'en aperçoit. (ii. 151)

Huysmans, the Goncourts and others would draw attention to Greuze's inveterate lubriciousness,[20] but Diderot preferred to see him as the uphholder of bourgeois morality. Greuze himself obviously enjoyed falling in with this misinterpretation, asking Diderot at one stage to suggest to him a moral-seeming subject involving a nude female. Diderot obliged with the idea for a 'modèle honnête', all innocent eyes and bashful looks (*Salons*, iii. 109 f.); but the picture was eventually composed, appropriately enough, by the painter Baudouin, Boucher's son-in-law and an artist reprimanded in the *Salons* for his libertine tastes. Diderot's refusal to acknowledge Greuze's salaciousness allowed him to present the latter's proclivity for showing lush and scantily clad young women clutching symbols of lost innocence as part of a drive to regenerate the nation and restore its lost sense of virtue in the wake of Boucher's rococo fripperies. Yet the dual meaning that both he and Greuze could impose upon the single figure of a reclining woman illustrates the sheer difficulty of convincingly establishing 'proper' norms. Either the body's messages are unclear, or the onlooker declines to see them clearly. Diderot admits that accompanying props and attendant circumstances can make a world of interpretative difference, but cannot allow that equivocality may have been deliberately built into a physiognomy, an attitude or an entire work. 'Sans ce secours, restent-elles [les physiognomies] indécises? Il faut bien qu'il en soit quelque chose' (*Salons*, ii. 151). A 'maternité' straightforwardly announces itself as moral and virtuous—or does it? The examples of Greuze's *La Mère bien-aimée* and La Grenée's *La Charité romaine* suggest that some scepticism may be in order.

Suggestiveness

In other cases the symbolic use of gesture may make a whole scene or portrait puzzling in its allusiveness. Diderot is sure about the meaning of an indecent sign made by the cupid in Vien's *La Marchande d'amours* ('il a la main droite appuyée au pli de son bras gauche qui, en se relevant, indique d'une manière très-significative la mesure du plaisir qu'il promet', *Salons*, i. 210), but how 'speaking', to take a familiar example, is the attitude of the girl weeping over her dead bird? Few contemporary critics, after all, read into Greuze's picture what Diderot saw. Perhaps a part of the attraction held by typologies of expression in the eighteenth century was the fact that they seemed to clarify what was actually vague and indeterminate, if not positively ambiguous; but writers and artists were well aware of how misleading such attempts at categorizing were. In other words, they acknowledged the relativism of those very appearances that the manuals of civility, moral writings and written or illustrated codifications attempted to reduce to rule.

One schema of particular relevance to painting, the 'têtes des passions' of the seventeenth-century artist Charles Le Brun, will be more closely examined in the next chapter. Another uncertain semantic area is that dealing with specifically erotic markers, and Diderot comments on their shifting values in his fiction and art criticism. As the history of fashion and culture reveals, certain erogenous zones vary from age to age, and what one period finds titillating or indecent will seem unexciting or unworthy of notice to the next. Diderot's France found nothing reprehensible in deep décolletages, and Diderot himself regularly fails to notice how Greuze's women burst out of their clothes as they partake in some supposedly moral activity; but the eighteenth century still thought it unseemly to bare part of the shoulder. The ankle, foot, hand, wrist and arm were more sexually perceived in the Enlightenment than they are today, at least in the Western world, and adorning part of the leg carried a stronger erotic charge—though any age would find suggestive the scene in *Jacques le fataliste* where Denise, having been presented with a garter by Jacques, massages his wounded leg until her hand reaches the critical point where he 'la baisa' (p. 779).

Somewhat surprisingly, Diderot often fails to extract the erotic maximum from a sexually charged situation, which makes his reader wonder whether he retains a bourgeois sense of inhibition about such matters. The only chapter in *Les Bijoux indiscrets* that actually depicts the erotic body on the rampage is one which Diderot himself is thought not to have written ('Le Bijou voyageur', with its explicit polyglot account of the courtesan Cypria's sexual exploits all over Europe, is generally attributed to Eidous). Even in the *Supplément au Voyage de Bougainville* the freely loving bodies of the natives, and eventually of the prudish chaplain, are left undescribed. Diderot's evocation of 'proper' and 'improper' bodies is almost never graphic—perhaps because of his affection for the sketch, which by leaving much unsaid provided space for the reader's or beholder's imagination to wander in, or perhaps because of his belief that the referential possibilities of language are severely limited.

What of his views on nudity, which was brought to his theoretical as well as practical attention in all the Salons he visited, and was necessarily affected by the claims of 'pudeur'? There may be modest and immodest nakedness, but certainly there are decent and indecent attitudes to it. A letter he wrote to Falconet in May 1768 underlines this point in connection with the difficulties Anna Therbusch encountered when, as a female artist statutorily excluded from male life-drawing classes, she tried to paint a nude man from life:

On permet au vice de regarder la nature, et on le défend au talent. Pourdieu, ne donnez pas là dedans. Mille femmes lascives se feront promener en carrosse, sur le bord de la rivière, pour y voir des hommes nuds; et une femme de génie n'aura pas la liberté d'en faire déshabiller un pour son instruction. (*Corr.* viii. 42)

The impulses of modesty may be aroused in predominantly sexual or predominantly social situations, or in both at the same time;[21] and as we have seen, shifts in perception make different kinds of exposure shocking, publicly as well as privately. The *Supplément au Voyage de Bougainville* observes that the practice of covering the body, however firmly prescribed by etiquette, may inflame the observer's imagination and excite his or her desires (p. 508). The nakedness of Carle Van Loo's Graces is decent, but the attempt to clothe some of it is not. The garland that feebly veils 'les parties que la pudeur ordonne de voiler' merely draws attention to them, and does so with a suggestive insistence.

Une figure toute nue n'est point indécente. Placez un linge entre la main de la Vénus de Médicis et la partie de son corps que cette main veut dérober, et vous aurez fait d'une Vénus pudique une Vénus lascive, à moins que ce linge ne descende jusqu'aux pieds de la figure. (*Salons*, i. 197)

Diderot returns to this theme in his commentary on another version of the Graces by Van Loo, in which the scraps of drapery loosely applied to the goddesses' buttocks and thighs illustrate how 'c'est une femme découverte, et non pas une femme nue qui est indécente. Une femme indécente, c'est celle qui auroit une cornette sur sa tête, ses bas à ses jambes, et ses mules aux pieds' (ii. 63; also iii. 94). The falsity in such depictions, he declares in his 1761 notice on Hallé, derives from the mores of the so-called civilized present, and is the product of its obsession with superficial propriety.

Nous ne voyons jamais le nu: la religion et le climat s'y opposent. Il n'en est pas de nous ainsi que des Anciens, qui avaient des bains, des gymnases, peu d'idée de la pudeur, des dieux et des déesses faits d'après des modèles humains, un climat chaud, un culte libertin. (i. 116)

Clothes

We may be reminded of Coleridge's remark on the refusal of Bernardin de Saint-Pierre's Virginie to take off her clothes when the sailor tries to save her from shipwreck by making her swim ashore: according to James Northcote, Coleridge found this 'a proof of the prevailing tone of French depravity, and not of virgin innocence. A really modest girl in such circumstances would not have thought of any scruple.'[22] Nor, according to Diderot, are the clothes of the civilized likely to promote an ideal of beauty matching what the Ancients knew, because 'nos ajustements corrompent les formes. Nos cuisses sont coupées par des jarretières, le corps de nos femmes étranglé par des corps, nos pieds défigurés par des chaussures étroites et dures' (*Salons*, ii. 116). His complaint is one heard in other writers of the time. Soemmering, who conclusively demonstrated the differences between the female and the male skeleton, wrote a work on the damaging effects of stays which showed how corsets and tight lacing caused anatomical deformities of the thorax and abdomen.[23] There was even a theory that corsets themselves put so much pressure on the abdominal organs that the uterus was squeezed out through the vagina.[24] But long before Soemmering Rousseau's *Emile* had inveighed against the wearing of this particular straitjacket, and his admirer Stanislas de Girardin erected a tomb in his memory at Ermenonville decorated with images of children merrily burning them on bonfires. The corset's purpose, of course, was to enhance the erotic form by making the breasts more prominent, partly through displacing the activity of the lungs in an upward direction so that the respiratory movement drew attention to the bosom—the 'pouter-pigeon' effect.[25] The anti-corset faction saw the staymaker as an artist in corruption, whose manifest plan was to inflame desire by creating a superior kind of body-sculpture.

Alphonse Leroy's *Recherches sur les habillements des femmes et des enfants* of 1772 attacks all the fashionable ligatures that prevent the body from assuming its natural forms, remarking that the compression which corsets cause under the armpits turns the arms and hands purple and makes them swell.[26] 'Un air négligé sied bien mieux à la beauté; le charme est d'autant plus puissant qu'il semble plus naturel' (p. 241), and the woman who wants to captivate her lover does not await his arrival dressed in this ridiculous armour. But it may well have been Diderot in his *Encyclopédie* articles 'Panier' and 'Perruque', and de Jaucourt in 'Vêtement', 'Mode' and 'Chaussure', who most effectively drew attention to the idiocies of extremist fashion.[27] If clothing was a sign of moral degeneracy, as Diderot observes in the *Essais sur la peinture*, it was also a cause of physical deformity. So the search began for ways to free the body from needless restriction—not just the burning of corsets and swaddling-clothes, but the casting off of collars, girdles, cuffs, garters and tight-fitting breeches. What is the point, Diderot asks, of 'nos culottes en fourreau [...], nos jarretières sous le genou, [...] nos souliers pointus' (p. 714)? De Jaucourt's *Encyclopédie* article 'Chaussure' alludes to the high-heeled footgear favoured by women, noting how it distorts the bones of the feet and makes them excessively arched 'à cause de la soudure non naturelle ou anchylose forcée de ces os, à-peu-près comme il arrive aux vertèbres des bossus'. People thus shod, he rather unnecessarily adds, find it extremely difficult to descend mountains, and cannot walk fast, 'étant alors obligées ou de se balancer a-peu-près comme les canards, ou de tenir les genoux plus ou moins pliés et soûlevés, pour ne pas heurter des talons de leur *chaussure* contre terre'. Not surprisingly, they cannot jump as well as people in low heels.

After escaping from the convent and finding refuge with Mme Madin, Suzanne Simonin acquires a trousseau which includes some corsets to take on to her new situation with the marquis de Croismare, because the world requires a different style of dress from the cloister (*La Religieuse*, p. 86). The clothes Diderot prescribes for 'la chaste Suzanne' in La Grenée's *La Charité romaine* are of a simplicity that matches her lack of coquettishness: 'Le luxe de draperie seroit un ridicule [...]; qu'elle soit vêtue simplement, et d'une étoffe grossière et commune' (*Salons*, ii. 95). Not that simplicity of costume necessarily indicates that one is free of worldly artifice, as the Mme de La Pommeraye episode of *Jacques le fataliste* illustrates: the 'dévote''s uniform that the mother and daughter d'Aisnon are obliged to wear as accomplices to Mme de La Pommeraye's plot is wholly misleading, since they are fallen women. Perhaps the daughter would have preferred in more normal circumstances to ornament herself in order to attract men, if not the kind of men who frequent her mother's house of assignation, but the marquis des Arcis, like Diderot, professes a preference for beauty that makes no concession to feminine ornament. This does not, however, make such ornament an undesirable artifice, devalued because it somehow embodies false pretences. (Orou's daughters and the other 'natural' women of the *Supplément au Voyage de Bougainville* do not spurn it when they wish to attract males.) What may perhaps be regrettable is the fact that men do not similarly enhance their looks by contrivance; that they are able, like Diderot in his famous dressing-gown, to profess a kind of intellectual and moral honesty through dressing carelessly. But that is a different matter altogether. The simple life to which those tired of civilized ways turned in the eighteenth century often entailed the adoption of correspondingly artless dress, or of a costume whose art concealed itself. So Rousseau started wearing an Armenian outfit because it was loose and flowing enough not to add to the discomfort caused by his urinary complaint, and also, no doubt, because it looked suitably savage. Diderot wore his 'robe de chambre'.

The *Correspondance littéraire* of 1 February 1769 contains a report on a visit which the Polish prince Adam Czartoriski paid Diderot in the company of Grimm, and describes how they found the philosopher 'paré d'une robe de chambre de ratine écarlate, neuve du jour' (viii. 276). Grimm writes that 'Je ne pus m'empêcher de me récrier sur sa magnificence. Quelques jours après, le philosophe sermonné m'envoya le morceau que vous allez lire', namely the 'Regrets sur ma vieille robe de chambre'. Wanting to thank Diderot for some service he had done her, Mme Geoffrin had allegedly replaced his old furniture and his entire wardrobe, including his dressing-gown, without, she hoped, contravening the essential simplicity he lived by, a simplicity that kept him at a distance from her salon kingdom in the rue Saint-Honoré. But Diderot complained that wearing the new clothes had reshaped his whole personality. The old dressing-gown 'moulait tous les plis de mon corps sans le gêner; j'étais pittoresque et beau. L'autre, raide, empesé, me mannequine'[28] as though he had been posed by Marcel, like some of the polite, dead figures in paintings criticized in the *Salons*. The dustiness of the cast-off garment, which he had regularly used to wipe the covers of books or blot ink with, was a reflection both of his cherished bohemian ways and of his free literary spirit. At present, however, 'j'ai l'air d'un riche fainéant', as misleadingly moneyed in appearance as the simpering portrait by Michel Van Loo had made him look. There he had been depicted in a 'luxe de vêtement à ruiner le pauvre littérateur si le receveur de la capitation [venait] à l'imposer sur sa robe de chambre' (*Salons*, iii. 66 f.).

The coquette's air he complains of in the Van Loo portrait has the same perfumed falsity he attributes to the courtesan of the 'Regrets sur ma vieille robe de chambre', whom he imagines himself first eyeing and following, then turning away from in disgust. His real tastes are quite different:

Je puis supporter sans dégoût la vue d'une paysanne. Ce morceau de toile grossière qui couvre sa tête; cette chevelure qui tombe éparse sur ses joues; ces haillons troués qui la vêtissent à demi; ce mauvais cotillon court qui ne va qu'à la moitié de ses jambes; ces pieds nus et couverts de fange ne peuvent me blesser. (p. 944)

This is because she presents the image of an estate he respects, and because he profoundly pities all the wretchedness her condition imposes upon her. The courtesan's tawdriness is altogether different: her torn cuffs, dirty silk stockings and worn shoes show him 'la misère du jour associé à l'opulence de la veille'.

This is not the garb of the civilized body, but the apparel of the *demi-monde* that merely approximates to politeness. Diderot's own tatters, by contrast, are distinguished, proclaiming a proud independence despite their owner's appearance of destitution. In his old, 'disgracieux' attire the philosopher looks like a man who commands his person rather than the other way about, refusing to be imprisoned by concepts of civility, manneredness (instead of mannerliness, though that is perhaps bad enough) and 'politesse'. So he silently argues for the right to establish social values in a defiantly individual way.

At this stage it may be worth summarizing the points made so far. Diderot's conviction that nothing can be explained without the body was the product of a loose materialism that did not exclude metaphysical sympathies, but firmly subordinated them to the physical. His freedom from philosophical dogmatism allowed him to investigate different kinds of dualism in his fictional writings, but never weakened his belief in the unitary coherence of human beings. A thinker and writer whose interest in sensibility as a psycho-physical phenomenon had far-reaching implications, he was encouraged to examine its influence in areas as diverse as the creation and reception of art and the development of a moral sense in man; and his alertness to the related issue of how different organs affect our apprehension of the world made him desire a closer acquaintance with the inner as well as outer structure of man, a desire that finds expression in works like the *Eléments de physiologie* and *Le Rêve de d'Alembert*. Both these texts, too, pursue the theme of the origin and growth of the human organism, a preoccupation whose pervasiveness in *Le Rêve de d'Alembert* makes that dialogue a compendium of arguments for monism and the psycho-physiological interpretation of life.

All this illuminates Diderot's scientific as well as philosophical concern with the corporeal. His view of the body as a *governable* entity is the product of humanism, while his belief that it is *governed* arises in large part from his materialist determinism. His humanism accounts for the way he sees real people's bodies as differing from mechanical ones, and bodily responses as things that can and should be learnt (as the little savage of *Le Neveu de Rameau* may be educated out of his Oedipus complex). His regard for the natural does not work against this preoccupation with good learning, as opposed to the absorption of artificial civilized doctrines, but actually reinforces it.

It also moulds the theories about bodily expressiveness to which we shall now turn: in the wake of constraint and propriety comes an emphasis on the freedom of expansive movement. Of course matters are less simple than that, and Diderot's corporeal eloquence suffers from certain restrictions. But in reflecting on body-language (as opposed to language about the body) in his imaginative writings, he put a new emphasis on physicality and the concept of the non-verbal but articulate self.

Notes to Chapter 3

1. On these general questions see Vila, *Enlightenment*, 1 and *passim*.
2. See Francis Barker, *The Tremulous Private Body* (Ann Arbor: University of Michigan Press, 1995), 10 f.
3. See Basil Munteano, 'Survivances antiques: l'abbé Du Bos esthéticien de la persuasion passionnelle', *RLC* 30 (1956).
4. On these general matters see Angelica Goodden, *'Actio' and Persuasion: Dramatic Performance in Eighteenth-Century France* (Oxford: Clarendon Press, 1986), 33.
5. *La Religieuse*, in *O.Rom.* 247.
6. See Vila, *Enlightenment*, 171, on the way this jerkiness hints at a potential pathological sensibility.
7. See Jean Starobinski, 'Sur la flatterie', *Le Remède dans le mal* (Paris: Gallimard, 1989), 61 f.; also Peter France, *Politeness and Its Discontents* (Cambridge: Cambridge University Press, 1992).
8. See Roger Chartier, *Lectures et lecteurs dans la France d'ancien régime* (Paris: Seuil, 1987), 48 ff.
9. See Alan Charles Kors, *D'Holbach's Coterie* (Princeton: Princeton University Press, 1976).
10. Quoted in Chartier, *Lectures et lecteurs*, 74.
11. Nicolas Faret, *L'Honnête Homme, ou l'art de plaire à la cour* (Paris: Du Bray, 1630), 6, 15 f., 25.
12. Jean-Baptiste de La Salle, *Les Règles de la bienséance et de la civilité chrétienne, à l'usage des écoles chrétiennes de garçons* (Reims: Florentin, 1736), 1–2.
13. See Stafford, *Body Criticism*, 12.
14. See also *Paradoxe sur le comédien*, in *O.Esth.* 581 ff.
15. See Arthur O. Lovejoy, '"Nature" as Aesthetic Norm', *Essays in the History of Ideas* (New York: Brazillier, 1955).
16. See Maurice Tourneux, *Diderot et Catherine II* (Paris: Calmann-Lévy, 1899), 75 (Grimm to Nesselrode, also quoted in Bil'basov, *Didro v Petersburge* (Cambridge: Oriental Research Partners, 1972), 58).
17. Extract from *Mélanges de d'Escherny*, quoted in *Œuvres complètes de Diderot*, ed. Assézat and Tourneux, xx. 138.
18. See Jean-Claude Bologne, *Histoire de la pudeur* (Paris: Orban, 1986).
19. See Georg Simmel, *On Women, Sexuality, and Love*, trans. Guy Oakes (New Haven and London: Yale University Press, 1984), 136.
20. See Bernard Ribémont, 'A la croisée des regards: la peinture de Greuze dans la critique de Diderot, des frères Goncourt et de Huysmans', in *Le Regard et l'objet*, Delon and Drost (q.v.), ed., 103.

21. See James Laver, *Modesty in Dress* (London: Heinemann, 1969), 9.
22. See William Hazlitt, *Conversations of James Northcote*, ed. Edmund Gosse (London: Bentley and Son, 1894), 224.
23. See Roberts and Tomlinson, *Fabric of the Body*, 366.
24. See Michie, *Flesh Made Word*, 21.
25. See David Kunzle, 'The Corset as Erotic Alchemy: From Rococo Galanterie to Montaut's Physiologies', in *Woman as Sex Object*, ed. Thomas B. Hess and Linda Nochlin (London: Allen Lane, 1973), 93 ff.
26. Alphonse Leroy, *Recherches sur les habillements des femmes et des enfants* (Paris: Le Boucher, 1772), 230 f.
27. See Daniel Roche, *The Culture of Clothing*, trans. Jean Birrell (Cambridge: Cambridge University Press, 1994), 463.
28. 'Regrets sur ma vieille robe de chambre', *Œuvres de Diderot*, ed. André Billy (Paris: Gallimard, 1951), 943.

CHAPTER 4

Eloquent Bodies

Body-language

Charles-Augustin Vandermonde was the first keeper of a collection of automata bequeathed to the French nation by Vaucanson, which opened in 1783. But he was also the author of an *Essai sur la manière de perfectionner le genre humain* (1756), a work that expresses a new kind of preoccupation with training the human body.[1] There is no longer any intention to ensure its 'proper' self-presentation, nor much concern with improving deportment and fitting the individual for life in a postured world. Vandermonde's aim is to cultivate the body's physical resources, and so restore the kind of tone that a tradition of social refinement has softened. Physical strength, he believes, is the 'premier soutien de la vie', a basis for civic and domestic order that past obsessions with 'politesse' had neglected. He follows Buffon's chapter 'De l'âge viril' in the *Histoire naturelle de l'homme* (pp. 109 ff.) in his account of the well-developed body as a balanced assemblage of muscle and bone whose fortitude owes absolutely nothing to 'belles manières'. This revolutionary power-dynamic represents what Georges Vigarello has called an 'ordre de vigueurs' calculated to renovate and restore a society that had been 'marcélisé' to the point where empty graces seemed to count for more than solid, purposeful deeds.

David's famous painting *Le Serment des Horaces* epitomizes the ground-breaking psycho-physiology that Vandermonde's essay seeks to formulate, and it is in one respect indebted to Diderot's theories.[2] The assertive arrangement of male bodies in the painting (the yielding female figures are relegated to one side) encapsulates the stern physical and moral principle that infused politicized neo-classical art in the years before the Revolution, and although the picture was completed after Diderot's death in 1784 there can be little doubt that David's conception of body-language had been influenced by him. The two men were regular guests at the *soirées* held by Sedaine in his lodgings at the Louvre, which he, as an architect as well as a playwright, shared with David from the late 1760s until 1775. *Le Serment des Horaces* in some respects embodies Diderot's observations on a new acting style in the *Entretiens sur 'Le Fils naturel'*: 'Il faut que l'action théâtrale soit bien imparfaite encore, puisqu'on ne voit sur la scène presque aucune situation dont on pût faire une composition supportable en peinture' (p. 89). David's picture does not actually translate a moment from an existing play, and the precise sources of the painted scene are disputed; but Corneille's tragedy *Horace* was certainly an inspiration.[3]

In its silent eloquence the picture also recalls Diderot's words on expressive pantomime in the *Lettre sur les sourds et muets*, where he remarks that he looks at paintings as though they were conversations between deaf mutes:[4]

considérez que celui qui se promene dans une galerie de peintures fait, sans y penser, le rôle d'un sourd qui s'amuseroit à examiner des muets qui s'entretiennent sur des sujets qui lui sont connus. Ce point de vue est un de ceux sous lesquels j'ai toujours regardé les tableaux qui m'ont été présentés; et j'ai trouvé que c'étoit un moyen sûr d'en connoître les actions amphibologiques et les mouvemens équivoques. (p. 52)

Diderot was exceptional among critics of his time in the attention he paid to the human body, though his opinion that the body—not merely the face—was the index of inner states of feeling had been current since antiquity.[5] When, much earlier in the century, Dubos had remarked in his *Réflexions critiques sur la poésie et sur la peinture* that the passions were all reflected in outward movement and expression, and that body-language was in theory capable of conveying the finest shades of meaning to the onlooker, he was echoing the ancient orators' views on how feelings may be translated through the speaker's attitude, action and physiognomy. *Actio*, the classical theory of corporeal eloquence, was employed at the Bar and in the law-courts as a way of persuading the mind by convincing the eye, and a central underlying assumption was that a close relation existed between inner state and outer show. The *Eléments de physiologie*, rather uncritically, echo and develop this notion:

Toutes les passions affectent les yeux, le front, les levres, la langue, les organes de la voix, les bras, les jambes, le maintien, la couleur du visage, les glandes salivaires, le coeur, le poumon, l'estomac, les arteres et veines, tout le sisteme nerveux, frissons, chaleur. (p. 267)

The theory of elemental bodily response also underpins the fascination of Diderot's age with more popular arts like dance and pantomime, which he himself saw as ideally suited to furthering the dialogue of emotion that his new acting methods were intended to generate: they were all silent objections to the bombast, stiffness and stylization characteristic of non-comic dramatic performance in his day. He was abreast of the expressive theories of Condillac and Rousseau, who emphasized the non-verbal origin of human communication, and his attraction to the idea that overwhelming experiences are best conveyed without any recourse to language[6] explains why an alternation of pantomime and dialogued scenes is proposed in the *Entretiens sur 'Le Fils naturel'*. But primitive gesticulation is one thing; vital movement that conveys the passage of thought as well as feeling is another. What form should it take? Diderot believed that dance, divested of its established formalized pattern, might translate the interaction of body and mind as effectively as articulated dialogue allied with the actor's natural bodily movements could do. Indeed, he wrote in the *Pensées détachées sur la peinture* about the extreme difficulty of accurately conveying feeling by more conventional means: 'Le sentiment est difficile sur l'expression; il la cherche, et cependant, ou il balbutie, ou il produit d'impatience un éclair de génie. Cependant cet éclair n'est pas la chose qu'il sent; mais on l'aperçoit à sa lueur' (p. 755). And the 1763 *Salon* asserts that 'Il y a des passions bien difficiles à rendre; presque jamais on ne les a vues dans la nature. Où donc en est le modèle? où le peintre les trouve-t-il? qu'est-ce qui me détermine, moi, à prononcer qu'il a trouvé la vérité?' (*Salons*, i. 121). Yet the suggestive language of the body can transcend these limitations. Dance, being even further removed from the domain of conventionalized expression than the actor's mute 'jeu', might paradoxically communicate with greater directness, if infinitely less specificity; but this was only possible if, as many eighteenth-century thinkers believed, it actually had something to imitate and hence convey. The more closely it adhered to the habits of civility and social dressage, the less likely this was.

At its most elemental, according to Dubos, dance was a form of bodily therapy as well as a more complex expressive mode, because it exteriorized and so governed human passions by the rhythmic representation of actions they engendered. As such, it had clear affinities with the other naturalistic kinds of bodily movement that fascinated Diderot. The importance of 'geste' (loosely understood as body-language in general) in his theory of action reflects the central place occupied by 'sensibilité' in a philosophy concerned with the way the unseen workings of the human organism are made visible. Diderot's assumption that this was best done freely and spontaneously looks uncontroversial in the context of his times, but raises problems connected with the possibility of *learning* effective movement that would exercise acting theorists influenced by Diderot in the later eighteenth and the nineteenth centuries.

Leaving that question aside for a moment, we may note that the principle of fluidity implied by his *Lebensphilosophie*, of which the philosophy of acting is merely a part, draws Diderot close to Montaigne. But he gives the notion of impermanence a sharper aesthetic emphasis than his forebear. It is because the present moment is transitory that imitative art has to capture its constant becoming, which means that the forms best suited to conveying human movement—in the eighteenth century, enacted drama and its silent offshoots—must set about translating the principle of mutability by rejecting congealed and lifeless convention. Extending Locke's philosophy in a vitalist direction, Diderot took sensation, which was at the origin of all thought, to be representative of the same type of movement as was manifested by external phenomena. First the mind mimicked a feeling, then its own motion was reproduced in gesture. The process was direct and immediate, and no intervening word or sound was needed to transmit it.

This may partly explain why Diderot so often feels it necessary to detail his bodily response to experiences like those provided by art, as well as the responses he thinks proper in artists themselves. A visually arousing phenomenon, he believed, should provoke a physical movement reflecting the flux of passion.[7] So the 1767 *Salon* describes the effect on him of one of Vernet's 'sites': 'je poussai un cri d'admiration, et [...] je restai immobile et stupéfait [...]. Quelquefois mes yeux et mes bras s'élevaient vers le ciel, quelquefois ils retombaient à mes côtés comme entraînés de lassitude' (*Salons*, iii. 151–2). The gestures are spontaneous, uncontrollable reactions to a sublime spectacle, or so Diderot would have his reader believe. Nor are such physical responses confined to the aesthetic realm. A letter to Sophie Volland of 18 October 1760 details his reaction to witnessing acts of justice:

Alors il me semble que mon coeur s'étende au dedans de moi, qu'il nage; je ne sçais quelle sensation délicieuse et subtile me parcourt partout; j'ai peine à respirer; il s'excite à toute la surface de mon corps comme un frémissement; c'est surtout au haut du front, à l'origine des cheveux qu'il se fait sentir; et puis les symptômes de l'admiration et du plaisir viennent se mêler sur mon visage avec ceux de la joye, et mes yeux se remplissent de pleurs. (*Corr.* iii. 56)

It should follow from all of this that Diderot feels hostile towards any attempt to reduce 'geste' to rule. In fact, however, he does allow a degree of prescriptiveness: after all, the *Paradoxe sur le comédien* calls the actor a 'pantin merveilleux'. But the *Entretiens sur 'Le Fils naturel'* stress the need to allow him to improvise when the mood takes him, at least if he is a sufficiently sensitive performer. Rules are for the ordinary man or woman to abide by, not the genius. Diderot never loses his rooted dislike of regulations like the ones issued in François Riccoboni's 1750 treatise *L'Art du théâtre*, which describes the proper way for an actor to kneel, bring the foot forward, walk, raise the arms and so on—instructions that recall the conduct-books of Faret and La Salle. Diderot wrote to Mme Riccoboni, François's sister-in-law, of the

maussade jeu [...] qui défend d'élever les mains à une certaine hauteur, qui fixe la distance à laquelle un bras peut s'écarter du corps, et qui détermine comme au quart de cercle, de combien il est convenable de s'incliner! Vous vous résoudrez donc toute votre vie à n'être que des mannequins? [...] Vos règles vous ont fait de bois, et à mesure qu'on les multiplie, on vous automatise. (*Corr.* ii. 94)

We have already noted Diderot's view of Mme Riccoboni's own deficiencies as a performer, despite what the *Réfutation d'Helvétius* describes as her constant study and consulting of the best authorities. Perhaps the standard training was partly at fault, though the *Paradoxe sur le comédien* does not consider that performers should simply be allowed to 'jouer d'âme'. At the same time, there is no suggestion in that dialogue that successful actors have learnt formalized precepts like the ones in François Riccoboni's handbook, even if they have so mastered their 'jeu' that they can reproduce it at will.[8]

Condillac had been the first to insist that gesture constituted the greater part of the 'langage d'action' that lay behind every 'langage d'institution'. None the less, the famous image in the *Traité des sensations* (1754) of the statue becoming sentient may have been borrowed from Diderot: the *Lettre sur les sourds et muets* imagines breaking a man down into as many individual creatures as he has senses (a process which Diderot calls an 'espèce d'anatomie métaphysique', p. 45) in order to establish what he owes to each. Given Diderot's own visual gifts, it is a little surprising that sight is called the most superficial sense; perhaps it is so because he believed—rather intermittently—that it could easily be deceived. He goes on, however, to suggest that the eyes are best equipped to judge the merits of an actor's performance, and that the ears derive no essential information from it, at least when the play's dialogue is already familiar to the listener. Remembering his fondness for going to the theatre as a young man, he notes provocatively that

Aussitôt que la toile était levée, et le moment venu où tous les autres spectateurs se disposoient à écouter; moi, je mettois mes doigts dans mes oreilles [...] et je me tenois opiniâtrement les oreilles bouchées tant que l'action et le jeu de l'acteur me paroissoient d'accord avec le discours que je me rappellois. (p. 52)

To the curious enquiries of other members of the audience 'je répondois froidement "que chacun avoit sa façon d'écouter, et que la mienne étoit de me boucher les oreilles pour mieux entendre"'.

Previously in the *Lettre* he had commented on the effect of a silent *actio* that no verbal expression could match, still less surpass—the scene in which Lady Macbeth walks silently and with closed eyes, 'imitant l'action d'une personne qui se lave les mains, comme si les siennes eussent encore été teintes du sang de son Roi qu'elle avoit égorgé il y avoit plus de vingt ans' (p. 47).[9] (Diderot does not mention that immediately after this powerfully silent moment Lady Macbeth starts speaking one of Shakespeare's most memorable lines.) In a letter to Voltaire of 28 November 1760 he had remarked on the ability of the actress Mlle Clairon, whom he disparages elsewhere, to inspire through pantomime an intensity of emotion no words could convey. The occasion which provoked this thought was a performance of Voltaire's *Tancrède*:

Ah! mon cher maître, si vous voyiez la Clairon traversant la scène, à demi renversée sur ses bourreaux qui l'environnent, ses genoux se dérobant sous elle, les yeux fermés, les bras tombants, comme morte; si vous entendiez le cri qu'elle pousse en apercevant Tancrède, vous resteriez plus convaincu que jamais que le silence et la pantomime ont quelquefois un pathétique que toutes les ressources de l'art oratoire n'atteignent pas. J'ai dans la tête un moment de théâtre où tout est muet, et où le spectateur reste suspendu dans les plus terribles alarmes. (*Corr.* iii. 272–3)

Of course, taking pantomime to be a universal and uniquely expressive language that transcended cultural and intellectual barriers might lead to the absurd conclusion that silent stage action should be preferred to every type of conventionally dialogued and articulated drama. At his most polemical or enthusiastic Diderot does seem to suggest this possibility, but in more sober mood he withdraws from its implications. The *drames Le Fils naturel* and *Le Père de famille* are notoriously verbose, despite the annoyed observation of the *Entretiens sur 'Le Fils naturel'* that 'Nous parlons trop dans nos drames: et, conséquemment, nos acteurs n'y jouent pas assez' (p. 100).

It may have been after seeing Garrick perform that Diderot was prompted to write the *Lettre sur les sourds et muets*:[10] at any rate, it was composed in the same year as the actor's first visit to France. Diderot remained an enthusiast for Garrick's acting style, writing for the *Correspondance littéraire* the (negative) review of Sticoti's pamphlet *Garrick ou les acteurs anglais* that would develop into the *Paradoxe sur le comédien*, and noting in the 1759 letter to Mme Riccoboni Garrick's opinion that there was no effect pantomime could not achieve even when completely divorced from speech (*Corr.* ii. 94). The same letter comments on the dumbshow Garrick performed with a cushion (masquerading as a child) to persuade sceptics of his point. It may seem a long way from this to the apparently more ritualized activity of dance, of which the third *Entretien sur 'Le Fils naturel'* remarks that it is an art still awaiting the man of genius; but the man in question, Noverre, was as greatly influenced by Garrick's mute performances as Garrick was by his, witness the fact that he accepted Garrick's invitation to dance at Drury Lane in 1755 and 1756. However, Noverre was equally close in spirit to Diderot. Just as the latter's writings on the theatre stressed the need for dramatic performance to become more pictorial and to base itself on 'les conditions' of ordinary life, so Noverre's *Lettres sur la danse* (1760) remark:

Que de tableaux diversifiés ne trouvera-t-il [the dancer] pas chez les artisans! Chacun d'eux a des attitudes différentes, relativement aux positions et aux mouvements que leurs travaux exigent. Cette allure, ce maintien, cette façon de se mouvoir, toujours à leur métier et toujours plaisante, doit être saisie par le compositeur; elle est d'autant plus facile à imiter qu'elle est ineffaçable chez les gens de métier.[11]

When Noverre comments on the instructiveness of watching 'la multitude de ces oisifs agréables, de ces petits-maîtres subalternes qui sont les singes et les copies chargées des ridicules de ceux à qui l'âge, le nom, ou la fortune semblent donner des privilèges de frivolité, d'inconséquence et de fatuité', he seems almost to be anticipating the discussion at the end of *Le Neveu de Rameau* of the positions people adopt in everyday life in order to curry favour with others. (In choreography, 'position' simply meant a way of placing the feet relative to one another.) To adopt a position, Diderot's dialogue suggests, is to forfeit the autonomy that only free spirits, like geniuses, are able to preserve.

Noverre robustly denied one actor's assertion that *Le Fils naturel* and *Le Père de famille* could not be well performed, though he acknowledged that acting mute scenes was a touchstone of excellence few could achieve (p. 262). The actor referred to may have been Grandval, the 'sociétaire' of the Comédie-Française who apparently sent *Le Fils naturel* back to the duc d'Orléans when the latter was trying to arrange performance at the theatre. His opinion was probably the consequence of Diderot's demand that the *drame* be acted as though in a private house, which entailed unheard-of innovations such as the performers turning their backs on the audience. (The impropriety of making such a demand is one of the themes of Mme Riccoboni's discouraging letter to Diderot of 18 November 1758 about the new acting style he envisaged.) Noverre's references to the *automata* who were bound to fail in the attempt to act the *drames* satisfactorily recalls the language of Diderot's reply to Mme Riccoboni, where the principle of avoiding machine-like regulation is unequivocally stated.

A degree of formalism may be requisite in choreography, but it does not have to be of the kind envisaged by the minuet-master. Noverre's revolutionary action ballets conveyed emotional states as Diderot wanted the 'jeu' of the actor to do—they were, after all, ballets with something to represent, unlike society dances and the 'grands ballets' of seventeenth- and eighteenth-century opera. Virtuoso effects were not entirely excluded from the dancer's repertoire; Noverre simply criticized the cultivation of purely technical accomplishment when it contributed nothing to the larger artistic concern that was the action ballet itself, believing like Diderot that isolated display interrupted the unfolding of continuous action mirroring the motions of life. But the activities of dance are not part of day-to-day existence, and it was inevitable that the action ballets should retain some of the stylization Diderot wanted to exclude from the dramatic stage.

Expressiveness

Yet Noverre left in practice, as Diderot left in theory, a tradition of unforced bodily movement whose expressiveness was enhanced by the relative imprecision of its 'meaning'. Attempts to reduce expression to the sort of rule that would make interpretation easier were still widespread, and Diderot was still occasionally tempted to follow the conventionalized patterns thus generated (for example, in some of the facial expressions described in *La Religieuse*).[12] But his fondness for the imprecise and half-formulated, which is declared throughout his aesthetic writings, meant that his work too offered the kind of latitude for interpretation that he associated with spontaneous and unregimented performing techniques. They activated the observer's projective capacities, like the sketch in visual art, and this seemed to him an unquestioned advantage. Loosely expressive bodily arts such as pantomime were preeminently suited to producing the suggestive sense of the *non finito* that so appealed to the eighteenth-century mind. 'Je vois dans le tableau une chose prononcée, combien dans l'esquisse y supposai-je de choses qui y sont à peine annoncées', Diderot remarks in the *Salon* of 1765 (ii. 154); and in the commentary on Greuze's *La Mère bien-aimée*, 'plus l'expression des arts est vague, plus l'imagination est à l'aise' (ii. 154). Equally, 'Le négligé d'une composition ressemble au déshabillé du matin d'une jolie femme; dans un instant, la toilette aura tout gâté' (*Pensées détachées sur la peinture*, p. 823).

Diderot's need to be physically moved by a painting is closely bound up with his rejection of the softly mannered art of the rococo, whose lack of elemental feeling is implicitly contrasted in the *Essais sur la peinture* with the 'quelque chose de sauvage, de brut, de frappant et d'énorme' (p. 714) that the new ethos of passion requires. The latter is certain to be compromised, if not excluded altogether, when bodily depictions are mannered, and when a 'système de mesquinerie' is allowed to cheapen artistic production. But it might be objected that to do as Diderot proceeds to do and answer one kind of system with another equally dependent on imitation and classification is to compound the error. Diderot may have disliked Le Brun's cataloguing of the essentially mobile and often ambiguous facial translations of feeling, which were first set out in a series of lectures at the Académie royale de peinture et de sculpture and then published with illustrations in 1702,[13] but he remained attracted to the principle it embodied. He was so drawn to its absolute categorization, indeed, that he became curiously blind to the very possibility of ambivalence. As the *Essais sur la peinture* declare, 'L'homme entre en colère, il est attentif, il est curieux. Il aime, il hait, il méprise, il dédaigne, il admire; et chacun des mouvements de son âme vient se peindre sur son visage en caractères clairs, évidents, auxquels nous ne nous méprenons jamais' (p. 696). This may remind us of Suzanne's changing expressions as detailed in *La Religieuse*: 'à mesure que j'avançais, la frayeur, l'indignation, la colère, le dépit, différentes passions se succédant en moi, j'avais différentes voix, je prenais différents visages et je faisais différents mouvements' (p. 242). Although Diderot allows that 'une grande imagination de peintre est un recueil immense de toutes ces expressions' (*Essais sur la peinture*, p. 697), he does not conclude—at least at this point—that the vastness of the store may cause the artist to depict passionate states whose meaning is unclear.

In 1759 the comte de Caylus instituted at the Académie royale de peinture et de sculpture a prize in expression, for which the first subject was 'Affliction' as posed by Mlle Clairon. (Clairon was famous for her ability to convey every shade of emotion through facial expression.) Caylus's prize was part of a drive to make artists observe and render passion with a directness that befitted the emotional energy of the age, though the fact that an actress was the original sitter casts some doubt on the degree of naturalism envisaged and achieved. Ironically, de Jaucourt's *Encyclopédie* article 'Passion (peint.)' urges practitioners to observe Le Brun's models at the same time as it regrets the loss of expressiveness in the faces of the French nation generally. Caylus's intention, precisely, had been to overcome the a priori nature of Le Brun's prescriptions[14] by encouraging the observation of living models, though the artist's purpose had actually been to establish a set of rules which, once learnt, could be applied beyond his own limited number of examples.[15] And the prize certainly helped to develop the artistic interest in expression, though it may also have encouraged artistic *exaggeration* of expression: in the course of the late eighteenth century David, Vincent and Ménageot would all be winners.

According to Jacques Proust, Diderot's work offers an entire symbol-system of gestures and looks.[16] Some of the symbols of course derive from Le Brun's Académie lecture scheme: its influence can be detected in the *Lettre sur les sourds et muets*, the *Essais sur la peinture*, the *Salons*, at least some of the novels and the dramas. But Le Brun's system itself was not particularly original: it was based on the pathognomic theories of Descartes, who believed that since the passions were controlled by the brain, the face was the most accurate index to them. This notion was never accepted as completely authoritative, however. Descartes himself had observed that some people make the same face when they are happy as others when they are sad; Dubos would remark that the meaning of particular expressions and gestures varies from one culture to the next; and *Le Neveu de Rameau* contains references both to a cunning man with the face of an idiot and to an intelligent-looking fool (p. 59).[17] Despite the statement in the *Essais sur la peinture* that 'Il lui [i.e., nature] a plu de nous faire bons et de nous donner le visage d'un méchant; ou de nous faire méchants et de nous donner le visage de la bonté' (p. 698), Diderot seems oddly unhappy with the flexibility of interpretation this implies—oddly, because in other respects he so mistrusts fixed categories. So the same *Essais* state roundly that 'L'expression est faible ou fausse si elle laisse incertaine sur le sentiment' (p. 698), while the *Eléments de physiologie* claim against the evidence presented by *Le Neveu de Rameau* that 'Un sot n'a jamais l'air d'un homme d'esprit' (p. 48). Buffon may have attacked this kind of absolute interpretation in the *Histoire naturelle de l'homme*, but Diderot seems to have been confused about its merits—remarkably confused, indeed, for a man who depicted a good number of dissemblers in his literary works. No matter that he portrays the sycophantic play-acting parasite Lui in *Le Neveu de Rameau*, the hypocritical nuns of *La Religieuse*, the vengeful Mme de La Pommeraye and her accomplices, and the devious père Hudson of *Jacques le fataliste*; he could still be credulous. This being so, there seems much to recommend the view of Jacques Proust that an often uncritical adherence to Le Brun's theories prevented Diderot from developing a coherent and advanced theory of expression.

'Seeing' Emotion

In his critique of Greuze's *Sévère et Caracalla* Diderot rather ungraciously suggests that the heads of the two secondary figures, Papinien and a senator, should be saved from the disaster of the whole canvas because of their admirable psychological depth and the 'speaking' nature of their depiction (*Salons*, iv. 106). But Sévère and Caracalla lack grandeur, and the son manifests none of the remorse in the face of his father's reproach for which Diderot wished there was a convenient shorthand ('Je voudrais que le remords eût son symbole, et qu'il fût placé dans tous les ateliers', he remarks in the *Essais sur la peinture*, p. 769). Nor did other canvases of Greuze's present this emotion with the straightforwardness Diderot the moralist would have liked, a fact that perhaps ought to have sounded a warning to him. There are almost no commentaries in the *Salons* on Greuze's fallen women—who clutch broken pitchers, hold baskets of smashed eggs and look at themselves in cracked mirrors in order to indicate that they have lost their virginity—mostly because few of them were shown at the exhibitions Diderot visited. In any case, many depict penitents who, in Mme Roland's words, look all set to perform the forbidden deed again. Diderot's observations in the 1765 *Salon* on the appeal of the sketch express a sentiment whose aesthetic attraction is considerable, but whose implications run counter to his equally strong urge for depictive clarity in the presentation of emotional states. As already noted, his interpretation of Greuze's *La Jeune Fille qui pleure son oiseau mort*—that the girl is bemoaning her lost virginity rather than the death of her bird—was not shared by other reviewers. This fact demonstrates the ambiguity which, in truth, the often equivocal art of painters like Greuze depended on.[18] Although expressions need to be seen in context, the artist often refuses to contextualize sufficiently to resolve uncertainties, or simply fails to see how his own portrayal gives rise to them. The identifying of emotional states is a much more complex process than the often superficial psycho-physiology of the eighteenth century implies: in Berkeley's words, they may not be 'immediate objects of vision'. One can describe the configuration of a set of features, but the concept of emotion they suggest cannot be seen in the same way. Sadness, for example, is not localized and demonstrable as a person's mouth is. Perhaps the solution is to invoke the Wittgensteinian notion of 'seeing-as': we use experience drawn from everyday life to understand something like the depiction of sorrow in visual art.

Although he demanded that painters be physiognomists, Diderot seemingly disapproved of Caylus's 'prix d'expression' because he (rightly) feared that it might lead to extremes of passionate depiction and a high degree of manneredness. But he also praised artists like Greuze for managing to convey true feeling in a faithfully realistic way—which is very far from how Greuze's more showy heads are 'read' nowadays. In the paragraphs he devotes to the 1763 *Piété filiale* he observes that the painter's critics are wrong to call the girl's father moribund, announcing that 'Le docteur Gatti dit que ces critiques-là n'ont jamais vu de malades, et que celui-là a bien encore trois ans à vivre' (*Salons*, i. 235). In other words, Greuze's sensitivity is far greater than that of those who dare to judge his work. Moreover, Diderot thought that Greuze excelled in the difficult art of blending expressions on a single individual's face. As we saw, one of the reasons why the *Salons* praise the portrait of Mme Greuze so extravagantly is that 'Jamais vous n'avez vu la présence de deux expressions contraires aussi nettement caractérisées' (that is, 'ce mélange voluptueux de peine et de plaisir', ii. 151). He admires Greuze's *L'Accordée de village* of 1761 because it introduces conflicting emotions into a joyous scene, showing an elder sister who 'crève de douleur et de jalousie de ce qu'on a accordé le pas sur elle à sa cadette. Elle a la tête portée sur une de ses mains, et lance sur les fiancés des regards curieux, chagrins et courroucés' (i. 142). To the modern eye this all looks very obvious, but to Diderot's age it indicated tact and a high degree of psychological finesse.

The case of Diderot's portrait by Louis-Michel Van Loo, a work he criticizes because it fails to convey the characteristic mobility of his expression, underlines the limitations of visual art in depicting feeling. The essence of emotion is movement, but the portrait freezes it.

J'avais en une journée cent physionomies diverses, selon la chose dont j'étais affecté [...]. J'ai un masque qui trompe l'artiste, soit qu'il y ait trop de choses fondues ensemble, soit que les impressions de mon âme se succédant très rapidement et se peignant toutes sur mon visage, l'œil du peintre ne me retrouvant pas le même d'un instant à l'autre, sa tâche devienne beaucoup plus difficile qu'il ne la croyait. (*Salons*, ii. 67)

Had Van Loo been a better artist, Diderot implies, he might have been able to persuade onlookers to re-examine the subject of the portrait with fresh curiosity, realizing that they had never known it properly: the artist of genius makes us contemplate everything anew. But the picture of Diderot, however attractive as an image, failed to convince as an *insight*—an insight into Diderot's essence as a man whose constant flux mirrored the movement of the universe.

We may leave aside for a moment the implications of the issue this predicament raises, that visual art is limited to a single moment in time: it explains why Diderot should have remarked in a letter to Falconet of 2 May 1773 that *literature* had the primary responsibility for depicting the passions (*Corr.* xii. 208 f.). All that needs noting now is the fact that the limitations of painting call into question Diderot's project of importing pictorial precepts into dramatic performance. (In this respect he is unpersuasive when he announces that 'Un comédien qui ne se connaît pas en peinture est pauvre comédien', *Essais sur la peinture*, p. 696.) When he wrote to the actress Mlle Jodin in 1766 that no decent paintings had ever been done from theatrical scenes because the actor's performing style was usually so artificial, he was scarcely consistent in advising her none the less to visit galleries in every town she passed through (*Corr.* vi. 168). Needless to say, Diderot wanted performers to do more than look at portrait *heads*, just as he wanted painters to do more than merely capture facial expression: he was as eager for actors to act with their whole person as for painters to attend to every detail of the human body. In this he was showing some critical originality. A letter of 21 August 1765 to Mlle Jodin encourages her to give a total bodily performance, remarking that 'C'est le visage, ce sont les yeux, c'est tout le corps qui doit avoir du mouvement'. Correspondingly, she is to avoid fragmenting her performance into a multitude of individual movements that draw attention to parts of her body rather than the whole. In fact she is to produce 'le moins de gestes que vous pourriez; le geste fréquent nuit à l'énergie, et détruit la noblesse' (*Corr.* v. 102).

He thinks that painters could benefit from the same sort of advice. When he remarks of the little boy who brings water to the paralytic old man in *La Piété filiale* that 'Il faut voir la douleur et toute la figure de celui-ci; sa peine n'est pas seulement sur son visage, elle est dans ses jambes, elle est partout' (*Salons*, i. 234), we may remember his observation on how an actor should show the involvement of his whole body in a particular emotional or physical state. The *Paradoxe sur le comédien* describes Garrick telling the actor Préville, who was pretending to be drunk, that he was not convincingly drunk *in the legs*. But because the doctrine associated with Le Brun still dominated Académie teaching in the mid-eighteenth century, facial expression remained the prime means of representing feeling.[19]

Diderot's concern with the whole expressive body, however, may have been partly inspired by his admiration for another seventeenth-century artist, Nicolas Poussin. The *Salons* of 1767 and 1769 praise the artist eloquently for showing emotion through the medium of the body, and attending to every detail of the 'speaking' attitudes that reveal states of mind and heart (e.g., iii. 83, 117, 286). His regard for Poussin, indeed, makes him harshly intolerant of the neo-Poussinists of the 1760s whose works fail to match the solemn impressiveness of their model—Carle Van Loo's *Auguste faisant fermer le temple de Janus* (*Salons*, ii. 61), which shows the unworthy emperor already referred to, Vien's *Marc-Aurèle faisant distribuer au peuple du pain et des médicaments* (ii. 88), where the figures are cold and expressionless, Hallé's *L'Empereur Trajan partant pour une expédition militaire* (ii. 82), where Trajan's lack of character and nobility belies his ancient model, and even the failed *Sévère et Caracalla*, which Diderot claims Greuze submitted to the Salon 'comme un morceau à lutter contre ce que le Poussin avait fait de mieux' (iv. 104), but where this painter of genre scenes appeared incapable of rising to the requisite heights of historical grandeur.

But at his proper level, according to Diderot, Greuze succeeded in making the human body a medium of true eloquence, every aspect of its language communicating with the spectator. This is not just the case with the *Accordée de village* and the *Piété filiale*, extravagantly though Diderot praises them. It also applies, in his view, to the sketches (now in the Musée de Lille) for the *Fils ingrat* and the *Mauvais Fils puni*, which Diderot describes in the 1765 *Salon*.[20] These highly wrought works are characterized by striking and emotive poses and gesticulations, which the finished canvases in the Louvre do not preserve. Diderot remarks on the raised arm, threatening hand and insolent attitude of the ungrateful son, the father trying to reach him, the mother desperately clinging to him, and the son's brutal shove as he fends her off. The picture may now look histrionic and overstated, but to Diderot and his contemporaries it simply expressed strong but appropriate emotion. The eloquence of the *Mauvais Fils puni* is even more extreme, every figure but that of the dead father on his bed gesturing with grief, misery and remorse. The finished version of the work suppresses some of the more emphatic details, like the son's loss of the leg with which he had kicked his mother away and the paralysis of the arm with which he had threatened his father. According to Diderot both sketches are wholly devoid of 'attitudes tourmentées'; instead they are filled with 'actions vraies qui conviennent à la peinture' and, particularly the second, infused with an 'intérêt violent, bien un, et bien général' (ii. 159).

Gesture, Meaning and Theatricality

Since this is unlikely to be the response of the modern observer, the question arises whether it is really necessary to take every gesture as significant, or to depict all the overt forms of bodily reaction a given situation might provoke. Surely there may be gestures which are devoid of any clear intention, but are hard to distinguish formally from other apparently more meaningful ones.[21] In the absence of the kind of internal evidence that discursive language can provide, signs made on canvas must normally be taken to be assertions rather than negations; so a tableau of the Greuzian type will opt for strong statements that make the storytelling intention as clear as possible. This does not, of course, mean that hints and double entendres have no place in Greuze's work; far from it. But it cannot be denied that he often resorts to theatrically obvious body-language, a form of emphasis which Diderot castigates when he sees it in dramatic performance or in painting that seems to him to imitate its worst excesses, but which he rarely detects in this particular artist.

According to the *Essais sur la peinture*, the kind of painterly contrast found in academic painting, where relationships are knowingly manipulated for reasons of effect, is reprehensible because unnatural: 'c'est une action apprêtée, compassée, qui se joue sur la toile. Le tableau n'est plus une rue, une place publique, un temple; c'est un théâtre' (p. 713). When the truth of nature is forgotten, Diderot remarks in the same work,

l'imagination se remplit d'actions, de positions et de figures fausses, apprêtées, ridicules et froides. Elles y sont emmagasinées; et elles en sortiront pour s'attacher sur la toile. Toutes les fois que l'artiste prendra ses crayons ou son pinceau, ces maussades fantômes se réveilleront, se présenteront à lui; il ne pourra s'en distraire; et ce sera un prodige s'il réussit à les exorciser. (p. 670)

But if this is true, and if it is true (as the *Essais sur la peinture* remark) that no theatrical scene has ever produced a tolerable painting, it is odd that Diderot should have recomposed Carle Van Loo's 1759 picture of Medea and Jason (with Mlle Clairon posing as Medea), a work he disliked for its theatrical décor, as a melodrama. Finding Jason too unimpassioned, he complains that 'Il fallait lever au ciel des bras désespérés; avoir la tête renversée en arrière; les cheveux hérissés; une bouche ouverte qui poussât de longs cris, des yeux égarés' (*Salons*, i. 64). Of course, Jason may simply be looking unmoved because the very composed Medea has just petrified him with a spell after butchering her children. Diderot disliked the attitudinizing of Clairon in general, calling her, the actress Mlle Dumesnil and Sophie Arnould 'des copies souvent gauches, toujours froides et maniérées de la nature'.[22] Here he calls Clairon-Médée 'roide' et 'engoncée', a 'Médée de coulisse'. However, the actress herself apparently considered Van Loo to have surpassed the art of the theatre in his painting, telling him that 'il faudra que l'original étudie longtemps sa copie'.[23]

Words and Images

It is perhaps surprising that Diderot's admiration for Poussin did not lead him to distance himself from painting which, like Greuze's, sought so intently for plastic effects.[24] Poussin thought that such a tendency implied too great a concern with the given, whereas the artist, in his opinion, should reject what was present and visible and aim instead at intellectual penetration. Rousseau was of the same mind, believing that the most powerful artistic as well as moral experiences were internalized: this view is argued in the fifteenth chapter of the *Essai sur l'origine des langues*. He considered, however, that his own century was obsessed with materializing all the operations of the soul. Diderot, conversely, was seduced by an eighteenth-century version of behaviourism, which meant reducing all mental predicates to a description or depiction of actual conduct. If this externalization risked making the stage or the canvas resemble a puppet-play, he seems to have been unaware of the danger.

A possible answer was to work deliberately for a countervailing kind of inwardness, an area of stillness unbroken by bustle or gesticulation. One such moment of repose appears to be provided by the tableau, which the *Entretiens sur 'Le Fils naturel'* oppose to the intrusive staginess of the *coup de théâtre*. Mme Riccoboni's letter to Diderot had included the observation that, however pictural the dramatic stage might be, it was a *tableau mouvant* in which bodies regrouped, adopted new attitudes and changed the rhythm of a scene.[25] His rejoinder was that the movement occurred only after the moment of rest which met the spectator's gaze when the curtain rose, and that the dynamics of performance then required the most energetic arrangement of bodies possible. Yet in his opinion the quiet, static canvas could also approximate to this energetic presentation, for the work of an artist like Greuze presents a high degree of 'on-stage' activity. This gives his painting a narrative flow that lends the time-bound medium of painting the expository possibilities of literature.

When Diderot imaginatively enters the world of Greuze's *Le Mauvais Fils puni* it is as though he is physically involving himself in a scene of intricate bodily movement. 'Imaginez un père qui expire au milieu de ses enfants,' he orders Mme Riccoboni in the letter of 27 November 1758; 'Voyez ce qui se passe autour de son lit: chacun est à sa douleur, en suit l'impression, et celui, dont je n'aperçois que certains mouvemens qui mettent en jeu mon imagination, m'attache, me frappe et me désole plus peut-être qu'un autre dont je vois toute l'action' (*Corr.* ii. 91). No more than in a painted picture should the figures in drama be 'symétrisés, roides, fichés, compassés et plantés en rond' (p. 90). Theatrical tableaux emphasize the rhetorical principle of *compositio* on a small scale,[26] and in so doing call on the actors' ability to convey through bodily attitude the same kind of unobtrusive, unstylized integration into a greater whole as Diderot demands of each component in a painting.[27]

The restricted space of the theatre he envisages for the performance of his *drame* (*Le Fils naturel* is supposed to unfold 'dans le salon de Clairville', one of the characters) means that it can in theory avoid the kinds of exaggeration entailed by the size of conventional playhouses. Painting dealing with action—the province of history painting in the eighteenth century, as well as of the genre scenes by Greuze that Diderot regarded as their equal in rank—must choose, in Lessing's phrase, the 'fruitful moment' to depict. The urge to overstate in order to ensure that meaning has been successfully conveyed is obvious. But drama, which moves in time, has words with which to reinforce its figural depictions: this theoretically lessens the temptation to exaggerate, though a performer such as Clairon still remained, in Diderot's words, 'emphatique' and 'empesée' (*Le Neveu de Rameau*, p. 54). As performed drama combined visual effects with speech, all the advantages of image and discourse were available to it: it could communicate with the directness that both Burke and Lessing associated with the visual arts, and it could suggest moods, thoughts and other intangible states that were beyond the easy reach of painting and sculpture.[28] Such a blend of directness and suggestiveness is difficult to achieve, and Diderot was far less successful at conveying it in his dramas than in dramatic dialogues like *Le Neveu de Rameau*, where debate on intangible values joins with a strikingly material rendition of human life.

The *Pensées détachées sur la peinture* describe the way the visual image actualizes and solidifies what in the conventional medium of language is denied direct presentation, and do so with reference to the body:

Pourquoi l'*Hippogriffe*, qui me plaît tant dans le poème, déplairait-il sur la toile? J'en vais donner une raison bonne ou mauvaise. L'image, dans mon imagination, n'est qu'une ombre passagère. La toile fixe l'objet sous mes yeux et m'en inculque la difformité. Il y a, entre ces deux imitations, la différence d'*il peut être à il est.* (p. 762)

The *Lettre sur les sourds et muets* expresses a similar notion, that bodies which appear unconventional or malformed are rendered inoffensive in non-representational art-forms whose medium is narrative or expository time, though they appear concrete in the form of visual images (p. 84). Here the difficulty of painting a majestic picture of Neptune emerging from the sea leads to the conclusion that painting, which shows the thing itself, lacks the suggestive resources of the 'hieroglyphic' arts of literature and music—literature merely describing the object, and music barely suggesting an idea of it. '[La] poésie nous fait admirer des images dont la peinture serait insoutenable [parce que] notre imagination est moins scrupuleuse que nos yeux' (p. 97). Representational painting, having scant use for metaphor (except in allegorizing or symbolic works), cannot be successful when deploying such a mode in combination with non-figurative bodies. This, Diderot says, is why Carle Van Loo's painting of *L'Amour menaçant* in the 1759 Salon makes a ludicrous impression.

[Je] ne sais, mon ami, si vous auriez remarqué que les peintres n'ont pas la même liberté que les poëtes dans l'usage des flèches de l'Amour. En poésie, ces flèches partent, atteignent et blessent; cela ne se peut en peinture. Dans un tableau, l'Amour peut menacer de sa flèche, mais il ne la peut jamais lancer sans produire un mauvais effet. Ici le physique répugne; on oublie l'allégorie, et ce n'est plus un homme percé d'une métaphore, mais un homme percé d'un trait réel qu'on aperçoit. (*Salons*, i. 111)

To work effectively, images of this sort have to be dematerialized and indirectly described through the resources of language.

Though Diderot knew the representational power of words to be limited, his description of the human body may be obscured for reasons of 'pudeur' (as was suggested in the previous chapter) or incomprehension (as with Suzanne Simonin), rather than because linguistic resources necessarily fall short of his ideal of presentational clarity. Despite the fact that language 'images', at best, only by conventional means, its ability to present what the seventeenth-century writer Bernard Lamy called a 'peinture sensible de la chose dont on parle'[29] was still prized in the Enlightenment. Trained in rhetoric by the Jesuits, Diderot was well acquainted with verbal techniques of visualization, like the *hypotyposis* which allowed a speaker to bring an object so clearly to his listeners' minds that they seemed to see what was being said;[30] and he was well aware of the sheer *enargeia* (vividness) of words themselves.

As a philosopher, furthermore, he was sympathetic to the notion championed by Locke and Hobbes as well as Descartes that the role of words was to evoke images: indeed, it clearly supported him theoretically as well as practically in his work as a Salon commentator. If language worked eidetically, it should obviously be possible for it to convey images with directness and clarity. But as a critic and imaginative writer as well as a philosopher, Diderot was constantly engaged by the question of how images and words respectively related to the world. Though the painter tries to show the thing itself, the non-depictive arts capture movement, and so suggest the restless indeterminacy of life. Language may fail to present certain types of sensuous image adequately, but its capacity to evoke the actions and passions of men fully compensates.

In *Le Neveu de Rameau* language succeeds in graphically depicting movement as well, paradoxically, as being converted into the same gesticulating pantomime it serves to evoke. The abstractions of the two interlocutors' discussion on the theme of genius must be translated by Lui, who complains that he cannot speak as effectively as Moi (p. 94), into the tangible discourse of the body. As a successful artist (rather than the mediocrity he knows he is) he would have a large house ('et il en mesuroit l'étendue avec ses bras'), a good bed ('et il s'y etendoit nonchalament'), fine wine ('qu'il goutoit en faisant claquer sa langue contre son palais'), a coach and four ('et il levoit le pié pour y monter'), beautiful women ('a qui il prenait deja la gorge et qu'il regardoit voluptueusement') and the satisfaction of a good night's sleep ('et en parlant ainsi il se laissoit aller mollement sur une banquette; il fermoit les yeux, et il imitoit le sommeil heureux qu'il imaginoit') (pp. 16–17). In one sense this bodily eloquence is the same language of dissimulation as Diderot associates with the refined gestures of the courtier: the whole being of the sycophantic 'adulateur de profession' described in the *Paradoxe sur le comédien* consists in a series of attitudes and postures demanded by his masters. The Nephew must prostitute himself with all manner of 'singeries' in order to amuse his morose patrons, while feeling uneasily how great a disservice such physical self-abasement does to his talent (p. 47). At such times the whole business of performing appears a second-rate way of masking an inner unrest—his painful awareness that he lacks the genius of his uncle and other great artists.

To reduce the concept of genius to body-language is of course to degrade it in ways incomprehensible to Moi, whose discourse remains at the level of abstraction. Moi, as Aram Vartanian has pointed out, never gesticulates.[31] But Lui's most solid form of reassurance is to reduce spiritual aspiration and achievement to the level of the basely material, and call all else vanity. So while Moi speaks of intangible values—duration, posterity, spiritual influence and the like—such as the ones Diderot himself upholds in his correspondence with the sceptical sculptor Falconet, Lui is bound to respond in terms of wine, women and song. Mind is triumphantly subordinated to body, or appears to be; but as the progression of the conversation reveals, the Nephew is actually haunted by a sense of failure, epitomized in his inability to translate his deepest insights into words or music. The rhythm of creation transmitted by the language of the body is inadequate to serve the cause of art.

But so, it appears, is the polished language of mind that the philosopher speaks. He feels elevated above this bohemian contortionist, this apparent automaton[32] of whom he says at one point that 'il resta immobile, stupide, étonné. Il tournoit ses regards autour de lui, comme un homme egaré qui cherche a reconnoitre le lieu ou il se trouve. Il attendoit le retour de ses forces et de ses esprits; il essuyoit machinalement son visage' (p. 85). Moi tolerates seeing him once a year because 'il restitue a chacun une portion de son individualité naturelle' (p. 5). But the philosopher does not evidently transcend the Nephew, being as impressionable by the illusory substance of Lui's orchestral performance, which consists simply in bodily gesture, as Lui is drained in the process of realizing it. Though he affects contempt for the Dionysian display, revolted by the shameless self-revelation and alarmed by the way the Nephew abuses his body (p. 26), he cannot deny the power of Lui's sensibility and its corporeal translation (p. 27).

Lui's pantomime is in some respects a form of liberation from his usual dependence on the material, and so becomes a kind of transcendence above the body that executes its gestures. But such a performance is not the spiritual endeavour this suggests, not an achievement of the art he aspires to create, so much as a finding of himself through the 'sensible' potential of his body. When he remarks to Moi that, as well as writing music 'que personne ne joue', he has created attitudes and positions unknown before him, he is laying claim to a prouder achievement than his interlocutor is prepared to allow. As a mime creating himself out of motion, he has converted music into another form of sense-impression, and so released the powers of feeling in his body that are otherwise uselessly expended on toadying and posturing before his social superiors. Moreover, as the power of gesture may transcend language and exceed its suggestiveness, it can be said to match what the *Lettre sur les sourds et muets* calls music's inimitable evocativeness. Lui's love of music and submission to it has passed into his body, which makes it inevitable that at the end of his corporeal display he should appear utterly consumed by its force: 'Assis sur une banquette, la tête appuyée contre le mur, les bras pendants, les yeux a demi fermés, il me dit: Je ne sçais ce que j'ai; quand je suis venu ici, j'etois frais et dispos, et me voilà roué, brisé, comme si j'avois fait dix lieues' (pp. 87–8). But the end of the dialogue shows him recovering ground, in a characteristically physical set of images. When he describes the positions which he says all are made to adopt in the standard motions of social life, he manages to impress Moi with an uncomfortable awareness of his own submission to bodily forces—a dependency on the flesh that governs even philosophers, who must eat (though at nature's ill-served table) and indulge their sexual appetites (though possibly alone, like Diogenes in his barrel).

The rhythm Lui prefers is that of activity 'à deux', or with his menagerie of comrades. Not for him the individualism to which Moi lays claim, or at least not consistently. Although it is a state in which one remains truer to oneself than do those who dance the beggarly dance, Lui is bound to others not just for the material sustenance he cannot do without, but also for the bodily gratifications that, while less sustaining, are still supremely pleasurable. Not that he remains any longer a spokesman for the purely animal instincts he had earlier defended; he now supports the claims of social living in at least a partly civilized form. It is for Moi, rather forlornly, to uphold the superior merits of the solitary Diogenes and life in the wild, which Lui regards as representative of pointless self-mortification: 'je suis dans ce monde, et j'y reste', and 'Je vais à terre' (p. 103).

The distance from corporeality that Moi appears to recommend is superficially similar to the detachment Suzanne Simonin attempts to preserve in *La Religieuse*. Her determination to describe her body's non-participation in the different schemes to appropriate it is striking: 'Quoique les religieuses s'empressassent autour de moi pour me soutenir, vingt fois je sentis mes genoux se dérober, et je me vis prête à tomber sur les marches de l'autel' (p. 239), she remarks at one stage of her calvary. When she appears at the altar to take her vows she is like a lifeless doll, her limp body effectively the property of others to dispose of as they will: 'je ne me trouvais plus de jambes; deux de mes compagnes me prirent sous les bras; j'avais la tête renversée sur une d'elles, et je me traînais' (p. 246), like a young victim being borne along for sacrifice. Her later interview with the obdurate Mme Simonin is described as though it were a tableau from a drama: sitting opposite one another in the carriage they remain wordless, until Suzanne falls at her mother's feet and rests her head in supplication on her knees. Mme Simonin angrily thrusts away a body that has become intrusive and burdensome, a new version of the unwanted appendage she had bundled into the convent in order to forget about her daughter's illegitimacy.

Even in a state of passivity, the body cannot help communicating; but its moves may be ambiguous. Its ability to tell a story is obviously heightened when supporting contextual information is available. In acting, this occurs most straightforwardly when dialogue is allowed to shore up and amplify the silent 'jeu'. The mimicry of Rameau's nephew may be at its most effective when it is based on the 'speaking' music of the Italians (which he praises for its expressive power) rather than the conventionalized and non-communicative melody of the French, or where it is fitted into a social situation (of pandering, eating, flattering or whatever) that complements it. In the case of less worldly-wise individuals, failure to gauge certain physical responses at their intended worth may result in complete bafflement. We have already noted this in the case of Suzanne Simonin; but the non-verbal language of Diderot's corporeally eloquent dramas seems also to have nonplussed at least some of its audience. In the *Mémoires d'outre-tombe* Chateaubriand describes attending a performance of *Le Père de famille* in his youth, and failing to realize either that the performance had taken place or that the action he witnessed had any meaning whatsoever to communicate:

J'aperçois deux hommes qui se promenaient sur le théâtre en causant, et que tout le monde regardait. Je les pris pour les directeurs des marionnettes, qui devisaient devant la cahute de madame Gigogne, en attendant l'arrivée du public: j'étais seulement étonné qu'ils parlassent si haut de leurs affaires et qu'on les écoutât en silence. Mon ébahissement redoubla lorsque d'autres personnages, arrivant sur la scène, se mirent à faire de grands bras, à larmoyer, et lorsque chacun se prit à pleurer par contagion. Le rideau tomba sans que j'eusse rien compris à tout cela [...]. Telle fut la première impression que je reçus de l'art de Sophocle et de Molière.[33]

If such a problem can arise with performed drama, it is plain that the visual and plastic arts may intensify them. Diderot seems, rather naively, to have taken all bodily attitudes and movements to be both communicative and charged with significance. But where the body's *hidden* operations were at issue, it was less easy to do so than in the case of straightforwardly externalized ones: some organic and pathological reactions demand to be understood differently from overtly behavioural ones. This may be one reason, as I shall suggest, why the art of medicine interested Diderot as greatly as it did: it excited his desire to know not only what symptoms meant, but also what apparently symptom-free states of bodily disequilibrium signified. When he remained on the surface of the organism both as an observer of expressivity and as a diagnostician of feeling, his theory of corporeal eloquence could appear strained and simplistic.

Notes to Chapter 4

1. See Georges Vigarello, *Le Corps redressé* (Paris: Delarge, 1978), 93 ff.
2. See Dorothy Johnson, 'Corporeality and Communication: The Gestural Revolution of Diderot, David, and *The Oath of the Horatii*', *Art Bulletin* 71 (1989), 109.
3. See Anita Brookner, *Jacques-Louis David* (London: Chatto and Windus, 1980), 69 ff.
4. See also Herbert Josephs, *Diderot's Dialogue of Language and Gesture* (Ohio: Ohio State University Press, 1969), 55.
5. See Goodden, *'Actio' and Persuasion*, 8 f.
6. See also Josephs, *Diderot's Dialogue*, 69.
7. See Vartanian, 'Erotisme et philosophie', 369.
8. On this general matter see Goodden, *'Actio' and Persuasion*, 139 ff.
9. See also Josephs, *Diderot's Dialogue*, 69 f.
10. See Roland Virolle, 'Noverre, Garrick, Diderot: pantomime et littérature', in *Motifs et figures* (Paris: Presses Universitaires de France, 1974), 202.
11. Jean-Georges Noverre, *Lettres sur la danse et sur les arts imitateurs* (Paris: Lieutier, 1952), 73.

12. See Jacques Proust, 'Diderot et la physiognomonie', *CAIEF* 13 (1961).
13. See Jennifer Montague, 'Charles Le Brun's *Conférence sur l'expression générale et particulière'*, unpublished Ph.D. thesis, 2 vols. (University of London, 1959).
14. See John Montgomery Wilson, *The Painting of the Passions in Theory, Practice and Criticism in Later Eighteenth-Century France* (New York and London: Garland, 1981).
15. See Montague, 'Charles le Brun's *Conférence'*, i. 159.
16. Proust, 'Diderot et la physiognomonie', 230–1.
17. See also Graeme Tytler, *Physiognomy in the European Novel: Faces and Fortunes* (Princeton: Princeton University Press, 1982), 140–3.
18. See B. R. Tilghman, *The Expression of Emotion in the Visual Arts. A Philosophical Enquiry* (The Hague: Nijhoff, 1970), 47 ff.
19. See Johnson, 'Corporeality', 92 ff.
20. See Johnson, 'Corporeality', 94.
21. See Ludwig Wittgenstein, *Bemerkungen über die Philosophie der Psychologie*, ed. G. H. von Wright and Heikki Nyman, 2 vols. (Oxford: Blackwell, 1980), i. 34 f.
22. Letter to Sophie Volland of 27 Jan. 1766 (*Corr.* vi. 31).
23. See *Lettre d'un artiste sur le tableau de Mlle Clairon* (Paris: 1759), in *Collection Deloynes*, 63 vols. (Paris, Bibliothèque nationale), vii, no. 90; see also Goodden, '*Actio*' and Persuasion', 92.
24. See Jacques Thuillier, 'Temps et tableau: la théorie des "péripéties"', in *Stil und Überlieferung in der Kunst des Abendlandes*, 3 vols. (Berlin: Mann, 1967), iii. 195.
25. Quoted in full in *Œuvres complètes*, ed. Assézat and Tourneux, vii. 396–9.
26. See Goodden, '*Actio*' and Persuasion', 88 f.
27. See *Pensées détachées sur la peinture*, 790.
28. See E. Allen McCormick, '*Poema pictura loquens*: Literary Pictorialism and the Psychology of Landscape', *Comparative Literature Studies* 13 (1976); Gita May, 'Diderot and Burke: A Study in Aesthetic Affinity', *PMLA* 75 (1960). See also Goodden, '*Actio*' and Persuasion', 38.
29. [Père Bernard] Lamy, *De l'art de parler*, 2nd edn. (Paris: Prulard, 1676), 74.
30. Lamy, *De l'art de parler*, 89–90; see also Pierre Zoberman, 'Voir, savoir, parler: la rhétorique et la vision', *XVIIe Siècle* 133 (1981), 410 ff.
31. See Vartanian, 'Dualist', 261.
32. See Josephs, *Diderot's Dialogue*, 175.
33. François-René, vicomte de Chateaubriand, *Mémoires d'outre-tombe*, ed. Maurice Levaillant and Georges Molinier, 2 vols. (Paris: Gallimard, 1951), i. 56.

CHAPTER 5

Fleshly Indulgence, Bodily Torment

Treating the Organism

Assigning ultimate meaning to the body, as Diderot did, meant paying keen attention to its state in sickness and health. This was a less straightforward matter than might at first appear, and its complexity helps explain his remark that it is impossible to think cogently about metaphysics or ethics without being an anatomist, a naturalist, a physiologist and a physician.[1] The quantity of medical articles in the *Encyclopédie* reflected a general Enlightenment preoccupation with understanding both how the human 'machine' functioned and how it might function better—for instance, by avoiding or palliating the hygienic dangers it was routinely exposed to. Physicians began to write more or less expressly for laymen in the eighteenth century because so few of those who needed their services had access to them, particularly in the country.[2] Samuel Tissot's self-help manuals, for example (on masturbation, the health of men of letters and the health of the worldly), were originally published in Latin, but rapidly translated into French and the major European languages. All became bestsellers. Aristocrats suffering from hypochondria, women tormented by the vapours or the 'fureur utérine', writers plagued by indigestion and complaining of a loss of tone, and adolescents (and others) tempted by Rousseau's 'dangerous supplement' obviously required serious medical assistance.

People were healthily as well as unhealthily preoccupied with the operations of their bodies. The enlightenment and advice dispensed to them were not necessarily reassuring, however: hardened masturbators and their minders, for instance, were as often alerted to the inevitable decline into madness and eventual death which the practice allegedly caused as actually counselled about ways to alleviate and resist its temptations. A rhetoric of admonition that at times developed into a rhetoric of terror[3] warned men and women of the medical dangers of their century, an age when the cultivation of sensibility posed a serious threat to mental and physical wellbeing,[4] and when the over-refined lives of the privileged weakened their constitutions. Few were prepared to adopt the radical solution recommended by Rousseau in cutting all ties with civilization, and Rousseau himself never went as far down this path as is often assumed; but his cautions about the hygienic as well as moral perils of culture still exerted great influence.

Other remedies, in some cases almost as drastic, were proposed. As part of a move to modernize medicine the old catch-all treatments of purgation and bleeding, which met with increasing disfavour in advanced circles, began to be replaced by a physic that respected the holistic nature of human life. In line with enlightened beliefs about the organically based dynamics of the body, the ancient Hippocratic notion that nature heals best was revived, inviting a prudent resort to the so-called non-naturals—air, food, drink, rest and motion, and other elements affecting the body from without. The mistrust of civilization that was particularly felt from the 1750s onward produced a new doctrine preaching the nefarious effects of an environment which generated stress and licensed sensory over-stimulation, and as a consequence a therapy directed at the Enlightenment goal of human 'perfectionnement' was developed. Its fundamental principle was to maximize the body's hygienic resources by eradicating its taste for sexual and sensual over-indulgence, toughening it through recommended forms of physical activity and convincing it that health depended on prudent self-regulation.

Diderot's fascination with medical matters is celebrated. 'Pas de livres que je lise plus volontiers que les livres de medecine, pas d'hommes dont la conversation soit plus interessante pour moi, que celle des medecins' (Eléments de physiologie, p. 299). One of his first literary undertakings was to collaborate with Eidous and Toussaint in translating Robert James's Dictionary of Medicine and Surgery, and he then enlisted the help of over twenty medical men for the different articles of the Encyclopédie. His workhorse de Jaucourt, for instance, had studied at Leyden under the great Boerhaave, the most celebrated medical teacher of his day, and taken a medical degree. Other notable contributors were the doctors Tarin, who had translated Haller's Primae lineae physiologiae into French, Vandenesse, the head of the Paris medical faculty, and Tronchin of Geneva, who wrote the article on inoculation. But Diderot composed some entries himself, even if they were not particularly original. The long article on the anatomy and pathology of the heart, for instance, may have been largely extracted from Sénac's *Traité de la structure du cœur* (1749), but it is still significant that Diderot should have wanted to compile it in the first place, and noteworthy that he should have done the pieces on 'Accouchement' and the 'Hôtel-Dieu': he was, after all, keenly interested in midwifery, and the Hôtel-Dieu in Paris was particularly closely associated with it.

He held strong opinions, besides, on a fraught issue of the day, the question of the relative status of physicians and surgeons. This was partly because he deplored the habit of disparaging 'métiers', such as the surgeon's, on the grounds that they involved merely mechanical skills: it ran counter to the *Encyclopédie's* project of being a 'Dictionnaire universel des sciences, arts et *métiers*'. Finding the hierarchical distinction between (theoretical) physic and (manual) surgery offensive, he wrote the *Lettre d'un citoyen zélé à M. D. M***** of 16 December 1748 in order to illustrate the respective strengths and weaknesses of practice and theory, making emblematic use of the human body to argue that the two professions should actually unite (*Corr.* i. 59 ff).

In the letter Diderot tells the parable of a man who, after slipping and falling into a bog, discovered that he could get no help from the fine phrases and lucid theory of a passing physician, who although he had excellent eyesight was one-armed; nor could he be aided by another passer-by, who despite having two good arms was blind. The first was cut off from experience, and the second (a surgeon) from speculation. As the *Lettre sur les aveugles* would argue, the world is nothing but the projection of the human body, which structures it according to its specific nature and affirms or denies realities according to the sensory equipment it possesses. Diderot's holistic solution is summed up in the man's call to both passers-by, 'unissez-vous pour me secourir: vous, honnête manchot, qui possédez des yeux excellens, dirigez un peu les mains de ce bon aveugle qui ne demande qu'à travailler'. Surgeons can be supplied with eyes and physicians with hands, that is, only by forming a confederation. As Diderot tells his surgeon correspondent (probably Sauveur Morand), 'S'il y eut un tems où l'ignorance des Chirurgiens et l'habileté des médecins sembloient condamner les premiers à monter derrière le carrosse de ceux-ci, il faut convenir que ce tems a bien changé; du moins s'il en faut juger par la confiance que les Chirurgiens ont obtenue du Public' (*Corr.* i. 67).

In other words, the objects of an earlier polemic—the barbers and barber-surgeons lampooned in humanist medical writings, or the unlicensed practitioners of the seventeenth century[5]—had become respectable, if less so than Diderot would have wished. The status of surgery had been elevated by the successful operation on Louis XIV for anal fistula in 1687, by Louis XV's endowment of five chairs in surgery in 1724, and by the creation of the Académie royale de chirurgie in 1731;[6] but the elitism complained of in Diderot's letter still persisted. One is bound to note that the surgeon espied by Jacques and his master in *Jacques le fataliste*, who confirms Jacques's observation on the complications of mending wounded knees, is described as 'une espèce de paysan' (p. 496). If any doubts remain about the general surgical advances made in the Enlightenment, and their effect on the regard in which surgeons were held, a look at the plates accompanying the *Encyclopédie* article 'Chirurgie' may intensify them. They are remarkably unreassuring. More than one, for instance, illustrates the 'cruel and imperfect' methods of breast amputation still prevalent, methods which according to the captions did more harm than good to the patient. Perhaps the intention was partly to underline the extent to which femaleness itself was a malady, a matter to which we shall be returning; but if the Enlightenment grounded its claims for fuller recognition of the surgeon's status on his empirically acquired knowledge of anatomy, which made his 'métier' into an art based on fixed, rational principles, there was still evidently work to be done. Yet the academic structure of the medical profession was becoming well established: Haller, after all, taught anatomy, surgery and medicine from the same Chair, and in France the dynamic school centred on Paris controlled surgical teaching and practice with authority.

Diderot was abreast of other current medical issues apart from this one. He admired Catherine II's campaign to inoculate her subjects against smallpox and her boldness in having herself injected before any of them; and he tried, apparently successfully, to persuade Sophie Volland's mother to undergo the treatment too.

Je n'ai pas eu le moindre doute que maman, bonne, humaine, bienfaisante, heureuse comme le sont presque toujours les personnes prudentes, n'acquiescât à la proposition que je lui faisois. J'en ai prévenu Gati qui attend son retour avec la même impatience que moi, et qui ne demande pas mieux que de l'initier dans toute cette petite pratique. (15 November 1768; *Corr.* viii. 221)

Mme Volland's chance meeting with a woman who had lost her sight through smallpox added to the force of Diderot's argument. Dr Gatti, he added, had inoculated sixty-one children in his little hospital without any of them suffering ill-effects. Many of Diderot's other medical friends were equally progressive in outlook. Théophile Bordeu, one of the most celebrated, had known Diderot since 1752 or 1753 at the latest, and was also a contributor to the *Encyclopédie* (for which he wrote the article 'Crise'). He was a member of d'Holbach's salon in the rue Royale, and Diderot frequently met him there.[7]

Medicine and the Human Condition

The letters to Sophie Volland of February and March 1766 describe Bordeu's attending Sophie's sister in a serious illness diagnosed by Diderot as whooping-cough (3 February 1766; *Corr.* vi. 47), on which he sent Tronchin some observations at about the same time. The details are as vivid as one would expect from a man so absorbed by medical matters, though not all seem to point unambiguously towards the condition Diderot thought he detected: Mme Le Gendre's vapours, aches and pains, fever and troubled nights could indicate depression or a characteristically female loss of tone. Tronchin was suffering from gout at the time[8] (rather surprisingly, given his promotion of the kind of wholesome diet that was meant to ward off this particular ailment), so the services of Drs Petit and Bordeu were called upon.[9] Eventually Tronchin sent a prescription, followed by a home visit in the company of Petit. Bordeu then paid a call. Not even this impressive network of attendants could reassure Diderot, however, and he continued to 'live' Mme Le Gendre's condition with a mixture of obsessive fussiness and deep practical sympathy. Indeed Viallet, another correspondent of Diderot's and an admirer of Mme Le Gendre, thought that the two must be involved with one another.[10]

Eventually Mme Le Gendre's condition seems to have been alleviated by Bordeu's prescription of goat's milk, though Diderot himself believed a different treatment would be appropriate[11]— something like the 'médecine de l'esprit' which his acquaintance Antoine Le Camus had written about in a 1753 book of the same title, and which Diderot would draw on in the *Eléments de physiologie*.[12] What this vaporous 'femme sensible' really needed, he concluded, was a treatment to anaesthetize her faculties of thought and feeling, which traditional medicine could do nothing about.

Sa tête, qui travaille sans cesse, s'entretenoit d'idées capables de déranger tout l'effet des remèdes. Cette méchante femme aime à s'affliger; et son âme sensible, ne pouvant avoir dans ce moment la sorte d'exercice qui lui plairoit si fort, qu'elle souhaite avec tant d'ardeur, ce seroit lui rendre un service important que de l'engourdir pour un ou deux mois. (*Corr.* vi. 132)

This sounds very like the therapy the real-life Julie de Lespinasse alternately craves and rejects in her correspondence with her disappointing lover the comte de Guibert, though there is little trace of such a tendency in the fictive dialogue she conducts with Dr Bordeu in *Le Rêve de d'Alembert*. The lesbian Superior of *La Religieuse*, who 'aime à pleurer' (p. 347) and anticipates being happy with Suzanne in proportion as the girl rehearses the detail of all her past suffering to her, may also come to mind. But perhaps she and Mme Le Gendre, albeit in slightly different ways, simply embody the sentimental mood of their times. The female impressionability to feeling, as we have seen, gave strong emotion—which might shade into erotic arousal—an autonomous value, though there was generally a tendency on the part of (male) commentators to disparage or caution against it. Diderot asks Sophie to dull her sister's emotionality for roughly the same hygienic reasons as Suzanne tries to dampen the Superior's, but with little hope of finding a remedy. In both cases, emotional suffering leads to sharp physical deterioration.

However great Diderot's respect for the doctors who attended Mme Le Gendre, he was still far from uncritical of their profession. In this he resembled Rousseau, who thought medicine an art more pernicious than the ills it tried to cure. The fact is that before the mid-nineteenth century clinical medicine had almost no beneficial impact on health, and may well, as Rousseau believed, have done more harm than good. On 26 September 1762 Diderot wrote to Sophie Volland apropos of his wife's ill-health that

Ce que je vois tous les jours de la médecine et des médecins ne me les fait pas estimer davantage. Naître dans l'imbécillité et au milieu de la douleur et des cris; être le jouet de l'ignorance, de l'erreur, du besoin, des maladies et des passions; retourner pas à pas à l'imbécillité; du moment où l'on balbutie, jusqu'au moment où l'on radote, vivre parmi des fripons et des charlatans de toute espèce; s'éteindre entre un homme qui vous tâte le pouls, et un autre qui vous trouble la tête; ne sçavoir d'où l'on vient, pourquoi l'on est venu, où l'on va: voilà ce qu'on appelle le présent le plus important de nos parents et de la nature, la vie. (*Corr.* iv. 169)

(A letter Diderot wrote to his daughter when she was expecting her first child actually blames Mme Diderot's years of ill-health on the fact that she did not keep to her bed for long enough after Angélique's own birth.)[13] In 1768 the agonizing and protracted illness of Damilaville, who was suffering from cancer, prompted in Diderot the reflection that death might be preferable to enduring months of agony for the sake of a few days' remission, and that a profession which could prescribe two antithetically opposed forms of treatment for the same disease, as in Damilaville's case, barely inspired confidence,[14] despite the fact that the representatives of the opposing views were Tronchin and Bordeu. The satire of the medical profession in *Jacques le fataliste*, much of it borrowed from Diderot's model *Tristram Shandy*, is of course timeless, as the narrator himself notes: 'Je vous fais grâce de toutes ces choses, que vous trouverez dans les romans, dans la comédie ancienne et dans la société' (p. 507).

But other works by Diderot deal with the subject more seriously. The real-life Le Camus is an important fictional character in *Ceci n'est pas un conte*, the man whose attentive treatment of Mlle de La Chaux in her illness commands her undying respect, but cannot earn her love. The equally real Gardeil, a Montpellier doctor who in 1801 would publish a *Traduction des œuvres médicales d'Hippocrate*, is the lover who deserts her despite her selfless support of him, and whose revulsion from her she claims is caused by a skin complaint she contracts. In the *Entretien d'un père avec ses enfants* (c.1771) Dr Bissei, a family friend of the Diderots, addresses the question whether a physician should try to cure a notorious criminal and leave punishing him to the law.

Le docteur Bissei, après un moment d'incertitude, répondit ferme qu'il le guérirait; qu'il oublierait le nom du malade pour ne s'occuper que du caractère de la maladie; que c'était la seule chose dont il lui fût permise de connaître; que s'il faisait un pas au-delà, bientôt il ne saurait plus où s'arrêter; que ce serait abandonner la vie des hommes à la merci de l'ignorance des passions, du préjugé, si l'ordonnance devait être précédée de l'examen de la vie et des mœurs du malade. (*O.Phil.*, p. 415)

And Dr Bordeu's role in *Le Rêve de d'Alembert* is central: his philosophical acumen parallels his medical expertise, and his physician's commonsense acts as a foil to Mlle de Lespinasse's sometimes poetic imaginings. Thus a Molièresque ballet of words occasionally develops between the two interlocutors:

MLLE DE LESPINASSE.— Il m'a semblé plusieurs fois en rêve...
BORDEU.— Et aux malades, dans une attaque de goutte...
MLLE DE LESPINASSE.— Que je devenais immense.
BORDEU.— Que leur pied touchait au ciel de leur lit. (p. 62)

As an experienced doctor he can pronounce on the implications of d'Alembert's racing pulse, excited breathing and profuse sweating, offer case-study illustrations of the organic structure of various 'monsters', comment on women's indispositions—the 'maladies des femmes' familiar to the eighteenth century, such as the menopause, hypersensibility and nervous weakness generally—and develop sexological theories more or less shocking to his female listener.

The specific illnesses suffered by literary men were of interest to Enlightenment writers such as Diderot, always alert to the condition of their own bodies, because corporeality was the material fabric of their identity. They were keenly conscious of how environment and habit affected the organism, and of how debilitating their own professional and social habits might be. According to James's *Dictionary of Medicine* (which here borrows from a 1682 work by Thomas Sydenham), the male version of hysteria, or the so-called hypochondriacal affliction, struck particularly hard at *littérateurs* who led desk-bound lives, giving them violent head-pains, weakened sight, anxiety, constipation, palpitating hearts and convulsive movements of the limbs. Tissot's *De la santé des gens de lettres* blamed the habits of excessive mental exertion and sedentariness for the typical writer's indispositions,[15] which included indigestion resulting from mechanical, preoccupied eating and poor posture; it recommended palliative physical exercise that engaged the whole body—real tennis, battledore and shuttlecock, pall mall, billiards, hunting, skittles and bowls. '[Mais] malheureusement ils sont tombés dans un si grand discrédit que, dans plusieurs endroits, les hommes qui s'appellent les *honnêtes gens* auraient presque honte de s'en amuser' (p. 136). Tissot played a major part in propagating the image of the intellectual that dominated the later eighteenth century[16]—an enfeebled semi-invalid whose constitution could barely withstand the rigours of ordinary life—and seemed to offer a negative answer to the Enlightenment's question whether the physical organism had a part to play in the general betterment of the human race.

Diderot acknowledges the reality of occupational indisposition in a letter of 7 November 1762 to Sophie Volland, where he observes that his rheumatism is exacerbated by his habit of bending over a desk all day. Chopping logs would be far better for his health, he comments. His physical robustness, it must be said, was much remarked upon. According to the comte de Cheverny he was 'taillé en porteur de chaises', and there was the story of Diderot, 'fort comme un Turc', seizing by the collar someone who had dared to contradict him and threatening to throw him from the stalls of the Opéra into the orchestra pit.[17] Humans, in the philosopher's view, were not made for reading, meditation, literature, philosophy and physical inactivity: all were forms of depravity that seriously endangered their health. It would, he thought, be far better to revert to the habits of the animal world, and 'Si je ne craignais pas de scandaliser Uranie [Mme Le Gendre], je vous dirais franchement que je me porterais mieux si j'étais resté penché sur une femme une portion du temps que je suis resté penché sur mes livres' (to Sophie Volland, 7 November 1762; *Corr.* iv. 213). A similar note, though not a scabrous one, had been struck two years previously by Dr Tronchin when Diderot consulted him by letter over his health.[18] According to Tronchin, the colic Diderot was suffering from was a spasmodic affliction to which literary men were particularly subject, because sitting down all day distorted their intestines. His prescription, naturally enough, was that Diderot should take more exercise, write standing upright, moderate his passions, and particularly avoid anything acidic: 'une goûte de jus de citron peut vous donner un spasme' (*Corr.* xvi. 25). But Diderot, it seems, had been following a lactic regime for years, a 'cruel remède' when combined with bread and water and nothing else. 'Du lait le matin, du lait à midi, du lait à goûter, du lait à souper. C'est bien du lait!'[19]

Gourmandise versus the Simple Life

The affliction of gout was associated not so much with the bookish life as with the self-indulgent one: the *bon viveur* Diderot was apparently a martyr to it, and in letters to correspondents as diverse as Hume, Falconet and Sophie Volland he describes its painful progression through his body, from arms to chest to stomach and intestines, and finally to his ears.[20] He used to mock the gouty, he wrote to Falconet on 16 September 1768, but no longer dared to (*Corr.* viii. 131). Fasting and abstinence from alcohol seem to have cured him, though Diderot claimed that an occasional orgy still did him good.[21] Mme Diderot, who is not known to have shared his self-indulgent tendencies, suffered from the same complaint,[22] though it afflicted more men than women. In turn, she martyred her husband, because 'Mme Diderot est du petit nombre de femmes qui ne sçavent pas souffrir'.[23] An apoplectic fit she suffered in July 1771 was explained by her husband as the consequence of bad temper, chagrin and an 'humeur rhumatismale et goutteuse'.[24]

In the eighteenth century gout assumed near-epidemic proportions, mostly because a degree of affluence and the leisure associated with a consumer society encouraged people to adopt protein-rich diets and a variety of physically self-indulgent habits.[25] The fact that males were the main sufferers sometimes prompted in them the resentful reflection that it was a far more inconvenient affliction for their sex because they were more active (whereas women were essentially bearers of children, which meant that their characteristic malady 'rightly' involved the womb—at least in the popular understanding of hysteria). Though various herbal and household remedies were recommended,[26] the commonest gout-treatment mentioned by Enlightenment writers was, unsurprisingly, moderation. Tissot as well as Tronchin was a champion of healthy abstinence, and both doctors enjoined it on a number of sufferers apart from Diderot (who was told to eat fruit as well as drink milk and water).[27]

The model of the simple, salubrious life puts us in mind of Rousseau, as Swiss as Tissot and Tronchin and equally convinced of the dietary benefits of eating dairy products and the dangers of highly seasoned meat dishes. But many other writers and medical men recommended the kind of self-restraint that Diderot found so hard to observe. Le Camus's *La Médecine de l'esprit* associates temperance in eating with other kinds of bodily control, and remarks that those who fail to practise it become like beasts. 'La continence est une vertu par laquelle on s'abstient des voluptés défendues, et l'on n'abuse point des permises.'[28] Tissot's recommendation to worldly sophisticates in his *Essai sur les maladies des gens du monde* (1770) is to eat like poor labourers—the coarsest bread and the simplest fat-free soups, along with cheese, beans and vegetables. The rich man, in contrast, indulges in succulent and well-hung meat, exquisite and concentrated dishes, sweetmeats, highly seasoned cheese and 'violent' wines.[29]

The eighteenth century's attitude to food was ambiguous. On the one hand, it was an age that promoted judicious abstinence, or at least called for a return to the plain fare associated with rustic life and the bourgeois kitchens of the past. On the other hand, it gloried in gourmandise, regarding the refinement of cuisine as a mark of human advancement, and the sharing of food as a profoundly social experience.[30] In the course of the century the focus of social and intellectual exchange shifted from the salon to the dining-room (a relative newcomer in worldly architecture),[31] and this move was reflected in the emergence of a new kind of 'écriture gourmande' for the discerning food-lover.[32] The number of food articles written for the *Encyclopédie* by Diderot may not imply any particular expertise on his part—he could cook little but gruel for his suffering wife, and happily plagiarized existing culinary sources[33]—but it does speak for a passionate interest as well as a weakness. He was rarely sensible about eating, preferring to binge and then purge. Sensible eating, as he knew, was the sort that satisfied the body without causing it discomfort or inducing in it a state of over-stimulation or torpor; but it never seemed very convivial. The letters to Sophie Volland about feasts at Grandval, d'Holbach's country home, exhaustively document his dietary excesses. He tells her on 1 October 1759, for example, that 'Nous dînons bien et longtems. La table est servie ici comme à la ville [i.e., in the rue Royale], et peut-être plus somptueusement encore. Il est impossible d'être sobre, et il est impossible de n'être pas sobre et de se bien porter' (*Corr.* ii. 264). His enthusiastic *Encyclopédie* entry on 'Abricots' may remind us that the fruit formed part of the very solid meal he ate just before his sudden death on 30 July 1784, along with soup, boiled mutton, chicory and some cherry compote.[34]

Diderot's letters at the time his father died describe the intensive feeding he underwent in the homes of the Langres townspeople, and express his regret at having had to refuse their wine on medical advice, the more so as everyone else drank so deeply. If de Jaucourt, who wrote many of the food articles for the *Encyclopédie*, could remark in 'Cuisine' that it was the pernicious art of making one eat more than was necessary,[35] Diderot's own view was (paradoxically) more temperate. His entry on 'Alimens' concedes that all excess is probably harmful to the constitution, but notes that some confirmed gluttons and hard drinkers live long and healthy lives despite their over-indulgence, and might conceivably have died sooner had they been more sober.

Perhaps this is special pleading, because there can be no doubt that Diderot himself was extremely greedy. He admits it freely, remarking that he eats fast, without chewing, and so gives himself stomach-ache.[36] Tissot writes in *De la santé des gens de lettres* that 'Rien ne soulage l'estomac autant qu'une mastication exacte', and says that literary men habitually neglect it (pp. 167 f.); his *Essai sur les maladies des gens du monde* observes, by contrast, that only the common people masticate properly, and that this greatly aids their digestion.

Elle se fera sans douleur, les aliments ne croupissant pas ne se corrompront point; ils n'auront aucune âcreté, ils n'agaceront ni l'estomac, ni les intestins; on n'éprouvera ni coliques, ni constipations, ni diarhées; ils formeront un chile doux qui passera dans les vaisseaux sans les irriter et sans donner la fièvre. (pp. 21–2)

Many of Diderot's letters, on the other hand, dwell on his indigestion, generally the result of a wholesale assault on his system. It seems altogether fitting that he was not the author of the sad *Encyclopédie* article 'Abstinence', but instead supplied the entries on 'Adéphagie' (the goddess of gourmandise) and 'Comus' (the god of feasts).[37] The following extract from a letter to Sophie Volland of 19 November 1760 sums up his dangerously festive nature:

Lundi [...], le ventre à table, le dos au feu, je causai, je disputai, je plaisantai, je bus, je mangeai, depuis une heure jusqu'à dix du soir. La nuit du lundi au mardi a été affreuse. J'ai cru que je mourrois. Le mardi, en dépit du docteur Dubourg, du chirurgien Louis, de mad^e Diderot, j'étois habillé à neuf heures et dans les rues à dix. Je n'en ai pas été plus mal. (*Corr.* iii. 253)

In other words, Diderot was blessed with a basically solid constitution, but tended towards violent self-abuse (usually in the 'good' cause of conviviality), and was correspondingly fond of surrounding himself with medical ministrants. Food and drink were always too tempting to resist, and the price paid for the after-effects of gluttony—two cups of tea and a period of complete fasting after the episode described above—never seemed too high. So it is all the more surprising that as a *writer* on food Diderot can be deeply unevocative, particularly when he is describing painted fare in the *Salons* rather than recreating actual banquets. Despite repeatedly alluding to the naturalistic quality of Chardin's edible displays, for instance, he conspicuously fails to convey their sensuous appeal in words: 'c'est qu'il n'y a qu'à prendre ces biscuits et les manger, cette bigarade l'ouvrir et la presser, ce verre de vin et le boire, ces fruits et les peler, ce pâté et y mettre le couteau' (*Salons*, i. 222). Equally disappointingly, 'Les biscuits sont jaunes, le bocal est verd, la serviette blanche, le vin rouge' (ii. 113). Perhaps only the reality of food makes him salivate, unless it is that gluttons cannot be gourmands too (the latter alone being capable of detached analysis). Or is Diderot simply a prisoner of the pictorial hierarchy that still held relatively firm, and which in assigning a lowly position to still life made its component parts seem beneath serious attention?

Yet if food concerned the eighteenth century as it had not previous ages, part of the reason was surely the new focus on corporeality: developments in the biological sciences directed attention to the way the human subject is physically modified by ingesting food. Chardin's canvases may suggest its connections with spiritual life (food in painting has standardly formed part of the *vanitas* theme, though Diderot never refers to it in this light), but the materialist temper of the time points in a different direction—towards its vital, terrestrial significance. *Le Rêve de d'Alembert* underlines the link between food and the process of bodily change, which makes it emblematic of the flux of life rather than representative of its stable essence:

DIDEROT.— ... en mangeant, que faites-vous? Vous levez les obstacles qui s'opposaient à la sensibilité active de l'aliment; vous l'assimilez avec vous-même; vous en faites de la chair; vous l'animalisez; vous la rendez sensible. (p. 5)

Not that nutrition was well enough understood in the eighteenth century for there to be a clear sense of how different foodstuffs might affect the body's shape;[38] nor was this likely to be a lively concern, at least by modern standards. Fatness was much less disapproved of, and hence much less worried over, than it has subsequently been. Given that corpulence might simply be taken to indicate that one had had enough to eat—a factor of some importance in a period when food shortages were rife and poverty was rampant—it was unlikely to be deprecated unless it seriously interfered with the body's functioning, or seemed to indicate too gross an unawareness of others' lack. If the comfortably-off starved themselves, it was more often because they associated fasting with purgation and other principles of hygiene than because they seriously wanted to lose weight. This was certainly true of Diderot.

But there were exceptions. Although Cardinal Bernis lived off boiled herbs and a morsel of stale bread, waving aside the gravy, butter, salt, cream, eggs, oil, meat and fowl that his more fortunate guests were offered by his famous chef, he was still inclined to corpulency.[39] Nicolas Beaujon endured a similar kind of starvation: a man who had made a colossal fortune through dubious speculation, he lived in the exquisite former home of Mme de Pompadour (now the Elysée Palace) surrounded by a seraglio of beauties, called his 'berceuses', whom he was quite unable to enjoy. He too ate nothing but a few vegetables. When Louise Vigée Le Brun was commissioned to paint his portrait in 1784, the year of Diderot's death, she had to so it in his sumptuous dwelling because the gouty and dropsical Beaujon was unable to move.[40] Yet in ordinary circumstances the trim man might be thought deprived rather than healthily spare. In his 'anatomical' letter to Diderot, Dr Petit observes that a lame person is normally skinny because of his disability: 'les efforts qu'il fait sans cesse pour marcher droit lui font faire une grande dépense d'esprits, ce qui le rend maigre' (*Corr.* xi. 75–6). Petit also believed that losing an arm or leg made one overweight 'par la même raison que les gens oisifs et les grands mangeurs sont tels. Les sucs qui étoient employés à la nourriture du membre coupé cessent d'avoir leur emploi, surabondent, surchargent et font ce que les médecins appellent *pléthore*, laquelle amène la pesanteur etc.' (p. 75).

The Philosopher's judgement on Rameau's nephew when he sees him as 'maigre et have comme un malade au dernier degré de la consomption; on compterait ses dents a travers ses joues; on diroit qu'il a passé plusieurs jours sans manger, ou qu'il sort de la Trape' (*Le Neveu de Rameau*, p. 4) is a predictably damning comment on his feckless lifestyle. It is less clear, though, that the alternative of fat sleekness is a wholly positive state: having the stomach of Silenus does not necessarily indicate happy prosperity, for 'l'humeur qui fait secher mon cher oncle engraisse apparemment son cher neveu' (p. 8). The uncle is the naturally skinny man about whom Petit (who still kept some faith with the ancient medical doctrine of the humours) expressed certain reservations, the nephew the essentially changeable figure alluded to in the epigraph to the dialogue (*Vertumnis quotquot sunt natus iniquis*).

Eating is an ambiguous leitmotif of *Le Neveu de Rameau*. The Nephew knows that it ought to be the background to fellowship: as he declares, the banquet is a 'renouvellement de l'antique hospitalité' (p. 57). In allowing body and mind to converge,[41] it bridges the divide created by dualist philosophy. As we have seen, Lui suffers from the separation of eating and conviviality that his patrons force upon him ('Il se taisoit et mangeoit de rage', p. 6). He rebels against such

unseemly constraint by organizing his own feasts, though they are
hardly occasions for the ideal combination of sensuousness and
spirituality that would demonstrate the unitary nature of man: for the
menagerie of derelicts and bohemians has animal appetites above all.
'Des loups ne sont pas plus affamés; des tigres ne sont pas plus cruels.
Nous devorons comme des loups, lors que la terre a été longtemps
couverte de neige; nous dechirons comme des tigres tout ce qui
reussit.' Their consuming passions are for food and human
reputations, and it is only in attacking and dismembering that their
mental and physical energy fully expresses itself: 'c'est alors qu'il se fait
un beau bruit dans la menagerie. Jamais on ne vit ensemble tant de
betes tristes, acariatres, malfaisantes et couroucées. Nul n'aura de
l'esprit, s'il n'est aussi sot que nous' (p. 57).

Yet Lui remains envious of the ease others enjoy, if not of their
intellectual productions. (He envies only the true genius.) So the
contrast between the rich man's diet and the poor man's must always
enrage him, oblivious as he is to the hygienic as well as nutritional
advantages of eating plainly. Lui's dominant organ is his stomach; the
digestion of food is his main preoccupation, and the Messer Gaster of
Rabelais is a person 'contre lequel je n'ai jamais boudé' (p. 63). In the
materialistic world he inhabits, this digestive existentialism[42] easily
translates into the assumption that the body, whether fed or not, is all
that there is, the site of a corruption that cannot be transcended. As
the dialogue demonstrates, Lui does try to rise above it in his manic
musical pantomimes; but as his music remains *embodied*, the sum total
of physical gestures, dances, spasms and paroxysms, one might argue
that he fails.

At all events, there is little evidence in this dialogue that sobriety in
eating and drinking might be thought desirable, both because the
Nephew's patrons are vulgarly ostentatious and because the parasites,
constantly fearing starvation, judge the value of food by its lavishness
and the complication of its preparation. To the instinctive but
frustrated sybarite, the ideal is to '[faire] d'excellents repas [...] , [boire]
d'excellentes liqueurs, d'excellents caffés' (p. 12). Yet given his
precarious social existence, the scandal remains: 'il n'est pas du bon
ordre de n'avoir pas toujours de quoi manger. Que diable
d'œconomie, des hommes qui regorgent de tout, tandis que d'autres
qui [*sic*] ont un estomac importun comme eux, et pas de quoi mettre
sous la dent' (p. 103 f.). It is simply perverse, in Lui's view, to *want* to
be an ascetic living off nuts and berries; and the reason why it matters

to 'aller aisement, librement, agreablement, copieusement tous les soirs a la garderobe' (p. 25) is that it proves one has put enough in one's belly.[43] Hence the Nephew's exclamation *o stercus pretiosum*: dung is indirectly valuable to urban parasites as it is directly valuable to farmers, being the result of nourishment in the first place and the ultimate source of nourishment in the second.

The Nephew associates food with desire because it sustains the starving man, stimulates the senses and gives him potency. It also represents the achievement of the social and economic sufficiency he craves, and so is emblematic of material success. From classical times the generic term 'concupiscence' designated two aspects of fleshly sin, sexual and gustatory lustfulness.[44] Concupiscence is the extension of what Lamarck, in 1778, would describe as two principal functions of the human body, digestion and reproduction; and in psychoanalytical parlance the category of orality subsumes the interaction of sexual and alimentary desire that Freud designated under the theory of the libido. The *Encyclopédie* subscribed to the classical wisdom concerning the body: in its catalogue of nutritional aberrations and excesses it isolated the 'faculté concupiscible' as a 'lésion imaginaire'. The doctrine of the humours held chyle and sperm to be the same substance, and Tissot linked eating disorders with sexual ones: food becomes erotically charged, and conversely the erotic body appears to resemble food. The *Encyclopédie* article 'Fraise', for instance, defines its subject as 'un petit fruit rouge ou blanc [qui] ressemble au bout des mamelles des nourrices'.[45]

Nourishment and Desire

The Mme de La Pommeraye episode in *Jacques le fataliste* provides an illustration of how the dinner-table acts as a locus of human interaction, but one whose object is here emphatically (if disguisedly) sexual. After endlessly goading the marquis des Arcis's appetite for the apparently untouchable Mlle d'Aisnon, Mme de La Pommeraye invites him to dine with her, the girl and the girl's mother. But the meal is far from the sensuous occasion he may have anticipated: following the hostess's carefully laid plan the women make him talk for three hours of religion, of *agape* rather than eros (pp. 634 f.). Mme de La Pommeraye's taunts are so overt that a less besotted man would have grown suspicious: '"Vous entendez toutes les subtilités de l'amour divin, comme si vous n'aviez été qu'à Saint François de Sales

pour toute nourriture"' (p. 635). The 'having' of the girl to which the
marquis obsessively refers becomes a far more pressing desire than any
other bodily appetite could be, his lust perversely sharpened by the
ascetic denial that Mlle d'Aisnon's life seems to represent. The ascesis
of the meal is thus a metaphor for the much greater bodily denial his
former mistress has planned for him. To her chagrin, however, he
achieves gratification none the less. His offer of marriage to Mlle
d'Aisnon does not lead to the humiliation Mme de La Pommeraye
had anticipated, since he forgives his new wife her past profession and
deception, and settles down happily with her.

Diderot's one-time friend Rousseau also knew about the dynamics
of appetite and desire,[46] if in less extreme form. In *Les Confessions* he
describes the anorexic state Grimm affected when his passion for a
Mlle Fel was thwarted, a condition that prevented him from eating
anything but some preserved cherries which Rousseau occasionally
placed on his tongue.[47] The episode lasted several days and made
Grimm immensely fashionable. Besotted with Mme de Warens, the
young Rousseau forced her to remove food from her mouth so that
he could swallow it himself (*Œuvres complètes*, i. 108); and Emile
behaves similarly with Sophie, seizing plates of cream she has dipped
her spoon into so that he can savour it as though he were savouring
her (iv. 806). Diderot is a different kind of literary sensualist, but
equally alert to the erotic charge carried by food. There is, for
example, an obvious connection between the feasts which the lesbian
Superior of *La Religieuse* provides for the convent to celebrate
Suzanne's arrival and her sensual nature.[48] When Lent is over, and
feasting replaces fasting, the exquisite dishes that are served
complement 'les choses les plus douces' that the Superior says to her
flock:[49] circulating among her favourites, she makes their collations
into excuses for flirtation, putting morsels into her own mouth before
passing the dishes round (p. 361). When she falls in love with Suzanne,
former irregularities over mealtimes—too much one day, too little the
next—disappear (p. 330). The Superior's 'goût' for Suzanne seems to
combine the edible and the erotic, and orality is its sign[50] (the
innocent girl repeatedly kisses her, and is described as being her bodily
as well as her spiritual sustenance). When she withdraws from her
lover, there can be only one result: the Superior's lovesickness makes
her thin and haggard (p. 353), the delicious repasts she used to arrange
cease (p. 375), and finally she herself refuses all food (p. 384).

Suzanne herself had survived near-starvation at her previous convent with a show of astonishing physical resilience, and on arrival at Arpajon was praised for her 'embonpoint'. At Longchamp she had been served 'shameful' food unfit for animals, let alone humans, and reduced to eating off the floor of the refectory.[51] Though we see her swallowing her friend Ursule's note, little real nourishment passes her lips;[52] and it is a paradox matching others in her character that fasting, which should have transformed her from sensuous body to wraith, is never allowed to damage her physical appeal.

The saintly mère de Moni had forbidden every kind of bodily mortification on the grounds that it simply served the cause of pride, and her first acts on becoming Superior at Longchamp had been to stop food being mixed with ashes and to confiscate all the scourges and hair-shirts in the community (pp. 266–7). Her successor, however, reintroduced these forms of penitence, as the Superior of Saint-Eutrope also does when she has been denied the nourishment of Suzanne's love. Although *La Religieuse* raises the question whether bodily deprivation as well as torture is more to be feared than sexual persecution or the other way about, Diderot seems to be bent on showing how readily they merge. He clearly implies that the vindictive cruelty of the Longchamp nuns, for instance, has been produced by a life of unwilling and incomplete sublimation of the corporeal: emotional energies and physical needs for which the cloister has no use are channelled in the wrong direction, and 'normal' female sensibility becomes pathological. The dynamic forces created and then expelled (according to an ancient hydraulic theory of sexuality that was still current in the eighteenth century) through the conventional modes of loving are diverted into the 'irregular' ways of homosexuality, which torments and ultimately kills the Superior.

Part of Diderot's intention in this novel is to alert the reader to the nature of sensibility as both a force for good and a threat to the body's balance, though his intermittent prurience compromises the purity of this aim. As the lesbian Superior's infatuation grows, the 'bien' that Suzanne had originally associated with her becomes more and more evidently a 'mal', and eventually she dies of it. But in fact this 'mal' is simply a more extreme version of the malady Suzanne had detected in her earlier, an emotional 'égarement' expressed in the Superior's 'troubles', 'défaillances' and other more or less contagious disorders. The physical signs of organic upset merge with those of sexual arousal: her wild eyes are symbolic of words she cannot utter and feelings she dare not express, her shaking knees suggest by contiguity an uncontrollable erotic desire.[53] There seems little to distinguish this state from the condition of alienation exhibited by various inmates of Suzanne's convents, a condition in which body and mind appear to have slipped the moorings that hold them to normality.

Convent-madness is recurrently described in the novel. Sometimes it is seen as the product of frustrated sexual desire, but sometimes it is presented as an extension of the religious 'enthousiasme' whose secular variant may be observed in Rameau's nephew. Sometimes, of course, the two strains blend. Suzanne witnesses the mental toll of the enclosed life at the convent of Sainte-Marie, where an insane inmate escapes from her cell: 'elle traînait des chaînes de fer; ses yeux étaient égarés; elle s'arrachait les cheveux; elle se frappait la poitrine avec les poings, elle courait, elle hurlait' (p. 241). Diderot, whose own sister had gone mad in a convent, writes both powerfully and melodramatically about the physical and mental effects of claustration and submission to unreasonable authority.

The psychosomatic nature of the illnesses this environment fosters is illustrated by the way Ursule 'catches' the disease Suzanne contracts there, though it is said to be a condition caused mainly by deprivation and torture: as Suzanne recovers, Ursule's health declines (p. 321). But more dangerous than infectious fever is the mental desperation that incarceration induces, and which is destructive in proportion as the individual's 'machine' is weakened by attrition. Some nuns 'déchirent leurs vêtements et s'arrachent leurs cheveux [...]; d'autres, après s'être tourmentées longtemps, tombent dans une espèce d'abrutissement et restent imbéciles; d'autres, qui ont des organes faibles et délicats, se consument de langueur; il y en a en qui l'organisation se trouble et qui deviennent furieuses' (p. 382). The lesbian Superior's alienation is made manifest in her physical appearance as she runs around her cell barefoot, foaming at the mouth, wild-haired, screamimg and hallucinating (p. 386). But how far is this state from the mystical seizures Suzanne witnesses in Mme de Moni, or from the erotic climaxes she also observes in the lesbian Superior? Diderot leaves the question unresolved. In the case of Rameau's nephew the otherness induced by 'enthousiasme' is ultimately less destructive, because, as he informs Moi at the end of their conversation, he has his feet planted on the ground. Yet however inevitable his eventual return to the material world, the transports he displays in the grip of a sublime fit that is close to delirium seem almost life-threatening to the hitherto disengaged philosopher. Lui's mimicry is an 'aliénation d'esprit [...] si voisine de la folie, qu'il est incertain qu'il en revienne, s'il ne faudra pas le jetter dans un fiacre, et le mener droit aux Petites Maisons' (*Le Neveu de Rameau*, p. 83). As the *Eléments de physiologie* observe, all forms of talent that presuppose 'enthousiasme' verge on madness, because enthusiasm is a kind of fever (p. 52).

According to Diderot, the physiology of madness is captured in a picture which Doyen exhibited in the 1767 Salon. *Le Miracle des ardents* depicts a frenzied man tearing at his own flesh and showing the consistent marks of possession from one end of his body to the other. '[La] convulsion y serpente de la tête aux pieds, on la voit et dans les muscles du visage, et dans ceux du cou et de la poitrine, et dans les bras, le ventre, le bas-ventre, les cuisses, les jambes, les pieds' (*Salons*, iii. 186). Is Lui's frenzy in any way comparable? His is an internalized *manía*, not one produced by invasive pathogens, whereas Doyen's plague-victim has succumbed to a disease that attacks from without. In other respects, too, and despite Diderot's conviction of the interaction between *psyche* and *soma*, Lui seems to rise above the condition that has temporarily gripped him. Although he emerges from his fit as though from a state of unconsciousness (*Le Neveu de Rameau*, p. 85),[54] his apparent unawareness—which Moi regards as an indictment of the frenzied bodily expression the Nephew has preferred to the supple abstractions of mental life—actually articulates the synthesis of imagination and corporeality. True, the realization of this unity is fleeting, and seems to be reduced to the level of parody as soon as it has been established. Irrational and pre-verbal energies threaten to overcome him again, and in sacrificing consciousness he once more becomes displaced from the world of solid values that both he and Moi, in their different ways, find it reassuring to inhabit. Lui in fact moves and exists inside and outside his body, living its movements and periodically dominated by its energies. Imagination and emotion, or the enthusiasm of the performer, have transformed the body into an instrument *both* alien *and* possessed, in the sense of self-possessed. Lui dominates his body at the same time as being dominated by it:[55] he is at once frenzied and controlled, as *psyche* and *soma* exhibit their complex relationship of mutual sustenance and destruction.

Diderot's medical doctrine vacillated between a 'classical' belief that the right frame of mind—a composure born of subdued passions and mental settledness, such as Moi displays—could master sickness and a countervailing conviction that the power of emotion was, at least in some cases, beyond control. In the *Eléments de physiologie* he remarks that all the passions have their own movements (a physiologico-pathognomical belief based on Descartes's and Le Brun's typologies), but also exhibit distinct and unhealthy symptoms. 'Il y a la fievre des passions comme la fievre phisique, toutes deux se manifestent au pouls [...]. Les crises des passions se font par des eruptions, des diarhées, les sueurs, des defaillances, les larmes, par le frisson, le tremblement, la transpiration' (p. 270). Bordeu's medical article 'Crise' for the *Encyclopédie* incidentally remarks that crisis is a 'sorte d'extase'.

The malady Suzanne feels herself catching from the Superior can be contained, it appears, only by isolation. She must deny the woman her presence, not only because her confessor has told her to, but also because the sensations she experiences in her company spell a loss of selfhood, a forfeiting of the autonomy she wants to regain. She is unsure whether her arousal, which she does not understand well enough to name, is a 'mal' or a pleasure, yet at least she is able to achieve a degree of detachment from the body as she contemplates it. The Superior cannot do likewise. Pathological sensibility increasingly destabilizes her, and as the 'benign' irruption of 'jouissance' on which she has come to depend is denied her, she is destroyed by the negative force of diseased emotion.

The sexualized religiosity of the convent allows ecstasy to wear different guises. Suzanne may mistrust the kind the lesbian Superior displays because it so insistently seeks companionship and collaboration, but the disguisedly erotic spirituality of Mme de Moni gathers force and then expends itself in private, so arousing none of Suzanne's suspicions. This Superior carefully asks the girl not to 'move' her, but to 'laisse[r] les sentiments s'accumuler dans mon âme; quand elle sera pleine, je vous quitterai. Il faut que je me taise: je me connais, je n'ai qu'un seul jet, mais il est violent, et ce n'est pas avec vous qu'il doit s'exhaler' (p. 262). And Suzanne is too innocent to perceive the extent to which even here her bodily presence is crucial to the Mother Superior's possession: 'elle avait les yeux fermés avec effort; quelquefois elle les ouvrait, les portait en haut, et les ramenait sur moi; elle s'agitait; son âme se remplissait de tumulte, se composait et s'agitait ensuite [...]. Elle me serrait quelquefois la main avec force.' Sitting by Suzanne's bed, she refuses to watch her dress herself because 'cela me distrairait. Je n'ai plus qu'un souci, c'est de garder de la modération dans les premiers moments'. These moments, however, are to be spent not with Suzanne herself, but with Mme Simonin.

Dom Morel's diagnosis of the lesbian Superior's condition, that she has been driven mad by the enforced conditions of an unsuitable profession (p. 380), does not extend to the proffering of a cure. She has moved beyond the point where her energies might have been diverted into safer channels, or her personality softened into compliance (p. 381). But other writings of the time, including some of Diderot's, suggest more practical ways of curing emotional or erotic possession. The remedy of physical work was often recommended for the convulsive or melancholic conditions to which women were thought to be particularly subject.[56] In Le Rêve de d'Alembert Bordeu describes how he advised a vaporous young woman to become a peasant, dig all day, sleep on straw and eat rough bread; she declined, but recovered her health by travelling all over Europe (p. 74). According to the Encyclopédie article 'Vapeurs', this neurotic seizure is caused by 'irritations' rising from the nervous fibres of the lower abdomen to the brain, and is a condition particularly affecting urban, aristocratic and bourgeois women.[57] But repressed or unrestrained sexuality, which was no respecter of class or milieu, was commonly believed to provoke the condition too.

Convulsions—the non-specific 'orgasme' of this and later periods—were thought to be far commoner in women than men, and in the former's case were standardly associated with sexual response. (When men were convulsive, it was normally said to be because they were alienated or maladapted: scholars and clerics who stood apart from society were thought to be particularly susceptible.) Diderot had been powerfully affected by the memory of the so-called Convulsionnaires, originally a group of invalids who appeared to have been mysteriously cured of infirmities after praying at the grave of the Jansenist deacon François de Pâris at the Saint-Médard cemetery in 1731. Diderot had lived near Saint-Médard between 1744 and 1746, and his second baby was baptized there. The Pensées philosophiques allude several times to the Convulsionaries, around whom a controversial sect had grown up professing a religion far more radical than conventional Jansenism. Their frenzied displays included beatings and apocalyptic visions, and the cemetery became a theatre where 'patients' and followers acted out religious scenes and pleaded for various forms of torture—stabbing, trampling underfoot, burning and even crucifixion. All this left them curiously unharmed. 'Sur les femmes' comments on

une de ces femmes qui figuraient en bourrelet l'enfance de l'Eglise, les pieds et les mains cloués sur une croix, le côté percé d'une lance, garder le ton de son rôle au milieu des convulsions de la douleur, sous la sueur froide qui découlait de ses membres, les yeux obscurcis du voile de la mort, et, s'adressant au directeur de ce troupeau de fanatiques, lui dire, non d'une voix souffrante: *Mon père, je veux dormir*, mais d'une voix enfantine: *Papa, je veux faire dodo.* (p. 952)

Booklets on the 'healings' of such patients were produced and peddled at fairgrounds, often by women.

The old link with womb-madness, at least in the popular mind, seemed to explain both the apparently greater incidence of such convulsive conditions in females and the fact that they looked indistinguishable from hysteria. The term 'convulsion' covered a variety of corporeal seizures, from simple agitation to the figuration of Christ's passion and the sufferings of martyrs, or mystical ecstasies and possession by the devil.[58] In many cases an erotic undercurrent was apparent. The *Encyclopédie* article 'Fureur utérine' (by d'Aumont) gives this state the alternative title of 'nymphomanie', and defines it in heavily sexual terms that suggest some analogies with the lesbian Superior's 'illness' in *La Religieuse*. 'Fureur utérine', however, is called a heterosexual condition, suffered by women in want of a man.

C'est une maladie qui est une espèce de délire attribué [...] aux seules personnes du sexe, qu'un appétit vénérien démesuré porte violemment à se satisfaire, à chercher sans pudeur les moyens de parvenir à ce but; à tenir les propos les plus obscènes, à faire les choses les plus indécentes pour exciter les hommes qui les approchent à éteindre l'ardeur dont elles sont dévorées.

Men, says d'Aumont, are not subject to the same constraints as drive women to this pitch of distraction, because they are less fettered by the demands of modesty and because they more regularly masturbate—though masturbation can apparently take a hideous revenge on addicts of both sexes.

The 'extraordinary' ideas peculiar to women, according to 'Sur les femmes', are all attributable to the uterus, the 'organe propre à [leur] sexe'. It is susceptible to frightening spasms, inner disruptions which are then externalized in 'émotions épidémiques et populaires' (p. 949) like those of the convulsionaries, all flailing bodies and uncontrolled sensibility. The *Paradoxe sur le comédien* calls sensibility (or the state in which one is prone to weep, shudder, faint, cry and lose one's reason, but also show a capacity to feel with and for others) the product of organic debility. Here the weakness is that of the diaphragm—roughly, the solar plexus—rather than the womb (p. 343). Bordeu is Diderot's source for the belief that the diaphragm is the root of human sensibility (*Le Rêve de d'Alembert*, p. 80), and in the *Eléments de physiologie* Diderot makes it the organ of all emotivity. 'Il y a une simpathie très marquée entre le diaphragme, et le cerveau. Si le diaphragme se crispe violemment, l'homme souffre et s'attriste. Si l'homme souffre ou s'attriste, le diaphragme se crispe violemment' (pp. 289–90). Whereas in *Le Rêve de d'Alembert* the operations of the diaphragm distinguish the great man from the 'sensible' individual, in the *Paradoxe sur le comédien* its activities separate great actors from poor ones and from spectators. The *Réfutation d'Helvétius* comments that 'La tête fait les hommes sages; le diaphragme les hommes compatissants et moraux' (p. 586), but does not call it a source of weakness. All depends on the degree of its flexibility, which according to the *Réfutation* no external authority can control.

When the *Paradoxe sur le comédien* observes that women are more 'sensible' than men it effectively means that they are unable to control themselves as well: their sympathetic nervous system, in other words, cannot be mastered by the cerebral system. Diderot still seems to believe in the psychosomatic effects of possessing a womb, which turns females into trembling, dishevelled, shouting Pythias. 'Rien de plus contigu que l'extase, la vision, la prophétie, la révélation, la poésie fougueuse et l'hystérisme', 'Sur les femmes' remarks (p. 953). His unease mingles with admiration: 'La femme dominée par l'hystérisme éprouve je ne sais quoi d'infernal ou de céleste. Quelquefois, elle m'a fait frissonner. C'est dans la fureur de la bête féroce qui fait partie d'elle-même, que je l'ai vue, que je l'ai entendue.'

The womb is at the origin of many standard female maladies in Diderot's day, first because 'pendant une longue suite d'années chaque lune ramènera le même malaise [of menstruation]', then because of childbirth, and finally because of the menopause—'une maladie longue et dangereuse'[59] that may cause cancer of the uterus or, less damagingly, the sort of psychological upset described by Bordeu in *Le Rêve de d'Alembert*:

j'ai connu une femme [qui] se rapetissait par degrés, et rentrait en elle-même

[...] au point de se sentir aussi menue qu'une aiguille. Elle voyait,—elle entendait, elle raisonnait, elle jugeait, elle avait un effroi mortel de se perdre; elle frémissait à l'approche des moindres objets. Elle n'osait bouger de sa place. (p. 62)

But the change of life can hardly explain the ill-health of Mme Diderot, then in her 60s, which Diderot mentions in a letter to Grimm in June 1772: 'ma femme pleure toujours, et quoiqu'elle en ait peu de sujet, je ne m'afflige pas moins de sa douleur' (*Corr.* xii. 78). The menopause might, of course, account for some of the earlier indispositions he noted in her, though he preferred to attribute them to her confinement in 1753: 'Elle doit à sa dernière couche', he writes to Angélique on 25 or 26 October 1773, 'et à une sortie peut-être un peu trop hâtée, tous les malaises qu'elle a sentis depuis. Il y a vingt ans de cela; elle n'en est pas quitte; et je crains bien qu'elle n'en ait pour le reste de sa vie' (*Corr.* xiii. 79).

'Femmes, que je vous plains!', 'Sur les femmes' announces. There is good reason for this pity,[60] not least because women are the unfortunate subjects of such sweepingly dismissive remarks as these:

n'oubliez pas que, faute de réflexion et de principes, rien ne pénètre jusqu'à une certaine profondeur de conviction dans l'entendement des femmes; que les idées de justice, de vertu, de vice, de bonté, de méchanceté, nagent à la superficie de leur âme; qu'elles ont conservé l'amour-propre et l'intérêt personnel avec toute l'énergie de nature. (*Œuvres*, pp. 956–7)

This judgement would hardly impress a woman like the learned Mlle de La Chaux, possessed of great intellectual stamina, firm moral principle and utter selflessness. After all, it is Gardeil's rejection that destroys her, with the force of a physical stroke:

une pâleur mortelle se répandait sur son visage; ses lèvres se décolorerent: les gouttes d'une sueur froide qui se formaient sur ses joues se mêlaient aux larmes qui descendaient de ses yeux; ils étaient fermés; sa tête se renversa sur le dos de son fauteuil; ses dents se serrerent; tous les membres tressaillaient; à ce tressaillement succéda une défaillance qui me parut l'accomplissement de l'espérance qu'elle avait conçue. (*Quatre Contes*, p. 91)

Gardeil, unmoved, simply repeats the traditional male view of the weak, over-reactive female organism promoted by 'Sur les femmes', but then adds a new notion: woman's body is not, in fact, beyond her conscious control. Women are like the cold and machine-like actress Clairon of the *Paradoxe sur le comédien*: 'elles font de leur corps tout ce qu'elles veulent'. Does this mean that woman's cerebral system governs her sympathetic one after all? It seems unlikely, given that de La Chaux's body at this stage is 'comme sans force et sans vie'. And the skeletal frame of Mme de La Carlière, the heroine of the short story who fades away when her husband strays from her, hardly confirms such a verdict either.

Sexual Release?

According to the medical orthodoxy of the time, marriage should have saved Mme de La Carlière from melancholy and hysteria, if these conditions are indeed what kills her. But marriage in this sense presupposes a sexually active relationship, which hers ceases to be once she has discovered Desroches's infidelity. The act of lovemaking, writes Ménuret de Chambaud in the *Encyclopédie* article 'Mariage (Médec., Diète)', causes a salutary release of the seed that accumulates in both sexes (in the view of Galen, Descartes, Maupertuis, Buffon, Diderot and others) and whose unnatural retention often leads to physical and mental illness. In the case of females, 'dans qui les aiguillons sont plus précoces, les passions plus vives', retention of the seed is particularly dangerous, and likely to lead to a 'délire chlorétique, également funeste à la santé et à la beauté'. Without release they suffer not just from melancholia and languor, but also from paroxysmic seizures. '[Les] impressions que la semence trop abondante et trop active fait sur les organes et ensuite sur l'esprit, sont si fortes, qu'elles l'emportent sur la raison.' This may be the condition which the lesbian Superior of *La Religieuse* is suffering from. The innocent Suzanne finds the symptoms of release she observes in the woman equally disturbing, particularly the way she foams at the mouth at the moment of climax. She may do so, of course, because Diderot has chosen to describe orgasm in terms almost identical to those which Robert James had applied to 'uterine fury' in the dictionary Diderot co-translated as a young man. In his *Encyclopédie* article 'Jouissance' it is more specifically detailed:

le coeur palpite; les membres tressaillent; des images voluptueuses errent dans le cerveau; des torrents d'esprits coulent dans les nerfs, les irritent, et vont se rendre au siège d'un nouveau sens qui se déclare, et qui tourmente. La vue se trouble, le délire naît; la raison esclave de l'instinct se borne à le servir, et la nature est satisfaite.

Marriage—the word Ménuret also uses to describe orgasm—would apparently have righted the state the Superior exhibits in her unrequited love, but is of course unavailable to her. The benefits of marriage, on this interpretation, are entirely bound up with the fulfilment of sexual desire. Ménuret argues that women are highly susceptible to the effects of physical pleasure, so that, once married, languishing, sick, pale and disfigured chloretics promptly regain their health. But this cannot in fact be a regular occurrence, because women are unlikely to reach orgasm through intercourse. At least, this is the contention of 'Sur les femmes', which remarks that 'Plusieurs femmes mourront sans avoir éprouvé l'extrême de la volupté'. 'Cette sensation, que je regarderais volontiers comme une épilepsie passagère, est rare pour elles, et ne manque jamais d'arriver quand nous l'appelons. Le souverain bonheur les fuit entre les bras de l'homme qu'elles adorent' (p. 950). Of course, given the belief then prevalent that orgasm precluded conception, this might be a distinct advantage for a society that wanted to increase its population. As the *Eléments de physiologie* clinically observe, comfortably justifying Diderot's latent sexism, 'Conception a lieu sans plaisir de la part de la femme, même avec aversion. Point de conception quoique avec le plus grand plaisir simultané des deux sexes' (p. 187).

Montaigne's essay 'Sur des vers de Virgile' had earlier supported this contention, claiming that 'un plaisir excessivement chaut, voluptueux et assidu altere la semence et empesche la conception',[61] but until the eighteenth century the opposite opinion had prevailed— that female orgasm was a precondition of conception.[62] So it was the Enlightenment, surprisingly enough, that ushered in an age of literal female degradation by denying woman the legitimate pleasure of intercourse, as it liked to deny her the more reliable release of masturbation. Tissot's *De l'onanisme* (1760) thunders against the latter practice in females, declaring that it exposes them to 'des accès d'hystérie, ou de vapeurs affreux; à des jaunisses incurables; à des crampes cruelles de l'estomac et du dos; à de vives douleurs du nez; à des pertes blanches, dont l'âcreté est une source continuelle de douleurs les plus cuisantes; à des chutes, à des ulcérations de matrice, et à toutes les infirmités que ces deux maux entraînent; à des prolongements et à des dartres du clitoris' (p. 47).

The passion of the anti-masturbation lobby's rhetoric in the eighteenth century derives principally from Tissot's work, which accumulates image upon image of the hideous, exhausted, scarred bodies of those who have over-indulged.[63] There were more temperate voices, it is true. Ménuret's *Encyclopédie* article 'Manstupration', which is largely based on Tissot, starts by attacking the practice, but then announces that infrequent and non-lustful masturbation, 'qui n'est pas excité par une image bouillante et voluptueuse', is not threatening. But when Ménuret adds that indulgence must be a response to need, he seems unclear about what constitutes a legitimate resort: is it a state of melancholy and vague erotic upset, or simply the pressing need for pleasure? Since masturbation is in itself pleasurable, may the claim that it is needful not simply be a pretext? These issues are of course difficult to settle. Ménuret determinedly sticks to the therapeutic interpretation, supporting it with the authority of Galen (who reported Diogenes as saying that he masturbated only to avoid the damaging effects of stagnating, unexpelled semen). But his ideal is still copulation with a partner of the opposite sex.

Diderot's attitude to the practice varied. In *Le Rêve de d'Alembert* he allows Bordeu to support it discreetly, even in the case of girls:

BORDEU.—Vous avez une fille sage, trop sage, innocente, trop innocente. Elle est dans l'âge où le tempérament se développe. Sa tête s'embarrasse; la nature ne la secourt pas. Vous m'appelez. Je m'aperçois tout à coup que tous les symptômes qui vous effraient, naissent de la surabondance et de la rétention du fluide séminal. Je vous avertis qu'elle est menacée d'une folie qu'il est facile de prévenir et qui quelquefois est impossible à guérir. Je vous en indique le remède. Que ferez-vous?
MLLE DE LESPINASSE.—A vous parler vrai, je crois... mais ce cas n'arrive point.
BORDEU.—Détrompez-vous. Il n'est pas rare, et il serait fréquent si la licence de nos mœurs n'y obviait. (p. 98)

But when he is writing to Catherine II he is careful to inveigh against its prevalence in schools, calling for constant surveillance in the 'lieux d'aisance' to keep it in check (*Mémoires pour Catherine II*, p. 133). On the other hand, he is fond of using words like 'branler' and 'décharger' even when the context seems to call for something less expressly sexual: an early draft of the *Eléments de physiologie* employs these verbs in connection with suckling babies, which Diderot claims mothers do only if the experience is sensually pleasurable (pp. 134–5).[64]

If he sometimes regards masturbation as a perverse indulgence in women, Diderot also seems fascinated by it. His 1767 commentary on a painting by Le Prince that appears to deal with the subject, *La Jeune Fille endormie, surprise par son père et sa mère*, provocatively recreates a scene which Diderot disingenuously claims not to understand. Carefully remarking on the girl's attitude, hand suggestively placed, legs apart, face flushed, he proceeds to consider the implications of her parents' silent contemplation: 'Se repose-t-elle d'une fatigue voluptueuse? Cela se peut' (*Salons*, iii. 215). Have the parents been alerted by her unguarded sighs? Do they realize that the time has come to marry her off? Why does the father motion the mother to keep quiet? Does he plan to surprise the girl another time with a lover? Does the basket of eggs in the foreground signify that a deflowering has taken place? Yes, Diderot says, for all that he can make of the work:

je ne suis pas plus malin. Mais d'autres ont d'autres idées; tous ces plis, l'endroit où ils se pressent... Eh bien, ces plis, cet endroit, cette main? Après? Est-ce qu'une fille de cet âge-là n'est pas maîtresse d'user dans son lit de toutes ses lumières secrètes, sans que ses parents doivent s'en inquiéter?... Ce n'est donc pas cela; qu'est-ce donc?

However unsure they appear about the precise need masturbation answers, Diderot and other writers of his time usually concede Bordeu's point in the third dialogue of *Le Rêve de d'Alembert* that 'c'est toujours une chose douce' (p. 96). Bordeu remarks in addition that 'les actions solitaires' preserve men (and women) from the perils of disease as well as the temptations of infidelity (p. 97). And sexually transmitted disease was feared in Diderot's time as much as at any other. In the gardens of the Palais-Royal—where the Philosopher of *Le Neveu de Rameau* pursued *imaginary* 'catins', his thoughts—was a 'cabinet' that displayed models showing the various symptoms of venereal disease, which made it a 'musée admirablement placé au milieu de ce lupanar émérité et dont la vue pouvait arrêter les imprudents au seuil des malheureuses "folles de leur chair" qui hantaient le fameux jardin', in one commentator's words.[65] Diderot's 1765 *Salon* has a commentary on Challe's *Hector reprochant à Pâris sa lâcheté* which observes that Helen looks like a 'catin usée et malsaine. Je veux mourir si je me fiois à cette femme; elle a des taches verdâtres et livides'. The Trojan elders, according to Diderot, are so alarmed that they advise Priam to consult the syphilis expert Keyser about Paris's health (*Salons*, ii. 110). Of course, it is perfectly possible that Challe's model was indeed a diseased prostitute. In *Le Neveu de Rameau* (p. 8) Lui is mischievously asked by Moi whether he is still well after he has announced that he enjoys consorting with courtesans like Phryne. But it is Moi who, following

Galen and Ménuret, claims that Diogenes masturbated when he was unable to have the services of such women: not because he was worried about contracting a disease, but in order to expel his stagnant seed as expeditiously as possible. For someone who was reputed to masturbate publicly before the citizens of Athens, 'pudeur' was evidently not an inhibiting factor. But one wonders whether Diderot himself regarded the failure to treat the so-called ills of seminal retention on the grounds of modesty as reprehensible or regrettable. His view, as always, seems flexible. Bordeu's recommendation to the worried mothers of unmarried daughters in *Le Rêve de d'Alembert* sounds sincere, but he insists that 'ce serait fouler aux pieds toute décence, attirer sur moi les soupçons les plus odieux, et commettre un crime de lèse-société, que de divulguer ces principes' (p. 98)—which underlines the essentially speculative nature of much of the doctrine expounded in the dialogue. Even if Diderot regarded this kind of repression as an evil, because it pointlessly condemned the sufferer to frustration and even madness, he was less sure about the desirability of avoiding the perils of lovesickness in other cases. Madness may strike wherever the preventive measures needed to avert it are seen as unacceptable: this is the fate of the lesbian Superior in *La Religieuse*. Her condition of 'crèvecœur' has become pathogenic.

In his writings Diderot treats the body as a bundle of physical symptoms as well as host to a variety of psychological processes. The phenomenological focus of *La Religieuse*, so detailed in its recording of material events, does not preclude narrative attention to the sub- or super-physical. Like other works of Diderot's, *Le Neveu de Rameau* and the *Paradoxe sur le comédien* in particular, it explores the notion that bodies are recalcitrant objects as well as biddable ones, machines liable to break down as well as vital organisms responsive to (some) remedies and palliative treatments. In documenting various corporeal realities, these texts also emphasize the hidden forces that either shore up or sap the body's energies, and show how organic weakness both feeds and exacerbates the mental infirmities which, from the classical period on, were taken to be the true cause of disease. Materialist though he was, Diderot acknowledged, celebrated and exposed the secret powers that made fleshly ease as precarious as it was desirable.

Notes to Chapter 5

1. *Réfutation d'Helvétius*, in *Œuvres complètes*, ed. Assézat and Tourneux , ii. 322.
2. See Matthew Ramsay, 'The Popularization of Medicine in France, 1650–1900', in *The Popularization of Medicine, 1650–1850*, ed. Roy Porter (London: Routledge, 1992), 99.
3. See Paul Hoffmann, 'Le discours médical sur les passions de l'amour de Boissier de Sauvages à Pinel', in *Aimer en France 1760–1860 (Actes du colloque international de Clermont-Ferrand)*, ed. Paul Viallaneix and Jean Ehrard, 2 vols. (Clermont-Ferrand: Faculté des lettres et sciences humaines de l'Université de Clermont-Ferrand II, 1980), i. 352.
4. See Vila, *Enlightenment*, 40 f.
5. See Christopher Lawrence, 'The History and Historiography of Surgery', in *Medical Theory, Surgical Practice*, ed. Christopher Lawrence (London and New York: Routledge, 1992), 2 ff.
6. See Ruth Richardson, *Death, Dissection and the Destitute* (London and New York: Routledge and Kegan Paul, 1987), 35.
7. See Herbert Dieckmann, 'Théophile Bordeu und Diderots *Rêve de d'Alembert*', *Romanische Forschungen* 52 (1938), 56 f.
8. See Diderot's letter to Sophie Volland, 14 Feb. 1766 (*Corr.* vi. 55).
9. See Diderot's letter to Sophie Volland, 23 Feb. 1766 (*Corr.* vi. 108).
10. See Diderot's letters to Viallet, end Apr. / beginning May 1766 (*Corr.* vi. 175 ff.) and undated, 1767 (vi. 181 ff).
11. See Diderot's letter to Sophie Volland, 27 Feb. 1766 (*Corr.* vi. 131).
12. See *Eléments de physiologie*, p. xlvii.
13. 23 Oct. 1773 (*Corr.* xiii. 77).
14. To Sophie Volland, 28 Aug. 1768 (*Corr.* viii. 101).
15. Samuel Tissot, *De la santé des gens de lettres* (Lausanne: Grasset, 1768).
16. See Vila, *Enlightenment*, 95.
17. See Louis Marcel, 'La mort de Diderot, d'après des documents inédits', *Revue d'histoire de l'Eglise de France* 11 (1925), 37.
18. Tronchin to Diderot, 31 Mar. 1760 (*Corr.* xvi. 23 ff., 25); see also Jean-Daniel Candaux, 'Consultations du docteur Tronchin pour Diderot, père et fils', *Diderot Studies* 6 (1964), 51 ff.
19. To Caroillon La Salette, 22 Sept. 1755 (*Corr.* i. 198). See also Arthur M. Wilson, *Diderot* (New York: Oxford University Press, 1972), 232, 252, 340.
20. To Hume, 22 Feb. 1768 (*Corr.* viii. 14); to Falconet, May 1768 (*Corr.* viii. 27).
21. To Sophie Volland, 4 Nov. 1768 (*Corr.* viii. 209).
22. To Sophie Volland, 28 Aug. 1768 (*Corr.* viii. 102).
23. To Sophie Volland, 8 Oct. 1768 (*Corr.* viii. 188).
24. To Grimm, 12 July 1771 (*Corr.* xi. 69).
25. See Roy Porter and G. S. Rousseau, *Gout: The Patrician Malady* (New Haven and London: Yale University Press, 1998), 49.
26. Porter and Rousseau, *Gout*, 41; also *L'Albert moderne* (Paris: Veuve Duchesne, 1773), 40.
27. See Jean-Paul Aron, 'Biologie et alimentation au XVIIIe siècle et au début du XIXe siècle', *Annales ESC* 16 (1961), 973.

28. Antoine Le Camus, *La Médecine de l'esprit*, 2 vols. (Paris: Ganeau, 1753), i. 127.
29. Samuel Tissot, *Essai sur les maladies des gens du monde* (Lausanne: Grasset, 1770), 18 f.
30. See Jean-Paul Aron, *Le Mangeur du XIXe siècle* (Paris: Laffont, 1970), 18 f.
31. See Beatrice Fink, 'Enlightened Eating in Non-Fictional Context and the First Stirrings of *écriture gourmande*', *Dalhousie French Studies* 11 (1987), 9 ff.
32. See Beatrice Fink, 'Diderot face au manger', in *Interpréter Diderot aujourd'hui: Colloque de Cerisy, juillet 1983*, ed. Elisabeth de Fontenay and Jacques Proust (Paris: Le Sycomore, 1984), 206.
33. See Georges May, *Quatre Visages de Denis Diderot* (Paris: Boivin, 1951), 21 ff.
34. See Mme de Vandeul, *Mémoires*, p. lvii.
35. See also Jean-Louis Flandrin and Massimo Montanari, *Histoire de l'alimentation* (Paris: Fayard, 1996), 697 f.
36. To Tronchin, 31 Mar. 1760 (*Corr.* iii. 28).
37. See Fink, 'Diderot face au manger', 206 f.
38. See Pat Rogers, 'Fat is a Fictional Issue: The Novel and the Rise of Weight-Watching', in *Literature and Medicine During the Eighteenth Century*, ed. Marie Mulvey Robbs and Roy Porter (London: Routledge, 1993), 168 ff.
39. See Lady Anne Miller, *Letters from Italy in the Years 1770 and 1771*, 2 vols. (London: Dilly, 1776), ii. 193; also Angelica Goodden, *The Sweetness of Life: A Biography of Elisabeth Louise Vigée Le Brun* (London: Deutsch, 1997), 105.
40. See Elisabeth Vigée Le Brun, *Souvenirs*, ed. Claudine Herrmann, 2 vols. (Paris: Editions des femmes, 1986), i. 239 ff; also Goodden, *Sweetness*, 43 ff.
41. See Michel Jeanneret, *Des mets et des mots* (Paris: Corti, 1987), 9.
42. The phrase is Aram Vartanian's ('Dualist', 263).
43. See Elisabeth de Fontenay, *Diderot ou le matérialisme enchanté* (Paris: Grasset, 1981), 184.
44. See Paris IV, 'Discours sur le sexe et sexe du discours', in *Aimer en France*, ed. Viallaneix and Ehrard (q.v.), ii. 302.
45. See Jean-Claude Bonnet, 'Le réseau culinaire dans l'*Encyclopédie*', *Annales ESC* 31 (1976), 891.
46. See Jean-Claude Bonnet, 'Le système de la cuisine et du repas chez Rousseau', *Poétique* 22 (1975), 246.
47. *Les Confessions*, in *Œuvres complètes*, i. 370.
48. See Henri Lafon, 'L'aliment dans le roman', *Dix-huitième Siècle* 15 (1983), 177.
49. See Beatrice Fink, 'Des mets et des mots de Suzanne', in *Diderot: Digression and Dispersion*, ed. Undank and Josephs (q.v.), 101.
50. See Fink, 'Des mets', 102.
51. See Lafon, 'L'aliment', 182 n. 5.
52. See Fink, 'Des mets', 101.
53. See Deneys-Tunney, 'Ecritures', 162.
54. See also Michel Foucault, *Histoire de la folie à l'âge classique* (Paris: Gallimard, 1972), 363 ff.
55. On this general matter see Theodore M. Brown, 'Descartes, Dualism and Psychosomatic Medicine', in *The Anatomy of Madness*, ed. W. F. Bynum, Roy Porter and Michael Shepherd, 3 vols. (London and New York: Tavistock, 1985), i. 42 f.

56. Reading, writing and listening to music were also counselled: see G. S. Rousseau, 'Medicine and the Muses', in *Literature and Medicine*, ed. Robbs and Porter (q.v.), 35.

57. See Lindsay Wilson, *Women and Medicine in the French Enlightenment* (Baltimore and London: Johns Hopkins University Press, 1993), 127.

58. See *Les Convulsionnaires de Saint-Médard*, ed. Catherine-Laurence Maire (Paris: Julliard, 1985), 14.

59. 'Sur les femmes', 954. See also Lindsay Wilson, *Women and Medicine*, 5, and Elisabeth de Fontenay, 'Diderot gynéconome', *Digraphe* 7 (1976), 46.

60. Fontenay (*Matérialisme*, 114) analyses this statement in detail.

61. Michel de Montaigne, *Essais*, ed. Jean Plattard, 5 vols. (Paris: Rocher, 1931), v. 94.

62. See Laqueur, *Making Sex*, 4.

63. See Théodore Tarczylo, *Sexe et liberté au siècle des Lumières* (Paris: Presses de la Renaissance, 1983), 99 ff.

64. See Théodore Tarczylo, 'Moral Values in *La Suite de l'entretien*', in *'Tis Nature's Fault: Unauthorized Sexuality During the Enlightenment*, ed. Robert Parks Maccubbin (Cambridge: Cambridge University Press, 1987), 56.

65. A. Chereau, in A. Dechambre, *Dictionnaire encyclopédique des sciences médicales* (Paris, 1866), quoted by Le Breton, 205.

CHAPTER 6

Sexing and Gendering

At this stage it may be helpful to return to the main themes discussed so far. Diderot's philosophical interest in mind–body relationships built on the 'static' doctrines of anatomy and the 'mobile' ones of physiology, leading him to examine the degree to which humans could control their organism by acts of intention and will. His preoccupation with corporeal eloquence was expressed both in an aesthetic of *attitude*, often drawing on sources in painting and sculpture, and in one of *movement*, based on the dynamic properties of literature and performing arts such as dance, pantomime and acting. His speculations on bodily communication were hampered, however, by a residual allegiance to conventionalized theories current in the seventeenth century and earlier, which unintentionally qualified the naturalism he had hoped to introduce to stage performance. His work shows why the body's freedom was further curbed, in a different sense, by the hygienic factors that began to concern eighteenth-century thinkers, in particular its proneness to succumb to disabling socially conditioned ailments or to be seized by overwhelming and often sex-specific forces generated by body and mind together. But he also suggested ways of combating such apparently intractable conditions and bringing about the body's 'perfectionnement'.

All this implies a sharp awareness on his part of the body's complex structure and the waywardness of its instinctual drives, which could be contained—if at all—only by the adoption of a range of defensive strategies. Yet to say this is far from suggesting that Diderot consistently favoured such manipulation: his spontaneous, reactive self and his responsible bourgeois being, epitomized in the opposing characters of plays like *Le Fils naturel* and dialogues like *Le Neveu de Rameau*, fight each other as impulse and orderliness inevitably do. Sometimes, but by no means always, this tension is shown as deriving from sex categories: the essay 'Sur les femmes' and the *Paradoxe sur le comédien* declare irrationality and confusion to be definitive of the female, and intellectual rigour and self-governance of the male. Yet Diderot also describes cerebral women (Mlle de La Chaux, the philosopher Constance of *Le Fils naturel*) and emotional men (the diaphragmic Dorval, the wretched Tanié in *Ceci n'est pas un conte*). Indeed, this variability contains an implicit reflection on gender issues as well as sexual demarcations, and leads Diderot to draw some provocative conclusions. For instance, he comes close to admitting that the concept of stable bodily identity is questionable, and that sexual categories are in many cases provisional.

Gender Categories

It would be pointless to deny that Diderot's preoccupation with the body is partly a function of his enthusiasm for sex: he was famously impatient with attempts to curb the body's impulses or subordinate them to allegedly higher things. But his sexology is neither exclusively genital nor 'merely' corporeal in other ways. He believed that if sexuality helped define a person's identity, it did so in a complex fashion involving the non-material as well as the material being. Various writings of his argue human sexual response to be necessarily a product of spirit as well as of body, and to be valuable in virtue of that fact.[1] This does not mean that he refuses to attribute prime importance to the structure and functioning of the physical body in his imaginative and theoretical writings; but he also insists on going beyond anatomical and physiological data to find other less obvious truths about humans.

The degree of the material body's flexibility is obviously relative, and certain 'givens' are incontrovertible. Woman is sexually defined by her possession of a uterus, the organ maligned in natural philosophy throughout history,[2] still feared in the eighteenth century because of its popular association with hysteria, but also redeemed by its link with motherhood in an age that often liked to exalt the family. Yet woman does not forfeit her sex if her womb is removed, even though what many cultures (including the *Supplément au Voyage de Bougainville*'s Tahiti) regard as her prime function disappears with it. In any case, Diderot often emphasizes the anatomical similarities between men and women. In so doing he sets himself in a tradition reaching back to classical antiquity, of which we shall have more to say.

Rousseau seems to be aligning himself with this tradition when he remarks in *Emile* that men and women are equivalent in all but 'le sexe'.[3] But the exception is an enormous one: men and women are inherently alike, according to Rousseau, in all but reproductive systems, secondary sexual characteristics, orgasmic capacity and genetic and morphological structure. In *Le Rêve de d'Alembert* Bordeu informs Mlle de Lespinasse that 'la femme a toutes les parties de l'homme', and points out all the consequences that flow from this:

La seule différence qu'il y ait, est celle d'une bourse pendante en dehors, ou d'une bourse retournée en dedans; qu'un fœtus femelle ressemble, à s'y tromper, à un fœtus mâle; que la partie qui occasionne l'erreur s'affaisse dans le fœtus femelle à mesure que la bourse intérieure s'étend; qu'elle ne s'oblitère jamais au point de perdre sa première forme; qu'elle garde cette forme en petit

and that this part, the clitoris, is also the 'mobile de la volupté' (p. 57). The *Eléments de physiologie* repeat the idea that the clitoris resembles the penis, though eighteenth-century thinkers would not have thought of denying that except in extraordinary circumstances it is considerably smaller. Obviously, too, it performed the same function in micturition, and was sexually responsive in a comparable way. Tissot's *L'Onanisme* alerts its reader to an alarming female abnormality, the 'taille surnaturelle d'une partie très-petite à l'ordinaire' which some 'imperfect women' try to put to the same use as the penis. 'Ce dernier genre mérite d'autant plus d'attention, qu'il est fréquent de nos jours [...]. L'on a vu souvent des femmes aimer des filles avec autant d'empressement, que les hommes les plus passionnés.' This opinion dates at least from the Renaissance, when it was believed that women with very large clitorises could penetrate other women, either anally or vaginally.[4]

Although 'Sur les femmes' and the *Paradoxe sur le comédien* seem intent on defining woman as physically 'other', works like *Le Rêve de d'Alembert* and the *Eléments de physiologie* tell a different story. Diderot's view in the latter texts is that anatomical differences are less than might be assumed, and also that what may appear to be a radical difference is simply an example of reversal. He was attracted to Galen's opinion that a woman's sexual parts differed from man's merely in being internal rather than external, though he might not have agreed with Galen that this was because females lacked sufficient heat (the immortal principle of life, and a fundamentally male attribute) to propel the organs outward.[5] Following on this perception, he gave at least partial assent to the notion that the sexes cannot be distinguished from one another in terms of pre-given male and female entities—a concept familiar in the twentieth century from the work of Freud and Lacan.[6]

Diderot pointedly highlights the flexibility of what are now called gender categories in his description of Sophie Volland as part woman and part man (*Corr.* iii. 136), so acknowledging that while sex may be to an extent inborn[7] (woman has a womb, man a phallus), there are defining characteristics which are shaped by social, cultural and psychological factors. Such characteristics are not *essential* ones, as uterus and penis are.[8] Towards the end of the eighteenth century Cabanis would confirm this view, asserting that the sexes had not simply been differentiated 'naturally' by means of a single set of organs, the instruments of reproduction; there were other significant distinctions between men and women that related to the role they were allotted in life.[9] Although the concept of gender implies a belief that masculine and feminine attributes are always defined relative to one another,[10] it refuses the simple biological or essentialist understanding of male and female. Masculinity and femininity are not the same as maleness and femaleness,[11] for 'masculine' and 'feminine' are not fundamental characteristics of the sexes.

Rousseau's patron Mme d'Epinay attacked what she saw as the essentialism of the work that sparked off Diderot's 'Sur les femmes', Thomas's 1772 *Sur le caractère, les mœurs et l'esprit des femmes*, in a letter to abbé Galiani in which she asserts that Thomas attributes to nature what is actually the product of education or institutions. (Her argument anticipates that advanced by many modern feminists.)[12] The attempt to create a feminine character by insinuation or prejudice, a charge that could as readily be levelled at 'Sur les femmes' as at Thomas's work, is a deep-rooted part of woman's oppression, and the emancipated d'Epinay resented it. Diderot's expressed view in 'Sur les femmes' that Thomas had written as a hermaphrodite (or, depending on version, as a castrato) implies that to have written, desirably, as a man he should have explained exactly what the difference between the sexes actually was. Diderot remained convinced that such a difference existed, whereas Mme d'Epinay took it as axiomatic that men and women had the same constitutions. The corollary to this, in her words, was that

Les vertus qu'on a voulu donner aux femmes en général sont presque toutes des vertus contre nature, qui ne produisent que de petites vertus factices et des vices très réels. Il faudrait sans doute plusieurs générations pour nous remettre telles que nature nous fit.[13]

Diderot easily establishes the weakness of Thomas's position: he fails to particularize sufficiently as to the nature of women and so conveys the impression that he is incapable of loving them properly (or less capable than Diderot himself). But Diderot's own account of the essence of womanhood is remarkably uncritical, and couched in far more categorical terms than related discussions of his elsewhere. 'Sur les femmes' paints an unsubtle and sexist picture, alternately extremist in its presentation of woman's pathological character and flaccid in its delineation of the 'eternal feminine'. The itemizing of woman's characteristic weaknesses—her rhapsodic nature, violence, passionate-ness, inconsistency and instability—is thoroughly traditional, as is Diderot's listing of her contrasting positive qualities (devotion, patience and loving-kindness). It is a dismayingly conservative reckoning from a man who professed to want to educate his daughter in an enlightened and non-traditional way, and shows how oddly he remained imprisoned inside some of the assumptions of his age. This tendency is confirmed by some fragments he wrote on *Les Parents et l'éducation*: 'Peinture de la femme, molle, douce, Légèreté. Danse; peinture de l'homme, fier, nerveux, impétueux, Tyran, Course, Lutte. Education des garçons; Pisse comme un homme. Education des filles; Mademoiselle, on voit vos pieds'.[14]

The stereotypical view in 'Sur les femmes' of woman as a creature of overwhelming emotionality is only partly countered by a work such as *Le Rêve de d'Alembert*, which features a female (Mlle de Lespinasse) who is congratulated on her male intellectual fearlessness, but then damned for her readiness to abandon it and become emotional and shockable again. The occasion is a discussion with Bordeu about sex: 'Ah! Après avoir été un homme pendant quatre minutes, voilà que vous reprenez votre cornette et vos cotillons et que vous redevenez femme', Bordeu tells her (p. 100). How can a being who has within her an organ susceptible to 'terrible spasms' be trusted to think straight rather than be borne along by all manner of extraordinary ideas? This is as traditional as anything in 'Sur les femmes', but the dialogue does advance some more challenging views. One, voiced by Mlle de Lespinasse, posits a kind of physical comparability between the sexes: if woman is the monster of man, then man is the monster of woman (p. 57).

In that case, who takes precedence? The time-honoured opinion was that women *lacked* men's abilities and qualities: this had been Aristotle's belief, and it was echoed in St Thomas Aquinas's claim that the female was a defective male. Feminists might retort, of course, that a principal difference between the sexes is woman's possessing an ability (childbearing) that men are without, and that men are men in virtue of a *lack* of qualities (the ability to carry, give birth to and nurse a child).[15] But Bordeu's dominant role in the dialogue hardly conduces to a verdict favourable to the opposite sex, and the assumption that woman is a freakish version of the male is allowed to stand. (She is, after all, subject to all the disturbing and sex-specific ailments detailed in the last chapter.) Diderot's conviction, implicitly set against that of Mme d'Epinay, is that woman's is the problematic sex—a huge assumption based on the pathology of womanhood he had been developing since at least the time *La Religieuse* was drafted—and so subordinate to the male, a deviation from the stable norm of maleness. Woman's nervous structure condemns her to fluctuation and wildness; man's muscular solidity gives him physical and moral stability. An alternative view is that woman's hyper-sensitivity indicates an evolution beyond the male model, and her sexual anatomy likewise: though formed on the basis of the male's, it represents—as modern biological thought would concur—a stage further on.

Sexual Indeterminacy

The matter of sexual ambiguity or indeterminacy is one that keeps resurfacing in Diderot's work. Perhaps this insistency suggests that the comfortably imperialistic notion of woman's sexual distinctness from and subordination to man is less settled in his mind than it generally suits him to admit. He was certainly aware of stories told since antiquity about woman who had 'become' men when their testicles descended (*Eléments de physiologie*, p. 212), though like Galen and Pliny he had nothing to say about men who 'became' women, except in the artificial sense of their being castrated. He was fascinated by eunuchs, like other writers of his time, because their condition seemed to indicate the extent to which sexuality defined identity: Montesquieu's *Lettres persanes* report one of the eunuchs in Usbek's harem saying that castration has meant being separated from himself forever.[16] D'Aumont's *Encyclopédie* article 'Eunuque' relays a view familiar in the eighteenth century, and which the *Eléments de physiologie* repeat, that seminal fluid is body-building as well as essential to procreation, and therefore helps establish the difference in constitution between the sexes. According to the *Eléments*, which are simply recycling a theory presented in Buffon's *Histoire des animaux*, seminal matter that cannot be ejaculated spreads over the knees, hips and pelvis, giving them a characteristically plump and boneless look (pp. 136, 179). *Le Rêve de d'Alembert* adds that the organic loss results in other physical changes, so that Arab horsemen castrated by their habitual activity lose their beards, acquire rounded knees, squat to urinate, dress as women, consort with them and adopt female ways and customs (p. 58). Is it fanciful to see evidence of a castration complex in the same work's description of a Cyclops and other monsters ('l'animal sera sans nez', 'collez ensemble deux brins [...] les bras s'attacheront au corps')?[17] Perhaps; but the phenomenon continues to preoccupy Diderot. The *Supplément au Voyage de Bougainville*, like Bougainville's *Voyage* itself, describes castration as a cruel and superstitious practice (p. 460)—and in Diderot's case this is not merely because of a belief that ejaculation is necessary to health.[18]

The case of eunuchs might seem to settle the question to what extent bodily parts 'sex' the subject, but in fact matters are less clear than it suits Diderot to admit. What of the man-woman described in the *Eléments de physiologie*, which announce (p. 49) that she must be displeasing to both sexes (as the woman-man is also said to be)? Her 'poor organization' has given her a hairy chin and body, but there is no information on what constitutes this given condition. Diderot's unscientific view seems to be that females who menstruate irregularly or not at all acquire a virile aspect, to which he adds that women thought to be hermaphroditic have facial hair (p. 136). If this appears to him monstrous, the monstrosity is of a different order from that posited by Bordeu in his reference to anatomical similarities between the sexes.

The Enlightenment's attitude to hermaphrodites (which is perhaps all that the man-woman and woman-man are) underlines the difficulty of trying to establish femaleness and maleness, or femininity and masculinity, according to absolute criteria. De Jaucourt's *Encyclopédie* article 'Hermaphrodite' categorically states that their so-called condition is a 'chimère', because there are no examples of humans equally able to perform male and female sexual functions. (The case of the pregnant Prussian soldier whose 'monstrous' body was not equal to its maternal role illustrates the point.) External appearance, as with the masculine-looking woman and the feminine-looking man, may alert us to the sliding scale on which attempted definitions are based, but allows no radical conclusions about essential sexual markers to be drawn. ('Firm' or 'radical' in such a case almost invariably relates to the existence or otherwise of certain genital features.) Antinous looks effeminate in comparison with Hercules, but not when set against the ambivalent creatures of Fragonard's *Corésus et Callirhoé* (*Salons*, ii. 196 ff.): the high priest himself is the archtypal 'efféminé' of which Diderot's mincing portrait by Michel Van Loo is a very pale version. Diderot's *Encyclopédie* article 'Efféminé' rails against this type because 'L'expérience nous a fait attacher à chaque sexe un ton, une démarche, des mouvements, des linéaments qui leur sont propres, et nous sommes choqués de les trouver déplacés'.

Of course this is highly questionable, and in fact the article on *Corésus et Callirhoé* suggests a faintly prurient fascination rather than shock. It is Grimm, ironically enough, who remarks both in the fictive accompanying dialogue and in a real editorial interpolation on the sexual indeterminacy of Corésus and his acolytes—ironically, because elsewhere Diderot calls Grimm's own nature hermaphroditic. He explains in a letter to Falconet of July 1767 that this is because Grimm combines the strength of the male sex with the grace and delicacy (and, a later letter adds, the soft contours)[19] of the female (*Corr.* vii. 96). This cross between the Venus de' Medici and the Gladiator evokes in Diderot feelings of extravagant devotion that may surprise us, given the tone of the article 'Efféminé'. In a letter to Sophie Volland of 8 October 1759 he declares the passionate relief he felt when the friend he had been separated from for so long—'c'est qu'il y avoit huit mois que nous ne nous étions embrassés'—returned to Paris from Geneva:

je me levai et je courus à lui, et je sautai à son col. Il s'assit; il dîna mal, je crois. Pour moi, je ne pus desserrer les dents ni pour manger ni pour parler. Il étoit à côté de moi. Je lui tenois la main et je le regardois [...]. Après dîner, notre tendresse reprit, mais elle fut un peu moins muette. Je ne sçais comment le baron [d'Holbach], qui est un peu jaloux et qui peut-être étoit un peu négligé, regardoit cela [...]. On en a usé avec nous comme un amant et une maîtresse pour qui on auroit des égards. On nous a laissés seuls dans le salon. (*Corr.* ii. 268)

Elsewhere Diderot describes this devotion in terms that recall the ones Montaigne used of Etienne La Boétie:

Mon tendre, mon unique ami, vous qui l'avez toujours été, qui le serez toujours, même quand vous me tueriez de votre propre main [...]. Je me sens uni à vous d'une telle puissance, que je n'ai jamais séparé vos actions, bonnes ou mauvaises, des miennes; qu'il m'est impossible d'éprouver le plus léger mouvement de reconnaissance de vos bienfaits; que, quoi que vous pensiez, vous disiez, vous fassiez, c'est moi qui dis, qui pense et qui fais. Il y a vingt ans que je me crois un en deux personnes.[20]

Their relationship did not last forever, however. In the *Lettre apologétique de l'abbé Raynal à M. Grimm* of 1781 Diderot wrote to him that 'Vous êtes devenu [...] un des plus cachés, mais un des plus dangereux des antiphilosophes. Vous vivez avec nous, mais vous nous haïssez' (*O.Phil.*, p. 630).

Alternative Types

Le Rêve de d'Alembert constantly encourages its reader to reflect on the infinite variety of nature, and one consequence of this is that the traditional distinctions between species and sexes, norms and exceptions, become blurred. Diderot's interest in non-conformity had been apparent from his earliest work, but it marches ill with the occasionally highly prescriptive tone of his sexological pronouncements. Some of the examples of gender confusion he adduces in the *Eléments de physiologie*, for instance, show an inflexible attitude towards deviation from the norm that surprises in a writer who elsewhere welcomes irregularity and scorns the concept of the canonical. Generally speaking, the scientist Diderot more readily accepts non-conformism than the imaginative writer or lover, which may be why he can write detachedly and with great technical interest about hermaphroditism in the *Eléments*, but also inveigh against its apparent manifestations in other contexts. The matter of his passionate devotion to the sexually ambiguous Grimm is not one that can be cleared by reference to the sentimental affectations of his age.

The law that distinguished between the sexes and prescribed the union of man and woman was disposed to punish those whose sexual activities it regarded as 'against nature'—sodomy (between men and women and men and beasts as well as between men) and homosexual behaviour in general.[21] For a long time hermaphrodites were deemed criminal irrespective of the type of sexual activity they engaged in— if they did—or regarded as the offspring of crime. Sodomy, on the other hand, was permissible for those born in the upper classes;

'vulgar' sodomites were burnt to death in the place de Grève in Paris as late as the mid-eighteenth century.[22] Diderot's own tolerance of homosexuality may have been more theoretical or poetic than practical. He was concerned about Sophie Volland's relations with a sister who, according to her mother, 'aim[ait] les femmes', and wrote to Sophie of his fears on 17 September 1760:

Je vois [...] que madame Le Gendre est ou sera incessamment avec vous. Je suis devenu si ombrageux, si injuste, si jaloux; vous m'en dites tant de bien; vous souffrez si impatiemment qu'on lui remarque quelque défaut, que [...] je n'ose achever! Je suis honteux de ce qui se passe en moi, mais je ne sçaurois l'empêcher [...] il est sûr qu'elle vous aime beaucoup; et puis cette religieuse pour laquelle elle a eu tant de goût; et puis cette manière voluptueuse et tendre dont elle se penche quelquefois sur vous; et puis ces doigts singulièrement pressés entre les vôtres! (Corr. iii. 246)

The previous year, however, he had seemed untroubled by the evidence of the women's fondness for each other, writing to Grimm in April or May of 'Un spectacle qui vous toucherait sûrement, [...] la tendresse réciproque de ces deux soeurs' (Corr. iii. 125).

In La Religieuse he treats lesbianism sympathetically only to the extent that it is regarded as the product of an unnatural environment (p. 381); otherwise, his portrayal is lurid. (One wonders whether he might have found it a more acceptable sexual orientation if he had seen it as a product of female 'organisation' rather than something environmentally induced.) His theory of homosexual development may appear oversimplified,[23] owing much to his anatomical beliefs about substitutive functions: if the body lacks or loses a limb or organ it adapts, as the Eléments de physiologie declare, and if it lacks a 'proper' sexual outlet it will similarly find an alternative means of expressing itself. There is truth in this hypothesis, but it ignores the importance of psychic factors, quite apart from what would now be called genetic predisposition. However, the attempt to define sexuality in terms of the presence or absence of particular attributes is conditioned by the mores of individual cultures and times, which assign significance to different features. The lesbian Superior's 'type' does not correspond to the crude images of popular imagination (she is not mannish, and her voice becomes deep only when she approaches sexual climax), which might suggest that Diderot is not portraying her as organically a 'monster'.

Diderot had every reason to resist the usual sexual stereotypes. After all, he was reputed to be drawn towards Mme Le Gendre himself, and must have been aware that lesbians do not necessarily display characteristics conventionally thought of as masculine. (He was, for example, acquainted with Sophie Arnould, one of Greuze's most famous 'stunners'.) In other words, here as elsewhere his attitude is shifting, changing from the reactionary to the liberal—with heavy qualifications—and back again. In *Les Bijoux indiscrets* the sexual tastes of Fricamone (whose name evokes the 'fricatrices' described in Brantôme's *Les Dames galantes* 'qui font la fricarelle [frottement] en mestier de donna con donna')[24] are hinted at in a tone of slightly disdainful amusement, if without much censure: they too have apparently been produced by the segregated convent environment to be described in *La Religieuse*, which perhaps gives them a degree of circumstantial legitimacy. But the tolerance extended to homo-sexuality in *Le Rêve de d'Alembert*, which justifies same-sex relationships in terms of the harmless pleasure they afford lovers—

de deux actions également restreintes à la volupté, qui ne peuvent rendre que du plaisir sans utilité, mais dont l'une n'en rend qu'à celui qui le fait et l'autre le partage avec un être semblable, mâle ou femelle—car le sexe ici, ni même l'emploi du sexe n'y fait rien—en faveur de laquelle le sens commun prononcera-t-il? (p. 99)

—is not matched in the story of *La Religieuse*, however nuanced the early depiction of awakening attraction may be.

Diderot takes an obvious, voyeuristic pleasure in describing the lesbian Superior's attempt at seduction. It does not start overtly; it shades from indirect to direct *linguistic* approach, and then becomes a physical advance. Before all this begins we hear the hypocritical and seemingly non-erotic praise lavished on Suzanne by the other nuns: 'comme ce voile noir relève la blancheur de son teint! comme ce bandeau lui sied! comme il lui arrondit le visage! comme il étend ses joues! comme cet habit fait valoir sa taille et ses bras!' (p. 239). Dramatizing by concealing is nearly equivalent to the titillation by veiling that Diderot writes about in the *Salons*: it is because Suzanne's body is habitually shrouded that the (forbidden) process of uncovering it is so exciting. There follows the verbal denuding, the litany the Superior utters as Suzanne tells of her past convent life: first the reference to the whole 'machine délicate' of the girl's body, the assemblage of 'tous ces petits membres', then the individual elements—the arms, mouth, cheeks, brow, neck, shoulders—and lastly the bosom, which the Superior uncovers. This 'anatomy' in some respects recalls the dismembering of saints in the Christian tradition, but in the Superior's case the veneration of fragments has nothing to do with gaining access to God.

One cannot list every aspect of a body, though Diderot/Mme de ∗∗∗'s mounting excitement suggests that the attempt will be made. (Monique Wittig's *Le Corps lesbien* perhaps comes closest to a complete account, with its detailing of the beloved's skin, bones, organs, muscles, nerves and secretions, lifting the flesh off layer by layer, dissecting the body and making an écorché.) It is in the nature of description to be synecdochal:[25] here it lights on the body's fragments in order to apply an unspoken sexual fantasy to the whole. Mme de ∗∗∗ remakes Suzanne's body as she divides it up in a paean of praise. Suzanne herself comments:

En vérité je serais bien belle, si je méritais la plus petite partie des éloges qu'elle me donnait [...] si c'était mon front, il était blanc, uni et d'une forme charmante [...]; si c'étaient mes joues, elles étaient vermeilles et douces; si c'étaient mes mains, elles étaient petites et potelées; si c'était ma gorge, elle était d'une fermeté de pierre et d'une forme admirable; si c'étaient mes bras, il était impossible de les avoir mieux tournés et plus ronds; si c'était mon cou, aucune des soeurs ne l'avait mieux fait et d'une beauté plus exquise et plus rare. (p. 340)

How impressed is Suzanne herself with all this? We have already noted her apparent determination to describe her body's non-participation in the different schemes to appropriate it, and her mental absence is further underlined when she enters the Arpajon convent, where detachment seems at first a form of protection. At a psychological remove from the Superior's endearments, she barely feels them as involving her own body. Is this implausible? No more so, perhaps, than her claims when Mme de ∗∗∗ starts caressing her that 'je n'y entendais rien, ni elle non plus; à présent que j'y réfléchis, qu'aurions-nous pu y entendre?' (p. 333). In both cases she is being disingenuous at a distance, an aspect of her narrative character that has often been commented on.

More interesting are the complex instances where she *thinks* of emotion at the same time as watching its birth in Mme de ∗∗∗: the kisses and caresses become transparent signs of attraction and excitement, and Suzanne's own arousal reflects the intention behind the Superior's gestures. This would by no means be reassuring to her if she really understood their meaning. Or does she in fact do so?

Elle m'avait tiré à elle; elle me fit asseoir sur ses genoux; elle me relevait la tête avec ses mains, et m'invitait à la regarder; elle louait mes yeux, ma bouche, mes joues, mon teint; je ne répondais rien, j'avais les yeux baissés, et je me laissais aller à toutes ces caresses comme une idiote. (p. 335)

Yet the Suzanne who confesses at the end of the narrative that she may have been playing flirtatiously with her intended reader Croismare—

Ces mémoires que j'écrivais à la hâte, je viens de les relire à tête reposée, et je me suis aperçu que sans en avoir le moindre projet, je m'étais montrée à chaque ligne aussi malheureuse à la vérité que je l'étais, mais beaucoup plus aimable que je ne le suis. Serait-ce que nous croyons les hommes moins sensibles à la peinture de nos peines qu'à l'image de nos charmes? [...] Je suis une femme, peut-être un peu coquette, que sais-je? Mais c'est naturellement et sans artifice. (p. 392)

—is not prepared to own up to any deliberate attempt to allure those around her. She repeats the Superior's besotted remarks without hinting that she might have grasped part of what they betokened, and tries to convey the woman's body-language neutrally, as though she was and remains ignorant of the fact that it foretold a seduction.

The Superior's exploration of Suzanne's body becomes an urgent message, a more and more overt attempt to alert her to an interest Suzanne wishes to ignore. Eventually, both as a result of her own observations and because she has been warned by her confessor, Suzanne withdraws her consent: her raised consciousness makes her body less accommodating as she 'reads' the Superior's purpose. The process somehow mirrors the sequence of opening up, unfolding and covering over which Mme de ***'s advances, her touching and removing of clothing and finally her concealing of the naked body again had set in train. Thus Suzanne's body, usually hidden beneath the narrative 'I', emerges clearly through the complex focalization of the *récit*, and she belatedly recognizes the fact. Far from having erased it, as her mother intended that she be erased on entering the convent, or as the nun's garb intendedly erases her body, she reinscribes it for the benefit of her male reader Croismare.

This is a bravura performance, an extended exploration of the meaning of passion and seduction by an observer (Diderot/Suzanne) who appears both apart from and involved in it. It is tempting to conclude that *La Religieuse* is written from a male heterosexual point of view that perceives intimacy between women as exciting and culpable at the same time (as Diderot's letters to Sophie Volland and

Grimm about his lover's relations with her sister suggest); but the implications of the narrative are far more complex. Although the author of 'Sur les femmes' can call sexual intercourse a morally neutral process, although Bordeu can state in *Le Rêve de d'Alembert* that 'Tout ce qui est ne peut être ni contre nature ni hors de nature' (p. 100), and although the *Supplément au Voyage de Bougainville* can warn against 'l'inconvénient d'attacher des idées morales à certaines actions physiques qui n'en comportent pas', Diderot still seems in two minds about the propriety of homosexual attraction between women (unless he can laugh it off with male bravado or the erotic insouciance that pervades *Les Bijoux indiscrets*). Clearly it carries a particular and forbidden erotic charge. Yet although he finds it easier to jibe at male same-sex tastes (though rather surprisingly he never alludes to d'Holbach's), the very Diderot who could write of Frederick the Great that

> Le galant et joli métier
> De plaire au sexe est peut-être l'unique
> Dont il dédaigne le pratique[26]

and of the 'sodomite' Fréron:

> Un bon homme
> Fit la rencontre de madame,
> De madame ou monsieur Fréron;
> Car le profès dans sa séquelle
> Est, comme on veut, mâle ou femelle[27]

can still admit to feeling or having felt stray homosexual attraction himself. As he explains to Sophie Volland, however, he does so with some repugnance:

On s'accuserait peut-être plus aisément du projet d'un grand crime, que d'un petit sentiment obscur, vil et bas. Il en coûterait peut-être moins pour écrire sur son registre: 'J'ai désiré le trône au dépens de la vie de celui qui l'occupe,' que pour écrire: 'Un jour que j'étais au bain parmi un grand nombre de jeunes gens, j'en remarquai un d'une beauté surprenante, et je ne pus jamais m'empêcher de m'approcher de lui.'[28]

Perhaps this is an entirely hypothetical situation, but it seems unlikely. In any case, it anticipates Mlle de Lespinasse's question in the third dialogue of *Le Rêve de d'Alembert* as to where 'goûts abominables' come from, to which Bordeu responds (with reference to male homosexuality): 'Partout d'une pauvreté d'organisation dans les

jeunes gens et de la corruption de la tête des vieillards. De l'attrait de
la beauté dans Athènes, de la disette des femmes dans Rome,—de la
crainte de la vérole à Paris' (p. 104). This, Mlle de Lespinasse makes
clear, is a subject she has no intention of returning to. The response
of Suzanne Simonin is somehow more reassuring, because (or
although) more confused. Through her ambivalent reaction to the
Mother Superior of Sainte-Eutrope, Diderot shows that below the
threshhold of moral censorship which Mlle de Lespinasse represents
the distinction between 'normal' and 'abnormal' is not always easy
to make. Rather, a zone of interchangeability exists, as it does in
secondary and even some primary sexual characteristics. Diderot's
uncontroversial belief is still that the heterosexual component in
humans is stronger, and—perhaps more controversially—that
substitution of another element for it is second-best, however natural
in particular circumstances.

Sexual signs

Diderot was also well aware that sexual characteristics can be
concealed. The *Supplément au Voyage de Bougainville* gives a routine
illustration of this in recounting how the sailors on Bougainville's ship
were deceived as to the sexual identity of a woman who had disguised
herself as a man in order to join the expedition, but that the natives
of Tahiti immediately recognized her for what she was. No
explanation for this is given, but a prime reason must be the differing
values attached by contrasting cultures to sexual markers: what for one
is a highly charged erotic signal will barely be attended to by another.
The pretty ankle or shapely arm that were prized feminine attributes
in civilized eighteenth-century France ('Là,' the dialoguist B tells A,
'pour être belle on exige un teint éclatant, un grand front, de grands
yeux, des traits fins et délicats, une taille légère, une petite bouche, de
petites mains, un petit pied', p. 488) may have meant little to the
Tahitians, who were more moved by the broad hips that seemed to
guarantee a woman's success at childbearing. As B remarks, 'Il n'y a
presque rien de commun entre la Vénus d'Athènes et celle de Tahiti;
l'une est Vénus galante, l'autre est Vénus féconde' (pp. 488 f.).
    Some forms of concealment may prove impossible, frustrating the
body's desire for reticence. An example of this is given by *Les Bijoux
indiscrets*, where Sultan Mangogul's ring forces admissions women
would rather not make by activating an eloquent part of their

anatomy. But as other writings of Diderot's make clear, every part of the female's body speaks sexually—her trembling voice, her soft or flashing eyes, her languid attitude, her blush, her bodily collapse. *La Religieuse* underlines the fact that a woman's sexuality is not confined to a single organ, and perhaps, despite appearances, this is also the conclusion of *Les Bijoux indiscrets*. Mangogul can obtain no response from Fricamone's 'bijou'; instead he hears of her love for Acaris by the conventional organ of speech (p. 156). The *Eléments de physiologie* make it clear that Diderot understood the role of the clitoris in female pleasure, but perhaps he also understood the part that non-genital contact plays in lesbian relationships: after all, the lesbian Superior reaches climax without the stimulation of her 'bijou', and Fricamone's intense response to Acaris occurs similarly. Possibly, too, Diderot wanted to focus on the psychological as well as physical component in love. The phallocentric discourse of 'Sur les femmes' does not give the full measure of his erotic philosophy. He acknowledges the varied focuses of woman's sexuality (in contrast to man's) at the same time as emphasizing the elusiveness of female sexual pleasure. Women, he thought, came in acceptably divergent forms, and it was unprofitable to try defining the 'best' ones too narrowly.

As far as his own robustly conventional tastes were concerned, the bourgeois Diderot shared Tahiti's admiration for maternal figures. In a letter to Sophie Volland of July 1762 he recalls how his acquaintance Saurin had detested the sight of pregnant women before his marriage, and comments, rather condescendingly, on how unnatural such a feeling is: 'pour moi, cet état m'a toujours touché. Une femme grosse m'intéresse. Je ne regarde pas même celles du peuple sans une tendre commisération' (*Corr.* iv. 83). Later that year, even more patronizingly, he writes to Sophie about the redeeming effect of maternity on otherwise faded women:

Les femmes semblent n'être destinées qu'à notre plaisir. Lorsqu'elles n'ont plus cet attrait, tout est perdu pour elles. Aucune idée accessoire qui nous les rende intéressantes, surtout depuis qu'elles ne nourrissent ni n'élèvent leurs enfants. Autrefois une gorge flétrie était encore belle. Elle avait allaité tant d'enfants...[29]

This is an astonishing and outrageous statement from the lover of the spinster Sophie Volland, with her 'menotte sèche' and steel spectacles.

Diderot's imaginative and critical writings present a full catalogue of the signs that define a woman sexually, even if they are not all

fundamentally distinguishing characteristics. (He is much less informative about the male.) Many are wholly predictable. The breasts
and buttocks whose proliferation in Boucher's painting he apparently
deprecates are still mentioned often enough to make it clear that his
own liking for female curves is uncomplicated, or complicated only
by his doubts about how moral it is to enjoy them. Different
characters speak for different ideals of feminity. Rameau's nephew
underlines the comeliness of the wife who was to have made his
fortune by reference to her small mouth, row of pearl-like teeth,
perfect skin, slim figure, fine rump and model-like contours (*Le Neveu
de Rameau*, pp. 108 f.). But Mme de La Carlière dresses to impose:
when she appears in public in order to reveal the crime of Desroches's
infidelity, people exclaim at her statuesque and slightly forbidding
beauty (which, she wishes to imply, deserved better): '"Non, Dieu ni
la nature n'ont rien fait, n'ont rien pu faire de plus imposant, de plus
beau, de plus noble, de plus parfait"' (*Quatre Contes*, p. 120). The
contrast between Mlle de La Chaux's physical appeal—her great black
eyes, her soft and infinitely moving voice—and the unalluring
physique of Gardeil shows the inconsistency of sexual attraction as
well as the inherent imbalance in human relationships, the paradox of
the ugly man's rejecting the beautiful woman who has toiled so
thanklessly for him rather than the beautiful woman's leaving the
exploitative and unprepossessing man. '*Ce Gardeil était donc bien
séduisant, bien aimable?*—Point du tout. Un petit homme bourru,
taciturne et caustique; le visage sec, le teint basané; en tout, une figure
mince et chétive; laid, si un homme peut l'être avec de la physionomie
et de l'esprit' (*Quatre Contes*, p. 84).

'Possession'

But men still hold the upper hand. In his *Salon* commentary on Greuze's
La Mère bien-aimée Diderot frames the scene as a story in which both
he and the figure of the returning husband feature as potent males who
know, as they self-congratulatorily survey the crowd of children
surrounding their mother, that 'C'est moi qui ai produit tout cela!'.[30]
Perhaps too—as the wife's ambiguous expression suggests—they think
they know that the male is responsible for a more transient physical
state, which can be decently hinted at because it has been made part of
a larger and more easily formulable meaning. After all, the female's
assumed lack of interest in sexual intercourse (though manifestly not

shared by many of the women in *Les Bijoux indiscrets* or *Jacques le fataliste*) was supposedly proof of her fundamental frigidity, and useful in terms of actually conceiving children. One of Diderot's letters to Sophie Volland comments with apparent equanimity on her *occasional* desire for him, contrasted with his *perpetual* desire for her (*Corr.* iv. 188; 7 October 1762). 'La mère bien-aimée' is an anomaly: she has both produced plenty of children and shown that she has intense sexual feelings. But the joy in maternity masks, if it does not contradict, the joy in sex. Elsewhere, however, Diderot pushes the logic of frigidity further. When 'Sur les femmes' details woman's fear of sex it is confirming an orthodoxy that had prevailed since the heyday of humoral medicine: woman is cold, man hot. Mirzoza, Mangogul's favourite, 'avait peu de tempérament', which may, degradingly enough, explain why she passes the test of the magic ring. '[Elle] n'était pas toujours disposée à recevoir les caresses du sultan' (*Les Bijoux indiscrets*, p. 6), though he, equally, was not always 'd'humeur à lui en proposer'. But the female revulsion from sex, which 'Sur les femmes' takes as a sign of morbid 'pudeur' or frigidity, may actually point towards something else: her obsessive washing of her hands possibly indicates nothing more than a sense of defilement, but could also convey her pathological fear of becoming pregnant.[31] Greuze's 'mère bien-aimée' clearly has no such fear or inhibition, and so can enjoy the male's approach. The male organ's indulgence is only towards itself: it cannot be coerced into doing what it does not want to do. The very different case of the woman, theoretically ever-ready for lovemaking, may suggest one reason for her failure to achieve orgasm: she does not love, but rather resents, the man who is entering her body.

It is a resentment that Polly Baker, whose story is told in the *Supplément au Voyage de Bougainville*, would be fully justified in sharing, and we shall shortly see why. Her sex (and hers alone) is penalized by the opposite one, in its judicial guise, for extra-marital lovemaking and its aftermath. For that reason, as B observes,

lorsque la femme a connu, par l'expérience ou l'éducation, les suites plus ou moins cruelles d'un moment doux, son coeur frissonne à l'approche de l'homme. Le cœur de l'homme ne frissonne point; ses sens commandent, et il obéit. Les sens de la femme s'expliquent, et elle craint de les écouter. (p. 509)

It might be better, one would think, to be 'possessed' by a woman without much lasting physical consequence, but Diderot apparently does not agree. Indeed, the fact that he barely lingers over the more conventional possibility that Suzanne Simonin is raped by the perfidious monk with whom she escapes from her last convent, whilst devoting the most vivid pages of his novel to Mme de ✱✱✱'s attempted seduction of her, suggests at least a degree of anti-feminism. The rights of the 'testicule' appear to be paramount, and physical molestation by a man is more acceptable than physical molestation by a woman. Then there is the rather different case of the d'Aisnons, decent women called to Paris in pursuit of legal justice, ruined by their lawsuit and forced into prostitution. Diderot's sympathy for mother and daughter, whom he calls 'créatures', is curiously limited. Perhaps he thinks it better to be a Mlle de La Chaux, offering herself out of compassion and gratitude (but not love) to Dr Le Camus, or the courtesan Phryne invoked in *Le Neveu de Rameau*, who gave herself to Diogenes of her own free will. (In the *Regrets sur ma vieille robe de chambre* Diderot himself remarks that 'cette Laïs qui se vend si cher aux autres ne m'a rien coûté'—but this is simply a painted Laïs in a picture by Vernet.)

The problems generated by attempted sexual possession are further highlighted by the *Supplément au Voyage de Bougainville*, where the nefariousness of (male) sexual acquisitiveness is contrasted with the Tahitian disdain for ownership. The fear of appropriation that is woman's usual lot, and which is given new meaning in the lesbian world of *La Religieuse*, is Diderot's subject in a series of letters exchanged with Sophie Volland in the early 1760s. The point of departure is the story of a woman who wants a child but not a husband: she fears the fickleness of humans generally, worries that she might not wish to honour her marriage vows forever, does not want a tyrant to rule her life, cannot afford to support several children and has settled on an approach to a single man, relations with whom would cease when she became pregnant, in order to ensure that she does not produce a family. She may, of course, resent men for the reason that any self-respecting woman would have resented a man like Diderot, who could claim that women seemed made only for male pleasure.

In July 1762 Diderot tells Sophie about the woman's asking a worthy married man to whom she is unattracted for the service of impregnation: '"Je ne demande rien de vous qu'un atome de vie que je voudrois pouvoir recevoir autrement que nature ne l'a voulu"' (*Corr.* iv. 58 f.). Her lack of desire is strongly stated, and she insists that if the effect of the undertaking could be known after the first attempt 'je n'en permettrois pas un second pour ma vie'. Diderot, incidentally, seems to have believed that pregnancy may announce itself immediately after lovemaking, at least to judge by a statement in the *Eléments de physiologie*: 'Si après le coït la femme éprouve une espece de grouillement qui ressemble assez à de la colique, pour qu'elle s'y méprenne, et si ce mouvement est accompagné d'un peu de chaleur aux parties naturelles, elle se trompera rarement, lorsqu'elle se croira grosse'—though he also concedes that 'Elle peut être grosse sans avoir éprouvé ces deux simptomes: fremissement le long de la trompe, et espece d'evanouissement' (p. 194). In *Jacques le fataliste* the peasant woman Jacques stays with after the surgeon has dressed his wounded knee tells her husband as they lie together that 'je suis sûre que je vais être grosse! [...] cela n'a jamais manqué quand l'oreille me démange après, et je sens une démangeaison comme jamais' (p. 511). In the absence of such certainty, the woman discussed by Diderot and Sophie must help her purpose as best she can. But her motives as well as her distaste for the expedient she is forced to adopt are misunderstood by Diderot's lover, who believes that she will develop a taste for sexual pleasure and not want to stop indulging it.[32] However, Diderot is perfectly clear about the repugnance some women feel at having sexual relations with men. If the evidence of 'Sur les femmes' were not enough, there is also a letter to Sophie Volland of 29 August 1762 which describes how a 'defiled' wife sells herself to a detestable man in order to help her husband's professional advancement. She lies like a slab of marble awaiting penetration, is incised as though by a surgical instrument, and effectively suffers rape (*Corr.* iv. 121 f.).

The ill-used woman whose body is taken rather than given, who suffers rather than enjoys, and the woman who wants her body filled with a permanent life rather than the temporary thrust of a male organ, almost converge in the person of Polly Baker. As already suggested, her story exposes the injustice of a social system that penalizes women simply for being exploited by men. Seduced by an unprincipled male and then repeatedly got pregnant by others, the unmarried Polly raises all these offspring single-handedly, so contributing a stock of useful citizens to the New World colony she inhabits. Each time she 'falls' she is made to pay for her alleged immorality, and no account is taken of mitigating circumstances. We are not told whether she found her sexual experiences pleasurable, but in any case there is little likelihood of her ever having wanted sex without marriage. It is beyond doubt that sexual relations were forced upon her by men who regarded her as damaged goods and hence of little value.

This episode is not, or not primarily, about whether it is right, particularly in women, to confine sex to marriage. In the *Supplément au Voyage de Bougainville* Diderot makes it clear through the example of Tahiti that there is nothing wrong with sex without the catharsis of love; but the Polly Baker story demonstrates that the sex must not be taken, or imposed, by just one party (the male) on its own terms. The Tahitians insist that an element of commitment is still needed, though that is denied to Polly until her original seducer marries her: Tahiti's notion of commitment matches Polly's own, namely an undertaking to raise children with the love and attention required to make them into useful and productive citizens. The objection to men's having a largely sexual interest in women, valuing them principally for the bodily pleasures they afford, scarcely applies in a community like Tahiti, where woman-as-body is essentially, or ultimately, woman-as-mother. The fact that this is not also the case in Polly Baker's New World, Diderot implies, is shameful. The social attitude that condemns her is as inconsistent as it is morally indefensible, for in the environment she inhabits it is contraception rather than conception that should be punished. The scandal is that men have not treated her properly, not that she has loved 'freely' (that is, probably under duress) and been made pregnant several times.

The happy ending of Polly Baker's story, if that is what it is, consists in the fact that she may at last be able to take advantage of her position, after men have repeatedly taken advantage of her. If it is man's prerogative to be able to enjoy sex withot being encumbered with children, it is woman's to bear children who are undoubtedly her own—unless that strength is turned into a weakness by the inconsistent disapproval of a Christian moral tradition. Until Polly Baker marries her original seducer, her men have had it all their own way. They have taken advantage of their power over her and then abandoned her to the vengeance of a repressive social system. Yet if Polly turns the tables on them by abandoning them to their natural disadvantage of not knowing who their children are, we are not told so; and would they in any case care? Nor can we be certain that Polly really wants the children she has borne, though the care with which she raises them suggests that she does. At all events, it is in the New World's interests to ensure that all women who want to have children do have them, and are rewarded rather than punished for doing so; only then will the (different) desires of both parties be gratified. In Tahiti the woman's way is smoothed by the fact that so many public resources are poured into the upbringing of children, but in America private support like Polly's is all that can be counted on.

And what are the auguries for her lasting happiness? If she is reliant for it on her husband's fidelity—remembering that he, a magistrate, offers her marriage only after being publicly exposed as her seducer— or on her own unchanging feelings, she is likely to be disappointed. As Orou asks of the chaplain in the *Supplément au Voyage de Bougainville*,

Rien, en effet, te paraît-il plus insensé qu'un précepte qui proscrit le changement qui est en nous; qui commande une constance qui n'y peut être, et qui viole la nature et la liberté du mâle et de la femelle, en les enchaînant pour jamais l'un à l'autre [...]? (p. 48)

Diderot himself thought it natural for marriages to end, as his own did, in disaffection, boredom and infidelity. It is as normal for fidelity to cease, he believed, as for women to lose their looks, or men to become impotent (*Corr.* xii. 78, 144). Even less formal unions are subject to this law, for Diderot himself did eventually tire of the Sophie he repeatedly vowed (as his letters confirm) to love forever. But the type of desire he saw as underpinning worthwhile sexual relationships might prolong them beyond the average life-span of beauty or potency.

There is a delicate balance to be struck, then, between a purely sexualized concept of the other, whether male or female, and a humanized one. Desire as Diderot understands it in its best form (which is not the form familiar to the lesbian Mme de ***, the husband of 'Sur les femmes' and the effective rapist described in the letter to Sophie Volland) is part of an interpersonal response impregnated with emotion and thought. Desire in this sense is not self-contained, or assuaged without the willing involvement of the other; it presupposes that the other may be aroused and given pleasure, not that she (and it is usually a she) will 'naturally' be denied fulfilment because of the gendered nature of her bodily responses. The pursuit of intimacy is a necessary part of it, and reciprocation in some form is the goal.

When it fails, it may be because of the vulnerability entailed by being overcome in one's body by the other's presence: this is what the lesbian Superior of *La Religieuse* finds when Suzanne decides to reject her. There is no unity of the instinctual and the reflective natures. But the man who regards women as merely coincidental beings made for his pleasure is equally flawed, if not equally doomed to unfulfilment; for he is denying the other's irreplaceably individual nature by making her qualitatively equivalent to all other women in virtue of her sex alone. (This may not, of course, prevent him from achieving satisfaction with her.) The distinctive inner life is something that Diderot values even above the living body's sexual identity, however false he thought it was to attempt separating inner from outer, mind from body.

Categorization

Diderot's attachment to traditional concepts of gender difference is, finally, refreshingly provisional, for he no more shows the female as consistently passive and domesticated (consider Mme de La Pommeraye, or 'la belle Reymer' of *Ceci n'est pas un conte*, a woman who cruelly sends her lover away to make her fortune and is blithely unfaithful during his absence) than he depicts the male as necessarily roving and outward-reaching (consider Tanié's dismay at being despatched by la Reymer, or Dorval's private anguish in *Le Fils naturel*). And the comparative flexibility of his attitude to homosexuality—sensationalistically as well as compassionately treated in *La Religieuse*, happily tolerated on hedonistic as well as hygienic grounds in *Le Rêve de d'Alembert*—leaves him able to conclude that it is people, not programmed machines, who have erotic relationships, and that they differ from each other both within and outside the boundaries separating the sexes. These boundaries, too, are often depicted as open ones, and crossing them may be without great moral significance.

Lastly, his acceptance of the fact that people may not choose to aim at erotic fulfilment in their personal lives—though he still scorns Leibniz for being a mere thinking-machine—shows his philosophical humanism in a more flattering light than does some of his sociobiology. Equally, he sees all the injustice done to woman by social institutions that try to thwart her biological or sexual desire, taking it as unnatural when it is not constrained by society's own conventions. Pursuing motherhood without love is more defensible, he reasons, than pursuing sexual gratification without human consent.

Loveless pleasure-seeking may be a poor use to put the ever-indulgent organ to, though (other things being equal) the body's claims should be answered where possible. Useful impregnation, on the other hand, is wholly to be recommended, particularly given the appeal of pregnant women.

This conclusion mixes the liberal with the conservative, but it is far more satisfying to Diderot's modern admirer than the effusive condescension mingled with misogyny of 'Sur les femmes', a work that is a betrayal of the woman-lover who wrote it. His most representative reflections on the issues of gender and sexuality are to be found elsewhere, and they are far more adaptable than his response to Thomas suggests. When he allows Bordeu to lecture Mlle de Lespinasse on the apparently changeless nature of woman—a negative, inferior nature in comparison with man's—he is surely writing more ironically than a superficial reading suggests. 'Vous vous prêtez sans mesure', Bordeu tells his interlocutor, 'à la sensation d'une musique délicieuse; vous vous laissez entraîner au charme d'une scène pathétique; votre diaphragme se serre. Le plaisir est passé, et il ne vous reste qu'un étouffement qui dure toute la soirée' (p. 81). Does this mean that being (pathetically) female, for Bordeu and Diderot, is more a matter of organic endowment or organization than of cultural conditioning? *Le Rêve de d'Alembert* argues that Mlle de Lespinasse reacts in this way because of her necessary subjection to the diaphragm, rather than because her senses have been sharpened by exposure to sensorily affecting phenomena such as the strains of beautiful music. The implications of arguments like the former were examined in Chapter 1, and partially rejected: for if sensationalism is bound in this case to emphasize the way emotional response is conditioned by the possession of a particular organ, it also supports the notion that different experiences provoke different responses. In fact being female is neither a unified nor a stable notion, and a unidirectional organic psychology is something Diderot more readily associates with the male of the species. Bordeu's theory supports the idea that biology is destiny, but novels like *La Religieuse* suggest that this may be an inaccurate formulation. If *body* is destiny, then it must be allowed that bodies are contingent as well as absolute structures.

That being so, there is clearly a place in an anthropological system such as the one Diderot constructs for imprecision about gender issues. The body that can develop organs in accordance with needs, or lose an organ—such as the womb—once regarded as its primary sexual marker without permanent disruption to the entire organism, is by definition a flexible entity. Just as woman is not 'the' sex of tender compassion or vaporous disorder, or man 'the' sex of cool rationality or bodily strength, so female and male exist in interconnecting zones. The reason why it is inappropriate to adopt a single tone in discussing woman, as 'Sur les femmes' urges men to do, is that it is stupidly reductive, tantamount to the contention that because *some* women are gentle and maternal, or passionate and unreliable, *all* must be. To make this claim is not to attempt to eliminate or minimize sexual differences, though Diderot was fascinated by the extent to which men and women may share sexual characteristics. One of the major errors of 'Sur les femmes' is to suppose that what is a potential in women is in truth an unalterable fact, and it is precisely the point of gender-based arguments like Mme d'Epinay's to show that this is false.

Thus, to take another example, it cannot be accepted that because woman may be born weaker than man she should simply be left that way (the logic of 'perfectibility' that engaged people's minds in the second half of the eighteenth century challenges the notion), or that because a society destines her primarily for childbearing she may not do anything else with her body but bear children, rather than turning it and her faculties to any account she chooses. It is not interfering with natural arrangements to suggest that such biological conservatism should be queried, as women like Mlle Biheron effectively queried it: she manipulated bodies fearlessly, and not solely in order to demonstrate obstetric functions to ignorant women. Just as men's bodies can be weakened by the wrong kind of living, as doctors and lay observers in the age of Diderot more or less insistently argued, so women's can presumably be strengthened by the kinds of training examined in Chapter 3. It was after all Diderot's abiding conviction that to know the nature of something (what it is like physically and otherwise) is not to know what is best for it (how it should develop). That would be a reprehensibly static conclusion to draw.

The issue of body-identity, then, is far from straightforward. Even if men and women were born the same, or only marginally different from each other, there would be no reason to assume that the identity or the slightness of difference should be preserved. People change, as Rameau's nephew demonstrates, and do so physically as well as in other ways. The concept of the 'natural'—the natural woman of Tahiti, for example, all generous curves, sexual accommodatingness and blossoming maternity—is as open to debate as most other concepts. The 'good' savage body is not self-evidently good for another culture whose purposes are different, and it may change accordingly if transplanted there (so adapting its identity). The 'unnatural' proclivities of the convent lesbians are not self-evidently unnatural in the environment they inhabit, and but for the chastity they are supposed to observe it might make good sense to yield to them. There is no limit to the proper uses bodies may be put to—but what of improper ones? The debate about eugenics in the third dialogue of *Le Rêve de d'Alembert* suggests that it may be right to encourage unnatural couplings in order to create a race of creatures who will (relatively painlessly) save humans from being exploited and condemned to hard labour.

These examples of provisionality are convincing enough, but Diderot discusses others that call the fixedness of sex and gender roles into question: the woman who possesses a natural instinct for motherhood, but wants no partner (has she an unnaturally low sex drive?), the supposedly masterful male body which, like Tanié's, crumples up and perishes when it faces devastating sexual and emotional disappointment. Although Diderot seems to deny the contingency of the 'facts' about male and female identities in 'Sur les femmes', he acknowledges it in other writings—the probable contingency of sexual orientation in *La Religieuse*, for example, and even in the ancient Greece mentioned at the end of *Le Rêve de d'Alembert*. If at one time he appears to say that the male sex drive is stronger than the female, at others he denies it. Undoubtedly he had a vested interest in arguing for some form of sexual determinism, but an innate curiosity about human adaptability often caused him to qualify it. Although he had no desire to eliminate a relatively conventional sex-based culture, the practice of forcing men and women into preordained slots (anatomical, physiological, intellectual, moral) was not one he was happy to follow. That, apart from the obvious humanistic reasons, is why he could write with revulsion in the Polly Baker story about penalizing women for the loose sexual behaviour of men, and why he attacks infibulation as well as castration as outrageous abuses in the *Supplément au Voyage de Bougainville*.

But does he approve of the other checks on female sexual freedom described by the Tahitian Orou in the same work, justified with the argument that (woman's) sex is essentially for procreation? Despite his penchant for pregnant women, it does not seem likely. One can hardly justify certain types of differential treatment of bodies according to their reproductive potential—like distinguishing with coloured veils the Tahitian women who for one reason or another cannot conceive and so are forbidden sex—unless it be *generally* agreed that sex is only for reproduction. On the other hand, the fact that disapproval of so-called free love is always sex-related makes clear that tradition has sanctioned the principle of such a distinction. A mind as inquiring as Diderot's was unhappy with the confusion surrounding the respective roles of the two sexes in procreation, and knew that the possibility of male sterility had not been adequately investigated; so punishing *women* who wanted sex but could not have children probably struck him as unjust, at least when he was not describing all females as sex-objects, potential mothers and nothing else. The evidence does not seem to suggest that his attitude to all specifically female sexual issues was governed by the fact that he was a man. The letters he exchanged with Sophie Volland about the prospective single mother reveal a more emancipated view on his part than on his lover's, and the sympathy with which he tells the Polly Baker story is clear.

There is nothing surprising or unusual, finally, in Diderot's desire to see femininity as sharply distinct from masculinity, even though he tempered it in the case of one or two close friends and his lover. He had been conditioned to expect different things of women and men, and the differences were physical as well as mental. Yet his appalling statement—to Sophie Volland of all people—that women are devoid of all attraction when they are sexually uninviting condemns him, especially given that he wanted to educate his daughter to be unconcerned with the usual female vanities and teach her to rate the possession of a well-stocked mind and a moral conscience above superficialities. Seeing women as sex-objects is precisely what the magistrate and the other male lovers in the Polly Baker story are criticized for, after all. It is not enough, on this reading, to invoke Diderot's expressed preference for unadorned women over coquettishly made-up ones as though it demonstrated a redeeming taste for women as beauty-objects rather than sex-objects: the damage has been done. Since he never says whether the displeasing men-women mentioned in the *Eléments de physiologie* have compounded an alleged *natural* masculinity (facial hair, deep voices) by choosing to dress without the requisite feminine sense, it is unclear whether he is criticizing them for doing their best to offend male sensibilities, or—more unjustly—castigating them for possessing attributes they cannot easily alter.

No one, of course, would expect Diderot to make sex and sexual attractiveness low priorities, but one might have hoped that he would rate the possession of feminine charms as relatively unimportant when set against other significant factors. One such factor is the waning of sexual appeal (which, he claims, makes older women disgusting to the apparently ageless male) *that has been caused by the duties associated with motherhood.* He alludes to this in the letter to Sophie Volland that remarks on the wrinkling and sagging of breasts after years of suckling children, but fails to develop his thoughts further, beyond commenting that it is because women 'ont beaucoup de chair et de petits os à dix-huit ans qu'elles sont belles; et c'est parce qu'elles ont beaucoup de chair et de petits os que toutes les proportions qui forment la beauté disparaissent à quatre-vingts ans'. Yet if Gardeil's loss of love for Mlle de La Chaux had been caused by the damage to her looks resulting from her prolonged labours on his behalf it would have had to be deemed reprehensible (as the narrator refuses to deem it), though a distaste apparently arising from her having contracted a skin complaint is not.

At the end of *La Religieuse* Suzanne seems to criticize herself for a kind of female packaging that harms her moral cause: she has titivated herself with words, as a coquette does with cosmetics, and so demeaned herself. She justifies her procedure by reasoning that most women (perhaps particularly those who have fallen prey to other women) want to attract men, and, according to the logic of Diderot's statement to Sophie, must not make themselves more unappealing than they can help. But the point is that Croismare, her correspondent, is meant to be interested in her not for sexual purposes, but as a possible future companion for his daughter. Since their relationship is to be purely businesslike, she should not have used feminine wiles to advance her case. And yet, according to Diderot's psychology of woman, such conduct would have been a perversely negative mode of self-presentation (since it effectively denied the essential nature of her sex), and could not have served either Suzanne's cause or the cause of women generally. The fact remains—and has long outraged moderate as well as extreme feminists—that men do not need to package themselves in this way, and rarely have done, to achieve their desired ends. Indeed, all they need to do, according to Diderot, is preserve a shock of white hair and a healthily tanned skin.[33] This seems unfair as well as slightly ridiculous. Women have nothing comparable to resort to, he declares, and it appears that no moral or intellectual attractions they can boast will compensate. So in the end, and contrary to Gardeil's assertion, they are unable to do with their bodies 'tout ce qu'elles veulent'.

Notes to Chapter 6

1. See Roger Scruton, *Sexual Desire* (London: Weidenfeld and Nicolson, 1986).
2. See Schiebinger, 'Skeletons', 53.
3. *Emile*, in *Œuvres complètes*, iv. 163.
4. See Barbara Creed, 'Lesbian Bodies', in *Sexy Bodies*, ed. Elizabeth Grosz and Elspeth Probyn (London: Routledge, 1995), 89.
5. See Schiebinger, *Mind*, 163.
6. See *Feminine Sexuality*, ed. Juliet Mitchell and Jacqueline Rose (Basingstoke and London: Macmillan, 1982), 6.
7. For a different view see Jeffrey Weeks, *Sexuality and Its Discontents* (London and Melbourne: Routledge and Kegan Paul, 1985), 96 ff., 186.
8. See Janet McCracken, *Thinking About Gender* (Fort Worth: Harcourt, Brace, 1997), 12.
9. Pierre-Jean-Georges Cabanis, *Œuvres philosophiques*, 2 vols. (Paris: Presses Universitaires de France, 1956), i. 275; also Jordanova, *Sexual Visions*, 27.
10. See Jordanova, *Sexual Visions*, 4.
11. See Susan Rubin Suleiman, '(Re)writing the Body', in *The Female Body in Western Culture*, ed. Susan Rubin Suleiman (Cambridge, MA: Harvard University Press, 1985), 14.
12. See Michèle Duchet, 'Du sexe des livres, *Sur les femmes* de Diderot', *RSH* 168 (1977), 525 ff.
13. Mme d'Epinay to abbé Galiani, 14 Mar. 1772, in *Lettere inedite (1769–72)* (Bari: Laterza, 1929), 251, quoted by Duchet, 'Du sexe des livres', 534.
14. 'Les parents et l'éducation', in *Inventaire du fonds Vandeul*, ed. Herbert Dieckmann (Geneva and Lille: Droz/Giard, 1951), 196.
15. See Janet Radcliffe Richards, *The Sceptical Feminist* (Harmondsworth: Penguin, 1980), 162.
16. Montesquieu, *Lettres persanes*, ed. Paul Vernière (Paris: Garnier, 1960), 23.
17. See Deneys-Tunney, *Ecritures*, 176.
18. See Tarczylo, 'Moral Values', 45.
19. See *Corr.* viii. 118 (6 Sept. 1768).
20. *Corr.* xii. 62 f. (15 May 1772).
21. See Foucault, *Sexualité*, 52 f.
22. See Michel Delon, 'The Priest, the Philosopher, and Homosexuality in Enlightenment France', in *'Tis Nature's Fault*, ed. Maccubbin (q.v.), 122.
23. See Aram Vartanian, 'La Mettrie, Diderot, and Sexology in the Enlightenment', in *Essays on the Age of Enlightenment in Honor of Ira O. Wade*, ed. Jean Macary (Geneva and Paris: Droz, 1977), 365.
24. Quoted in the Herrmann edition of *Les Bijoux indiscrets*, in *Œuvres complètes de Diderot*, ed. H. Dieckmann et al., 25 vols. (Paris: Herrmann, 1975–86), viii. 147, from Brantôme, *Les Dames galantes*, ed. Maurice Rat (Paris: Garnier, 1965), 120.
25. See Michie, *Flesh Made Word*, 97.

26. Quoted in *Œuvres complètes de Diderot*, ed. Roger Lewinter, 15 vols. (Paris: Club français du livre, 1969–73), x. 864.

27. *Œuvres complètes*, ed. Lewinter, x. 866.

28. *Œuvres complètes*, ed. Lewinter, v. 666 (14 July 1762).

29. 15 Aug. 1762 (*Corr.* iv. 104).

30. See Brewer, *Discourse of Enlightenment*, 165.

31. See Vartanian, 'La Mettrie', 361.

32. Diderot to Sophie Volland, 26 Aug. 1762 (*Corr.* iv. 120).

33. Diderot to Sophie Volland, 15 Aug. 1762 (*Corr.* iv. 104).

CONCLUSION

It seems natural that Diderot's attitude to the body should have varied over the length of his writing career, since he mistrusted adherence to any settled opinion. In fact his thought is a mixture of consistency and inconsistency. Philosophically, he likes to argue the body's paramountcy in epistemological terms—nothing can be known except through the body, and the body may even enable everything to be known—but in his fictional work he has recourse to a dualist philosophy that sets mind apart from and above corporeal matter when it suits him. His attraction to physical explanations presupposing a belief in bodily agency, clearly apparent in the *Lettre sur les aveugles* of 1749, has not waned by the time he writes *Le Rêve de d'Alembert* in 1769, but is called into question when he starts composing *Jacques le fataliste* two years later. On the other hand, the *Réfutation d'Helvétius* of 1773–4 opens the door to a vitalist interpretation of the human organism, and so reintroduces the idea of a non-corporeal animating essence.

But much of Diderot's writing on the body is far less abstract than this implies. Although he was fascinated from early on by the philosophical implications of sensory knowledge, he investigated them in a thoroughly physicalist manner. In the *Lettre sur les aveugles*, for example, Saunderson insists that he must *touch* God if he is to be able to believe in him, and so converts spirit into bodily substance. This physicalism is a direct product of the empirical temper of Diderot's age, and its automatic tendency to make abstraction tangible is reflected over the range of his writings. Not that he is invariably successful in managing the transition between the two spheres. The dramas of the 1750s, for instance, and particularly *Le Fils naturel*, seem strangely intent on making a stage spectacle out of philosophy and preaching, despite the fact that the stage spectacle is supposed to emphasize bodily eloquence rather than verbal persuasion. As dramatic argumentation it is completely unconvincing. Constance's lecture to Dorval illustrates the point:

l'effet de la vertu sur notre âme n'est ni moins nécessaire, ni moins puissant que celui de la beauté sur nos sens; [...] il est dans le cœur de l'homme un goût de l'ordre, plus ancien qu'aucun sentiment réfléchi; [...] c'est ce goût qui nous rend sensibles à la honte, la honte qui nous fait redouter le mépris au-delà même du trépas

and so on. This runs counter to every notion of theatricality; yet Diderot's belief in the dynamic expressiveness of the body, declared as early as the *Lettre sur les sourds et muets* (1751) but reflecting a youthful interest in the mute 'jeu' of the actor, is maintained in the teeth of his extravagant verbal pieties. The aesthetic introduced by the *Entretiens sur 'Le Fils naturel'*, with their developed theory of *actio* and dramatic pictorialism, informs the works that follow—*La Religieuse, Le Neveu de Rameau* and the *Salons* of the 1760s. The *Paradoxe sur le comédien* of 1772 continues the idiom of the earlier works, while considerably developing their philosophy.

The barely mobile groupings of the stage tableau discussed in the *Entretiens sur 'Le Fils naturel'*, and the focus on static bodies in visual art, may look like a diversion from such concerns, but in fact reinforce them. Although Diderot chafes at the expressive limitations of painting and sculpture, resulting from their confinement to a single moment, he is quick to underline the power of unmediated bodily images and the impact of representational forms that show the 'thing itself'. Admittedly, where the thing itself is the human body, as in the artistic genres placed at the top of the academic hierarchy, certain difficulties might still present themselves. Diderot was no prude, but the directness of figural depiction posed a moral problem in his aesthetic (and possibly helps explain his fondness for the sketch in comparison with the finished work of art). Nudity did not offend him, but tampering with nudity—by draping it suggestively, for example—certainly did. It might appear a way of veiling explicit realities, but instead simply highlighted them.

His attitude towards other kinds of corporeal explicitness was equally ambiguous. He refused to acknowledge the part it played in the work of his beloved Greuze, presumably because the dual role of voyeur and moralist suited him, and found nothing wrong in allowing the body's supposedly shocking truths to be suppressed for reasons of propriety even when that evidence would have been useful to the observer. So he happily sent his daughter Angélique to anatomy lessons so that she could learn obstetric and other facts from inanimate models whose whole purpose was to be true to life, while condoning the omission to show her vital bodily parts like the genitals. (Perhaps the omission had been demanded by the mothers of other girls in Angélique's class.) Enlightenment, it seemed, must remain a relative affair. Elsewhere Diderot displays his own peculiar brand of body shame. The supposedly pornographic novel *Les Bijoux indiscrets* is remarkably coy about detailing the sexual encounters of the women whose anatomies are interrogated by Mangogul's ring, containing only one chapter of vivid description—but this description is polyglot, and few readers could decode it all. Perhaps this reticence is a proof of imaginative laziness (after all, Diderot did claim to have written the book in a matter of days), but more likely it reflects a sense of 'pudeur' mingled with frustration at the representational limitations of language. In any case, he would have quite enough trouble with the censorship when he published the *Lettre sur les aveugles* a year later, and a degree of reticence may have seemed advisable.

Linguistic constraint is a theme that runs throughout his writing, but there is little evidence of consistent evolution in his thought. The pompous periphrasis of *Le Fils naturel* occurs only six years after the *Lettre sur les sourds et muets* called for fearless directness in talk of sex and other indelicate matters, and is followed four years later by the scatological verbal exuberance of Lui's discourse in *Le Neveu de Rameau*. This dialogue was itself composed a year after the first draft of *La Religieuse*, with its mingled discretion and explicitness. The toning-down of the *Salons*' language by their editor Grimm, to whom Diderot gave *carte blanche* to alter whatever he thought fit, was undoubtedly prompted by concern for the sensibilities of subscribers to the *Correspondance littéraire*, though neither Frederick the Great nor Catherine II was known to be particularly prudish. In 1771 *Jacques le fataliste* calls for the unabashed openness in referring to bodily functions that Renaissance literature had shown, and follows the same path of technical explicitness as *Le Rêve de d'Alembert*. Yet much of the narrative is still veiled, spinning webs of 'politesse' around the physical activities it wanted to see freely declared.

Diderot is rarely very technical about lovemaking: this is particularly striking in the transposed erotic references of *La Religieuse*, which makes orgasm resemble the convulsion of hysteria. But his focus on the body is by no means always sexual, however tempting it may be to follow Leo Spitzer in detecting an erotic energy in all his writings. Although he felt his grounding to have been inadequate, Diderot developed an enthusiasm for anatomical study that informs works as diverse as the *Salons*, *Le Rêve de d'Alembert* and the *Paradoxe sur le comédien*. The study of physiology, too, was bound to attract a man whose literary *œuvre* so recurrently focuses on the body's movements, and the interest was enduring: he worked on the *Eléments de physiologie* from the 1760s to the end of his life. The 'scientific' body, of course, was no more separate from the sexual body than from the artistic one, and Diderot's concern with function embraces them all. Noticing how the muscles contract may aid the detailed understanding of erotic arousal as much as the evaluation of painted or sculpted nudes; knowing about the anatomical distinctiveness of the female frame may colour attitudes to gender issues as well as medical judgements or views on the most natural kinds of body-language on stage.

This preoccupation with function seems to have shaped Diderot's response to physical beauty too. It may be, of course, that statements like the one he made in a letter to Sophie Volland about utilitarian attractiveness (the deformity of the bandy-legged or hunchbacked man is appealing, not just inoffensive, because it is the consequence of productive labour) are entirely theoretical. Certainly, it is hard to imagine Diderot not preferring the useless beauty of a Venus de' Medici to the worn aspect of a middle-aged matron with sagging breasts. But theory always drew him strongly, however unpersuasively it might be worked out: his *Encyclopédie* article 'Beau', for example, aridly tries to argue that beauty inheres in relationships, which suggests the kind of symmetrical arrangement that utility–beauty repeatedly flouts. The tension between these two positions is more or less equivalent to that between Diderot's professed liking for moral art and his actual taste for images of voluptuous women, and it is tempting to wonder whether he would ever have enjoyed the angularity of stern neo-classical art as much as the softened, semi-rococo version of it he encountered in the work of Vien. Yet he would still have wanted to know why particular configurations of bone, flesh and muscle pleased the beholder more than others, and why judgements varied between different observers.

It seemed natural to Diderot to set the body up as a prime focus of literary, scientific, artistic, medical and philosophical investigation. The science of man could hardly avoid attending to the physical locus of biological and brain events, any more than artistic theory could subordinate the representation of the human figure to that of fruit, flowers or landscape. Eighteenth-century secularism dictated that the human factor be elevated above the non-human simply because it expressed man's developing sense of power over his environment. Of course that sense could easily be diminished by intrusive factors such as disease, uncontrollable emotion, mechanical breakdown, natural disaster and the like, and the philosophy of determinism ran counter to it when pushed to its furthest limits. But when even involuntary motions like passion could be construed as forces for good, as they were in the *Pensées philosophiques*, the concept of powerlessness was robbed of its threat. This might have unfortunate consequences, it is true. It could lead to an uncritical exalting of sensibility such as is described in *La Religieuse*, with all the disorderly forces that are released by it. But such dangers were rarely sufficient to call the practical and theoretical stature of the body, the locus of feeling and action, into question.

Diderot sees no purpose in tempering corporeal energies unduly, however careful he periodically is to underline the waywardness and unreliability of the flesh. He is much less inhibited than the ambivalent Rousseau, caught between Calvinist mistrust of the body and 'sensible' faith in its promises, and much less bloodless than the cynical Voltaire, who sees humans as ciphers and bodily energies as more or less certain to be thwarted. Not that Diderot uncritically praises the body's power either: the pointlessness of its frenetic activity is suggested in *Le Neveu de Rameau*, the misguidedness of its erotic thrust in *La Religieuse*. But even these works convey an abiding sense of the body's purposiveness and resistance to external forces, whether it be in the Nephew's—temporary—pantomimic transcendence above the contingencies of base material life, or Suzanne's success in physically withstanding starvation, torture, seduction and other forms of material assault.

Yet it would be mistaken to emphasize the transcendent body at the expense of the terrestrial one, even though the latter may often be caught in the various traps Diderot associates with corporeality. It is capable of asserting a degree of autonomy, showing that it is in charge of itself, performing and controlling. Undoubtedly, though, this sense of power is always liable to be checked by reflex actions and other barely governable responses. Diderot worked out the logic of this perception in characters like Mme de La Pommeraye, whose orchestrated vengeance by one body over another fails, the Philosopher of *Le Neveu de Rameau*, whose physical and moral intactness are shown to be less than he imagines, and the (symbolic) women of *Les Bijoux indiscrets*, who cannot stop their 'bijou''s chatter even though they might be able to curb its sexual indiscretions. But the answer to such vulnerability was not to confine action to spheres where no conceivable upset was possible. Diderot was always hostile to forces that tried to contain human individuality, and rigorous bodily dressage—in terms of aggressive hygiene, diet, social etiquette and other kinds of self-control—was anathema to him.

The body's freedom, then, is at a premium, but within limitations. Although Diderot disliked attitudinizing, certain *moral* postures seemed to him incumbent on humans. The male organ's indulgence towards its owner, for instance, has sometimes to be curtailed, as Polly Baker's story and at least one of Diderot's letters to Sophie Volland suggest. Correspondingly, the rights of a less self-assertive anatomy than the male must be respected. These rights are primarily ethical ones, though Diderot is well aware of how the physical and the moral shade into one another. The pregnant female body may be admired by men like him, but its condition is desperate when it has been left helpless and abandoned to a hostile society. Although it needs all its energy to support the lives that have been implanted inside it—often without its consent—, it may still be nearly destroyed by the rigours of a punitive social system that is itself primarily responsible for the female's predicament. This is not the case in an island paradise like Tahiti (a paradise for all except women who cannot conceive), because children constitute the community's wealth and the family's ease; but the civilized West knows little about such environments. Ruined by obloquy and social deprivation, fallen women in such a milieu either founder or accept the kind of half-salvation proffered to the mother and daughter d'Aisnon, helpless victims first of male passion and then of female plotting. With a few exceptions, Diderot is silent about the bodily exploitation such women suffer.

This is not because his interests are above all theoretical, allowing him to dissociate social bodies, and the circumstances that attend them, from bodies in art, drama or philosophy. On the contrary, his writings are markedly concerned with placing humans in a real environment. This is why he developed the theory of 'conditions' in the *Entretiens sur 'Le Fils naturel'*, favoured the genre painting of Greuze, enthused over naturalistic novel-writing when he eulogized Samuel Richardson, and called for greater realism in art generally. The cause may be, rather, a latent sexism that often finds expression in his eagerness to see the female body as principally a source of male pleasure. Luckily, he is not consistent in this attitude, but it still pervades his writing. Woman's independent desires, and her own yearning for pleasure, are seen as another matter altogether, and when she is either too hungry, like the lesbian Superior, or not hungry enough, like the woman who wants a child but no husband, she is likely to be disparaged or ruined.

Of course, as works like *La Religieuse* make clear, there are social, biological and psychological reasons for excessive or undue sexual desire, and 'Sur les femmes' hints at reasons for its absence in certain women. Diderot's account of the body does not always extend to explaining its impulses, though in works like *Le Rêve de d'Alembert* whose concerns are part-poetic and part-scientific the attempt at explanation is more boldly made than in scientific digests like the *Eléments de physiologie*. Yet there remains much about the human body that escapes Diderot's comprehension. Nor does he always want to gain or present a technical understanding that might obscure or exclude matters of essence. His imaginative writings as well as his correspondence often suggest, in the teeth of his mature philosophical reflection, that organisms are immaterial as well as material entities, shaped by social, cultural and psychic factors as well as by the hard realities of anatomy. He was preoccupied throughout his writing career with the way the human form encompasses intangible properties, and saw that they help to constitute it: thus thought and emotion are sensorily conceived before they are physically translated through gesture, movement and facial expression. In other words, there is not *a* thought or *an* emotion distinct from corporeality, as 'hard' dualists (denying all interaction between body and mind) would have it. Emotion and thought have their reality in physical expression, while remaining somehow separate from it.

This may not be a very profound message, particularly when it calls extremist brands of behaviourism to the fore. But it is often convincingly delivered, most memorably, perhaps, in *Le Neveu de Rameau*. The lesson is implicit in Diderot's theory of acting, in his (borrowed) doctrine of pictorial expression and even in his reflections on the symptomology of illness and disease. At the risk of being made to seem literally superficial, the psychosomatic ailments he repeatedly describes may be called mind–body compounds whose ultimate reality is in corporeal substance. If this were not the case they would remain detached from the person and incapable of marking him or her physically; but the Diderotian body is essentially an *overt* body, a body that translates inner into outer more often than the reverse. So the dry scholar is corporeally marked by his loss of tone, insomnia, indigestion and Leibnizian sexlessness, and the frustrated lesbian by the ravages of tormented passion. If this seems a rough-and-ready interpretation, the unsubtlety is of its time.

To say, as Diderot insists, that nothing is explicable without the body is effectively to say that nothing can be *unfolded* except against the body's background. The body is both the key to experience (as Locke had argued) and its representative medium. Just as a painting or sculpture is the embodiment of an emotion or set of emotions, Diderot believed, so an individual like Rameau's nephew is the source and the locus of the music he mimics, and even—because it remains mere mimicry—the music itself, music-as-embodiment.

When Diderot suggests that there is a non-corporeal essence, the more elevated in virtue of its incorporeality, he may be thinking of music. But he seems to qualify the notion, perhaps because of his fondness for music that is also a form of embodied expression (Italian opera rather than French). The fact that he, like others of his time, took all art-forms to be imitative is a mark of his empiricism; for this theory reduces artistic creation to what has been phenomenally perceived, and all perception occurs via the body. That makes Diderot's artistic credo a realist rather than an imaginationist one; even emotion is 'real' for him in this sense, being a body event. This is not to say that he loses his attraction to the artistic possibilities of immateriality, described in the *Lettre sur les sourds et muets*. Inasmuch as all art-forms are hieroglyphic, according to the *Lettre*, they are representative, and representative of imitable realities.

It is as a realist, then, that Diderot seems body-centred, reducing mental predicates to physical expression, emotion to organic occurrence, reflection to solid matter, stray impulse to tangible act. On this interpretation, bodily eloquence consists of far more than the pantomimic moves made by actors like Garrick and performers like Rameau's nephew: it subsumes every kind of expressivity, from the dynamics of disease (the skin eruption of the exploited woman scholar, the livid, blotchy flesh of the sick prostitute, the seizures of the hysteric, the ravaged body of the plague victim) to the involuntary motions of the impassioned (the love-racked, convulsive female, the indulgently erect male), via the moral angularity of the post-rococo human frame and the winsome appeal of the unformed child. Sight and touch are the principal agents by which these realities may be apprehended, unless it is the mind, guided by sensuous images, that activates the imagination. And it is by visual means above all that the body speaks for Diderot, bringing to the surface what has been harboured or nurtured beneath the skin. The body is both code and code-breaker, attitude and action, impression and expression, which makes it compendious enough to absorb even his wide-ranging intelligence.

SELECT BIBLIOGRAPHY

Manuscript Sources

Collection Deloynes, 63 vols. (Paris: Bibliothèque nationale).
DIDEROT, letter to John Wilkes (British Library, Add. Ms. 30 877 fol. 81).

Printed Sources

ADLER, KATHLEEN, and POINTON, MARCIA (eds.), *The Body Imaged* (Cambridge: Cambridge University Press, 1993).

L'Albert moderne (Paris: Veuve Duchesne, 1773).

ANDRIES, LISE, 'Cuisine et littérature populaire', *Dix-huitième Siècle* 15 (1983).

ARDENER, SHIRLEY (ed.), *Defining Females* (Oxford and Providence: Berg, 1993).

ARIÈS, PHILIPPE, *L'Homme devant la mort* (Paris: Seuil, 1977).

ARON, JEAN-PAUL, 'Biologie et alimentation au XVIIIᵉ siècle et au début du XIXᵉ siècle', *Annales ESC* 16 (1961).

—— *Le Mangeur du XIXᵉ siècle* (Paris: Laffont, 1970).

AUROUX, SYLVAIN, 'Condillac, inventeur d'un nouveau matérialisme', *Dix-huitième Siècle* 24 (1992).

BACHAUMONT, LOUIS PETIS DE, *Mémoires secrets*, 36 vols. (London: John Adamson, 1780–9).

BAERTSCHI, BERND, *Les Rapports de l'âme et du corps* (Paris: Vrin, 1992).

BARKER, FRANCIS, *The Tremulous Private Body* (Ann Arbor: University of Michigan Press, 1995).

BELLONI, LUIGI, 'Anatomia plastica', *CIBA Symposium* 7 (1959).

BENREKASSA, GEORGES, 'L'article "Jouissance" et l'idéologie érotique de Diderot', *Dix-huitième Siècle* 12 (1980).

—— 'Hystérie, "crises" et convulsions au dix-huitième siècle', *RSH* 208 (1987).

BLANCHARD, MARC ELI, 'Writing the Museum: Diderot's Bodies in the Salons', in *Diderot: Digression and Dispersion*, ed. Undank and Josephs (q.v.).

BOLOGNE, JEAN-CLAUDE, *Histoire de la pudeur* (Paris: Orban, 1986).

BONNET, JEAN-CLAUDE, 'Les manuels de cuisine', *Dix-huitième Siècle* 15 (1983).

BONNET, JEAN-CLAUDE, 'Le réseau culinaire dans l'*Encyclopédie*', *Annales ESC* 31 (1976).

—— 'Le système de la cuisine et du repas chez Rousseau', *Poétique* 22 (1975).

BOURDIN, JEAN-CLAUDE, *Diderot: le matérialisme* (Paris: Presses Universitaires de France, 1998).

BREWER, DANIEL, 'Diderot and the Image of the Other (Woman)', *Esprit créateur* 24 (1984).

—— *The Discourse of Enlightenment in Eighteenth-Century France* (Cambridge: Cambridge University Press, 1993).

BRISSON, MARIE, 'Dire l'inconnue: "Sur les femmes" de Diderot', *Esprit créateur* 29 (1989).

BROOKS, PETER, *Body Work: Objects of Desire in Modern Narrative* (Cambridge, MA: Harvard University Press, 1993).

—— *The Novel of Worldliness* (Princeton: Princeton University Press, 1969).

BROWN, THEODORE M., 'Descartes, Dualism and Psychosomatic Medicine', in *The Anatomy of Madness*, ed. W. F. Bynum, Roy Porter and Michael Shepherd, 3 vols. (London and New York: Tavistock, 1985), i.

BRUNOT, FERDINAND, *Histoire de la langue française des origines à nos jours*, new edn., 13 vols. (Paris: A. Colin, 1966–72).

BUFFAT, MARC, 'Diderot, le corps de la machine', *RSH* 47 (1982).

BUFFON, GEORGES-LOUIS LECLERC, COMTE DE, *De l'homme*, ed. Michèle Duchet (Paris: Maspero, 1971).

BUKDAHL, ELSA MARIE, 'Les symboles visuels et "la force de l'unité": classicisme et baroque dans le *Salon de 1767*', in *Le Regard et l'objet*, ed. Delon and Drost (q.v.).

BUTLER, JUDITH, *Gender Trouble* (London and New York: Routledge, 1990).

CABANIS, PIERRE-JEAN-GEORGES, *Œuvres philosophiques*, 2 vols. (Paris: Presses Universitaires de France, 1956).

CANDAUX, JEAN-DANIEL, 'Consultations du docteur Tronchin pour Diderot, père et fils', *Diderot Studies* 6 (1964).

CANGUILHEM, GEORGES, *La Formulation du concept de réflexe au XVIIIᵉ siècle* (Paris: Presses Universitaires de France, 1955).

CARTWRIGHT, MICHAEL, 'Diderot critique d'art et le problème de l'expression', *Diderot Studies* 13 (1969).

CHARTIER, ROGER, *Lectures et lecteurs dans la France d'ancien régime* (Paris: Seuil, 1987).

CHATEAUBRIAND, FRANÇOIS-RENÉ, VICOMTE DE, *Mémoires d'outre-tombe*, ed. Maurice Levaillant and Georges Molinier, 2 vols. (Paris: Gallimard, 1951).

CHOUILLET, ANNE-MARIE (ed.), *Colloque international: Diderot* (Paris: Aux amateurs des livres, 1985).

CHOUILLET, JACQUES, 'Des causes propres à l'homme', in *Approches des lumières: mélanges offerts à Jean Fabre* (Paris: Klincksieck, 1974).

CLARK-EVANS, CHRISTINE, *Diderot's 'La Religieuse': A Philosophical Novel* (Montreal: Ceres, 1995).

COHEN, HUGUETTE, 'La tradition gauloise et carnivalesque dans *Les Bijoux indiscrets et Jacques le fataliste*', in *Colloque international: Diderot*, ed. Chouillet (q.v.).

COLEMAN, W., 'Health and Hygiene in the *Encyclopédie*', *Journal of the History of Medicine* 29 (1974).

COULET, HENRI, *Marivaux romancier* (Paris: A. Colin, 1975).

COUNIHAN, CAROLE, and VAN ESTERIK, PENNY (eds.), *Food and Culture* (New York and London: Routledge, 1997).

CREED, BARBARA, 'Lesbian Bodies', in *Sexy Bodies*, ed. Elizabeth Grosz and Elspeth Probyn (London: Routledge, 1995).

CROCKER, LESTER, 'Diderot and Eighteenth-Century Transformism', in *Forerunners to Darwin*, ed. B. Glass, O. Temkin and W. L. Straus, Jr (Baltimore: Johns Hopkins University Press, 1959).

CUNNINGHAM, ANDREW, and FRENCH, R. K. (eds.), *The Medical Enlightenment of the Eighteenth Century* (Cambridge: Cambridge University Press, 1990).

DANIEL, GEORGES, 'Visages d'Uranie', *Diderot Studies* 23 (1988).

DAVID, JEAN-CLAUDE, 'La querelle de l'inoculation en 1763', *Dix-huitième Siècle* 17 (1985).

DECHAMBRE, AMÉDÉE (ed.), *Dictionnaire encyclopédique des sciences médicales* (Paris: Masson, 1866).

DELACOUX, A., *Biographie des sages-femmes célèbres, anciennes, modernes et contemporaines* (Paris: Trinquart, 1834).

DELON, MICHEL, 'The Priest, the Philosopher, and Homosexuality in Enlightenment France', in *'Tis Nature's Fault*, ed. Maccubbin (q.v).

—— 'Le regard détourné ou les limites de la représentation selon Diderot', in *Le Regard et l'objet* , ed. M. Delon and W. Drost (Heidelberg: Winter, 1989).

—— 'Violences peintes', *Recherches sur Diderot et l'Encyclopédie* 18–19 (1995).

DÉMORIS, RENÉ, *Chardin, la chair et l'objet* (Paris: Olbia, 1999).

—— 'Chardin et la cuisine', *Dix-huitième Siècle* 15 (1983).

—— 'Condillac et la peinture', in *Condillac et les problèmes du langage*, ed. Jean Sgard (Geneva and Paris: Slatkine, 1982).

DENEYS-TUNNEY, ANNE, *Ecritures du corps de Descartes à Laclos* (Paris: Presses Universitaires de France, 1992).

DIDEROT, DENIS, *Correspondance*, ed. Georges Roth and Jean Varloot, 16 vols. (Paris: Minuit, 1955–70).

—— *Eléments de physiologie*, ed. Jean Mayer (Paris: Didier, 1964).

—— *Lettre sur les aveugles*, ed. Robert Niklaus (Geneva: Droz, 1964).

—— *Lettre sur les sourds et muets*, ed. Paul Hugo Meyer, *Diderot Studies* 7 (1965).

—— *Mémoires pour Catherine II*, ed. Paul Vernière (Paris: Garnier, 1966).

—— *Le Neveu de Rameau*, ed. Jean Fabre (Geneva: Droz, 1963).

DIDEROT, DENIS, Œuvres, ed. André Billy (Paris: Gallimard, 1951).
——— Œuvres complètes, ed. Jules Assézat and Maurice Tourneux, 20 vols. (Paris: Garnier, 1875–7).
——— Œuvres complètes, ed. Herbert Dieckmann et al., 25 vols. (Paris: Herrmann, 1975–86).
——— Œuvres complètes, ed. Roger Lewinter, 15 vols. (Paris: Club français du livre, 1969–73).
——— Œuvres esthétiques, ed. Paul Vernière (Paris: Garnier, 1968).
——— Œuvres philosophiques, ed. Paul Vernière (Paris: Garnier, 1964).
——— Œuvres romanesques, ed. Henri Bénac (Paris: Garnier, 1962).
——— Quatre Contes, ed. Jacques Proust (Geneva: Droz, 1964).
——— Le Rêve de d'Alembert, ed. Jean Varloot (Paris: Editions sociales, 1962).
——— Salons, ed. Jean Seznec and Jean Adhémar, 4 vols. (Oxford: Clarendon Press, 1957–67).
——— and D'ALEMBERT, JEAN LE ROND (eds.), Encyclopédie, ou Dictionnaire raisonné des sciences, des arts et des métiers, 17 vols. (Paris: Le Breton et al., 1751–65).
DIECKMANN, HERBERT, 'The Autopsy Report on Diderot', Isis 61 (1950).
——— 'Théophile Bordeu und Diderots Rêve de d'Alembert', Romanische Forschungen 52 (1938).
——— (ed.), Inventaire du fonds Vandeul (Geneva and Lille: Droz/Giard, 1951).
DONNISON, JEAN, Midwives and Medical Men, 2nd edn. (New Barnet and London: Historical Publications, 1988).
DORVEAUX, PAUL, 'Les femmes médecins', in La Médecine anecdotique, historique, littéraire (Paris: Rousset, 1901).
DOYON, ANDRÉ, and LIAIGRE, LUCIEN, Jacques Vaucanson (Paris: Presses Universitaires de France, 1966).
DUCHESNEAU, FRANÇOIS, La Physiologie des Lumières (The Hague: Nijhoff, 1982).
DUCHET, MICHÈLE, 'Du sexe des livres, Sur les femmes de Diderot', RSH 168 (1977).
EAGLETON, TERRY, 'Edible Ecritures', in Consuming Passions, ed. Sian Griffiths and Jennifer Wallace (Manchester: Manchester University Press, 1998).
EDMISTON, WILLIAM F., Hindsight and Insight: Focalization in Four Eighteenth-Century Novels (Pennsylvania: Pennsylvania State University Press, 1991).
FARET, NICOLAS, L'Honnête Homme, ou l'art de plaire à la cour (Paris: Du Bray, 1630).
FEHER, MICHEL, NADOFF, RAMONA, and TAZI, NADIA (eds.), Fragments for a History of the Human Body, 3 vols. (New York: Zone, 1989).
FINK, BEATRICE, 'Des mets et des mots de Suzanne', in Diderot: Digression and Dispersion, ed. Undank and Josephs (q.v.).
——— 'Diderot face au manger', in Interpréter Diderot aujourd'hui, ed. Elisabeth de Fontenay and Jacques Proust (Paris: Le Sycomore, 1984).

—— 'Enlightened Eating in Non-Fictional Context and the First Stirrings of écriture gourmande', Dalhousie French Studies 11 (1987).

FISCHER, JEAN-LOUIS, 'L'art d'avoir de beaux enfants', Dix-huitième Siècle 23 (1991).

FLANDRIN, JEAN-LOUIS, and MONTANARI, MASSIMO, Histoire de l'alimentation (Paris: Fayard, 1996).

FONTENAY, ELISABETH DE, 'Diderot gynéconome', Digraphe 7 (1976).

—— Diderot ou le matérialisme enchanté (Paris: Grasset, 1981).

FOUCAULT, MICHEL, Histoire de la folie à l'âge classique (Paris: Gallimard, 1972).

—— Histoire de la sexualité I: La Volonté de savoir (Paris: Gallimard, 1976).

—— Naissance de la clinique, 5th edn. (Paris: Presses Universitaires de France, 1983).

FOX, C., PORTER, R., and WOKLER, R. (eds.), Inventing Human Science (Berkeley and London: University of California Press, 1995).

FRANCE, PETER, Politeness and Its Discontents (Cambridge: Cambridge University Press, 1992).

FRENCH, R. K., Robert Whytt, the Soul and Medicine (London: Wellcome Institute, 1969).

GALLAGHER, CATHERINE, and LAQUEUR, THOMAS, The Making of the Modern Body (Berkeley: University of California Press, 1987).

GARRISON, F. A., and STREETER, E. C., 'Sculpture and Painting as Modes of Anatomical Illustration', in Ludwig Choulant, History and Bibliography of Anatomical Illustration, trans. Mortimer Frank (New York and London: Hafner, 1945).

GAY, PETER, 'The Enlightenment as Medicine and as Cure', in The Age of the Enlightenment: Studies Presented to Theodore Besterman (Edinburgh and London: Oliver and Boyd, 1967).

GEFFRIAUD ROSSO, JEANNETTE, 'Jacques le fataliste': L'Amour et son image (Pisa and Paris: Goliardica/Nizet, 1981).

GELFAND, TOBY, 'Empiricism and Eighteenth-Century French Surgery', Bulletin of the History of Medicine 44 (1970).

—— 'The "Paris" Manner of Dissection', Bulletin of the History of Medicine 46 (1972).

GÉLIS, JACQUES, La Sage-femme ou le médecin (Paris: Fayard, 1988).

—— 'Sages-femmes et accoucheurs: l'obstétrique populaire aux XVIIᵉ et XVIIIᵉ siècles', Annales ESC 32 (1977).

GENETTE, GÉRARD, 'Discours du récit', Figures III (Paris: Seuil, 1972).

GENLIS, STÉPHANIE-FÉLICITÉ, COMTESSE DE, Mémoires inédits, 8 vols. (Paris and London: Coburn, 1825-6).

GIRARD, ALAIN, 'Le triomphe de la "cuisinière bourgeoise"', Revue d'histoire moderne et contemporaine 24 (1977).

GOLDBERG, RITA, Sex and Enlightenment (Cambridge: Cambridge University Press, 1984).

GOODDEN, ANGELICA, *'Actio' and Persuasion: Dramatic Performance in Eighteenth-Century France* (Oxford: Clarendon Press, 1986).

—— *The Sweetness of Life: A Biography of Elisabeth Louise Vigée Le Brun* (London: Deutsch, 1997).

GOUBERT, JEAN-PIERRE (ed.), *La Médicalisation de la société française 1770–1830* (Waterloo, Ontario: Historical Reflections Press, 1982).

GRIMM, FRIEDRICH MELCHIOR, RAYNAL, GUILLAUME-THOMAS-FRANÇOIS, MEISTER, JAKOB HEINRICH et al., *Correspondance littéraire, philosophique et critique*, ed. Maurice Tourneux, 16 vols. (Paris: Garnier, 1877–82).

GROSZ, ELIZABETH, *Volatile Bodies* (Bloomington, IN: Indiana University Press, 1994).

GUIFFREY, JULES, 'Le cabinet d'anatomie du chirurgien Desnoues', *Nouvelles Archives de l'art français* 6 (1890).

HAIGH, ELIZABETH, 'Vitalism, the Soul and Sensibility', *Journal of the History of Medicine* 31 (1976).

HANKINS, THOMAS, *Science and the Enlightenment* (Cambridge: Cambridge University Press, 1985).

HAVILAND, J. N., and PARISH, L. C., 'A Brief Account of the Use of Wax Models in the Study of Medicine', *Journal of the History of Medicine* 25 (1970).

HAZLITT, WILLIAM, *Conversations of James Northcote*, ed. Edmund Gosse (London: Bentley and Son, 1894).

HILL, EMITA B., 'Materialism and Monsters in *Le Rêve de d'Alembert*', *Diderot Studies* 10 (1968).

HOBSON, MARIAN, 'Sensibilité et spectacle: le contexte médical du *Paradoxe sur le comédien*', *Revue de métaphysique et de morale* 82 (1977).

HOFFMANN, PAUL, 'Diderot et la beauté de la femme', *Dix-huitième Siècle* 9 (1977).

—— 'Le discours médical sur les passions de l'amour de Boissier de Sauvages à Pinel', in *Aimer en France*, ed. Viallaneix and Ehrard (q.v.), i.

HUET, MARIE-HÉLÈNE, *Monstrous Imagination* (Cambridge, MA: Harvard University Press, 1993).

IMBAULT HUART, MARIE-JOSÉ, 'L'Ecole pratique de dissection à Paris de 1750 à 1822' (doctoral thesis, Université de Lille III, 1975).

JATON, ANNE-MARIE, 'Du corps paré au corps lavé', *Dix-huitième Siècle* 18 (1986).

JEANNERET, MICHEL, *Des mets et des mots* (Paris: Corti, 1987).

JOHNSON, DOROTHY, 'Corporeality and Communication: The Gestural Revolution of Diderot, David, and *The Oath of the Horatii*', *Art Bulletin* 71 (1989).

JORDANOVA, LUDMILLA, 'The Popularization of Medicine: Tissot on Onanism', *Textual Practice* I (1987).

—— 'Sex and Gender', in *Inventing Human Science*, ed. Fox et al. (q.v.).

—— *Sexual Visions* (New York and London: Harvester Wheatsheaf, 1989).

JOSEPHS, HERBERT, *Diderot's Dialogue of Language and Gesture* (Ohio: Ohio State University Press, 1969).

JOUARY, JEAN-PAUL, *Diderot et la matière vivante* (Paris: Messidor/Editions sociales, 1992).

KEMPF, ROGER, 'Deux essais sur Diderot: 1. La présence et le corps chez Diderot', *RSH* 100 (1960).

—— *Sur le corps romanesque* (Paris: Seuil, 1968).

KORS, ALAN CHARLES, *D'Holbach's Coterie* (Paris: Presses Universitaires de France, 1976).

KUNZLE, DAVID, 'The Corset as Erotic Alchemy: From Rococo Galanterie to Montaut's Physiologies', in *Woman as Sex Object*, ed. Thomas B. Hess and Linda Nochlin (London: Allen Lane, 1973).

LA CROIX, J. F. DE , *Dictionnaire portatif des femmes célèbres*, 2 vols. (Paris: Belin et Volland, 1799).

LAFON, HENRI, 'L'aliment dans le roman', *Dix-huitième Siècle* 15 (1983).

LAIDLAW, G. N., 'Diderot's Teratology', *Diderot Studies* 4 (1963).

LAISSUS, YVES, 'Le jardin du Roi', in *Enseignement et diffusion des sciences au XVIIIe siècle*, ed. René Taton (Paris: Herrmann, 1964).

LA METTRIE, JULIEN DE, *L'Homme-machine*, ed. Maurice Solovine (Paris: Boissard, 1921).

LA SALLE, JEAN-BAPTISTE DE, *Les Règles de la bienséance et de la civilite chrétienne, à l'usage des écoles chrétiennes de garçons* (Reims: Florentin, 1736).

LAMY, [PÈRE BERNARD], *De l'art de parler*, 2nd edn. (Paris: Prulard, 1676).

LANDER, KATHLEEN F., 'The Study of Anatomy by Women Before the Nineteenth Century', *Proceedings of the Third International Congress of the History of Medicine, London 1922* (Antwerp: De Vlijt, 1923).

LAQUEUR, THOMAS, *Making Sex* (Cambridge, MA, and London: Harvard University Press, 1990).

LASSEK, ARTHUR M., *Human Dissection* (Springfield, IL: Thomas, 1958).

LAVER, JAMES, *Modesty in Dress* (London: Heinemann, 1969).

LAVERDET, AUGUSTE-NICOLAS, *Correspondance entre Boileau-Despréaux et Brossette* (Paris, 1858).

LAWRENCE, CHRISTOPHER, 'The History and Historiography of Surgery', in *Medical Theory, Surgical Practice*, ed. Christopher Lawrence (London and New York: Routledge, 1992).

LE CAMUS, ANTOINE, *La Médecine de l'esprit*, 2 vols. (Paris: Ganeau, 1753).

LEBRETON, DAVID, *La Chair à vif* (Paris: Métailié, 1993).

LEMIRE, MAURICE, *Artistes et mortels: les cires anatomiques* (Paris: Chabaud, 1990).

LEROY, ALPHONSE, *Recherches sur les habillements des femmes et des enfants* (Paris: Le Boucher, 1772).

Lettre d'un artiste sur le tableau de Mademoiselle Clairon (Paris, 1759), in *Collection Deloynes* (q.v.), vii. 90.

LOCQUIN, JEAN, *La Peinture d'histoire en France de 1747 à 1785* (Paris: Laurens, 1912).

LOGAN, PETER MELVILLE, *Nerves and Narratives* (Berkeley: University of California Press, 1997).

LOVEJOY, ARTHUR O., '"Nature" as Aesthetic Norm', *Essays in the History of Ideas* (New York: Brazillier, 1955).

LUONI, FLAVIO, '*La Religieuse*: récit et écriture du corps', *Littérature* 54 (1984).

LUPPOL, IVAN KAPITANOVICH, *Diderot, ses idées philosophiques* (Paris: Editions sociales, 1936).

MACCORMACK, CAROLE, and STRATHERN, MARILYN (eds.), *Nature, Culture and Gender* (Cambridge: Cambridge University Press, 1980).

McCORMICK, E. ALLEN, '*Poema pictura loquens*: Literary Pictorialism and the Psychology of Landscape', *Comparative Literature Studies* 13 (1976).

McCRACKEN, JANET, *Thinking About Gender* (Fort Worth: Harcourt, Brace, 1997).

MACCUBBIN, ROBERT PARKES (ed.), '*Tis Nature's Fault: Unauthorized Sexuality During the Enlightenment* (Cambridge: Cambridge University Press, 1987).

MAIRE, CATHERINE-LAURENCE (ed.), *Les Convulsionnaires de Saint-Médard* (Paris: Julliard, 1985).

MARCEL, LOUIS, 'La mort de Diderot, d'après des documents inédits', *Revue d'histoire de l'Eglise de France* 11 (1925).

[MARIN, FRANÇOIS], *Les Dons de Comus*, new edn., 3 vols. (Paris: Cellot, 1775).

MARMONTEL, JEAN-FRANÇOIS, *La Bonne Mère*, in *Œuvres complètes*, 11 vols. (Liège: Bassompierre, 1777), i.

MAY, GEORGES, *Diderot et 'La Religieuse'* (New Haven and Paris: Yale University Press, 1954).

—— *Quatre Visages de Denis Diderot* (Paris: Boivin, 1951).

MAY, GITA, 'Diderot and Burke: A Study in Aesthetic Affinity', *PMLA* 75 (1960).

MAYER, JEAN, *Diderot homme de science* (Rennes: Imprimerie bretonne, 1959).

—— 'Les êtres et les monstres dans la philosophie de Diderot', in *Colloque international: Diderot*, ed. Chouillet (q.v.).

MERCIER, LOUIS-SÉBASTIEN, *Le Tableau de Paris*, 12 vols. (Amsterdam: 1783).

MICHIE, HELENA, *The Flesh Made Word* (New York and London: Oxford University Press, 1987).

MILLER, LADY ANNE, *Letters from Italy in the Years 1770 and 1771*, 2 vols. (London: Dilly, 1776).

MITCHELL, JULIET, and ROSE, JACQUELINE (eds.), *Feminine Sexuality* (Basingstoke and London: Macmillan, 1982).

MONTAGUE, JENNIFER, 'Charles Le Brun's *Conférence sur l'expression générale et particulière*' (unpublished Ph.D. thesis, 2 vols., University of London, 1959).

MONTAIGNE, MICHEL DE, *Essais*, ed. Jean Plattard, 5 vols. (Paris: Rocher, 1931).

MONTESQUIEU, CHARLES-LOUIS SECONDAT, BARON DE, *Lettres persanes*, ed. Paul Vernière (Paris: Garnier, 1960).

MONTGOMERY WILSON, JOHN, *The Painting of the Passions in Theory, Practice and Criticism in Later Eighteenth-Century France* (New York and London: Garland, 1981).

MORGAN, MICHAEL J., *Molyneux's Question. Vision, Touch and the Philosophy of Perception* (Cambridge: Cambridge University Press, 1977).

MUCHEMBLED, ROBERT, 'Le corps, la culture populaire et la culture des élites en France', in *Leib und Leben in der Geschichte der Neuzeit*, ed. Arthur E. Imhof (Berlin: Duncker und Humblot, 1983).

MUNTEANO, BASIL, 'Survivances antiques: l'abbé Du Bos esthéticien de la persuasion passionnelle', *RLC* 30 (1956).

NOVERRE, JEAN-GEORGES, *Lettres sur la danse et sur les arts imitateurs* (Paris: Lieutier, 1952).

OLRY, RÉGIS, *Homo dissectus* (Paris: Editions du bien public, 1997).

O'NEAL, JOHN C., *The Authority of Experience* (Pennsylvania: Pennsylvania State University Press, 1996).

OUTRAM, DORINDA, *The Body and the French Revolution* (New Haven and London: Yale University Press, 1989).

PARIS IV, 'Discours sur le sexe et sexe du discours', in *Aimer en France*, ed. Viallaneix and Ehrard (q.v.), ii.

PERROT, PHILIPPE, *Le Travail des apparences* (Paris: Seuil, 1984).

PETIT, SUSAN, 'Sexualité alimentaire et élémentaire: Michel Tournier's Answer to Freud', *Mosaic* 24 (1991).

PLANTIÉ, JACQUELINE, *La Mode du portrait littéraire en France (1641–1681)* (Paris: Champion, 1994).

PORTER, ROY (ed.), *The Popularization of Medicine, 1650–1850* (London: Routledge, 1992).

—— and ROUSSEAU, G. S., *Gout: The Patrician Malady* (New Haven and London: Yale University Press, 1998).

—— —— 'Toward a Natural History of Mind and Body', in *The Languages of Psyche*, ed. G. S. Rousseau (Berkeley: University of California Press, 1990).

PREMNIA, L., 'The Waxwork in Medicine', *Images* 48 (1972).

PROUST, JACQUES, 'Diderot et la physiognomonie', *CAIEF* 13 (1961).

—— *L'Objet et le texte* (Geneva: Droz, 1980).

PYKE, E. J., *A Biographical Dictionary of Wax Modellers* (Oxford: Clarendon Press, 1973; *Supplement*, London, 1981).

RADCLIFFE RICHARDS, JANET, *The Sceptical Feminist* (Harmondsworth: Penguin, 1980).

RAMSAY, MATTHEW, 'The Popularization of Medicine in France, 1650–1900', in *The Popularization of Medicine*, ed. Porter (q.v.).

REVEL, JACQUES, and PETER, JEAN-PIERRE, 'Le corps', in *Faire de l'histoire*, ed. Jacques Le Goff and Pierre Nora (Paris: Gallimard, 1974).

RIBÉMONT, BERNARD, 'A la croisée des regards: la peinture de Greuze dans la critique de Diderot, des frères Goncourt et de Huysmans', in *Le Regard et l'objet*, ed. Delon and Drost (q.v.).

RICHARDSON, RUTH, *Death, Dissection and the Destitute* (London and New York: Routledge and Kegan Paul, 1987).

ROBBS, MARIE MULVEY, and PORTER, ROY (eds.), *Literature and Medicine During the Eighteenth Century* (London: Routledge, 1993).

ROBERTS, K. B., and TOMLINSON, J. D. W., *The Fabric of the Body* (Oxford: Clarendon Press, 1992).

ROCHE, DANIEL, 'Cuisine populaire à Paris', *Dix-huitième Siècle* 15 (1983).

—— *The Culture of Clothing*, trans. Jean Birrell (Cambridge: Cambridge University Press, 1994).

ROGER, JACQUES, *Les Sciences de la vie dans la pensée française du XVIIIe siècle* (Paris: A. Colin, 1971).

ROGERS, PAT, 'Fat is a Fictional Issue: The Novel and the Rise of Weight-Watching', in *Literature and Medicine*, ed. Robbs and Porter (q.v.).

ROUSSEAU, G. S., 'Medicine and the Muses', in *Literature and Medicine*, ed. Robbs and Porter (q.v.).

ROUSSEAU, JEAN-JACQUES, *Œuvres complètes*, ed. Bernard Gagnebin and Marcel Raymond, 5 vols. (Paris: Gallimard, 1959–95).

ROUSSEAU, NICOLAS, *Diderot: l'écriture romanesque à l'épreuve du sensible* (Paris: Champion, 1997).

SCHIEBINGER, LONDA, *The Mind Has No Sex?* (Cambridge, MA: Harvard University Press, 1989).

—— 'Skeletons in the Closet: The First Illustrations of the Female Skeleton in Eighteenth-Century Anatomy', *Representations* 14 (1986).

SCRUTON, ROGER, *Sexual Desire* (London: Weidenfeld and Nicolson, 1986).

SEGUIN, JEAN-PIERRE, *Diderot, le discours et les choses* (Paris: Klincksieck, 1978).

SIMMEL, GEORG, *On Women, Sexuality, and Love*, trans. Guy Oakes (New Haven and London: Yale University Press, 1984).

SPITZER, LEO, 'The Style of Diderot', in *Linguistics and Literary History* (Princeton: Princeton University Press, 1948).

STAFFORD, BARBARA MARIA, *Body Criticism* (Cambridge, MA, and London: MIT Press, 1991).

STAROBINSKI, JEAN, 'Le philosophe, le géomètre, l'hybride', *Poétique* 21 (1975).

—— 'Sur la flatterie', in *Le Remède dans le mal* (Paris: Gallimard, 1989).

SUË, JEAN-JOSEPH (le fils), *Eléments d'anatomie à l'usage des peintres, des sculpteurs, et des amateurs* (Paris, 1788).

SULEIMAN, SUSAN RUBIN, '(Re)writing the Body', in *The Female Body in*

Western Culture, ed. Susan Rubin Suleiman (Cambridge, MA: Harvard University Press, 1985).

SWINBURNE, RICHARD, *The Evolution of the Soul* (Oxford: Oxford University Press, 1986).

TARCZYLO, THÉODORE, 'Moral Values in *La Suite de l'entretien*', in *'Tis Nature's Fault*, ed. Maccubbin (q.v.).

—— *Sexe et liberté au siècle des Lumières* (Paris: Presses de la Renaissance, 1983).

TELFER, ELIZABETH, *Food For Thought* (London: Routledge, 1996).

THOMPSON, C. J. S., 'Anatomical Mannikins', *Journal of Anatomy* 59 (1925).

THUILLIER, JACQUES, 'Temps et tableau: la théorie des "péripéties"', in *Stil und Überlieferung in der Kunst des Abendlandes*, 3 vols. (Berlin: Mann, 1967), iii.

TILGHMAN, B. R., *The Expression of Emotion in the Visual Arts. A Philosophical Enquiry* (The Hague: Nijhoff, 1970).

TISSOT, SAMUEL, *De la santé des gens de lettres* (Lausanne: Grasset, 1768).

—— *Essai sur les maladies des gens du monde* (Lausanne: Grasset, 1770).

—— *L'Onanisme* (Toulouse: Laporte, 1775).

TOURNEUX, MAURICE, *Diderot et Catherine II* (Paris: Calmann-Lévy, 1899).

TOUSSAINT, FRANÇOIS-VINCENT, *Les Mœurs* (Amsterdam, 1748).

TRIBOUILLET, P.-H., *Diderot et la médecine* (Lyon: Imprimerie-Express, 1921).

TYTLER, GRAEME, *Physiognomy in the European Novel: Faces and Fortunes* (Princeton: Princeton University Press, 1981).

UNDANK, JACK, and JOSEPHS, HERBERT (eds.), *Diderot: Digression and Dispersion* (Lexington, KY: French Forum, 1984).

VAN DER CRUYSSE, DIRK, *Le Portrait dans les 'Mémoires' du duc de Saint-Simon* (Paris: Nizet, 1971).

VANDEUL, ANGÉLIQUE DE, *Mémoires pour servir à l'histoire de la vie et des ouvrages de Diderot*, in *Œuvres complètes de Diderot*, ed. Assézat and Tourneux (q.v.), i.

VARTANIAN, ARAM, 'Diderot the Dualist in Spite of Himself', in *Diderot: Digression and Dispersion*, ed. Undank and Josephs (q.v.).

—— 'Erotisme et philosophie chez Diderot', *CAIEF* 13 (1961).

—— 'La Mettrie, Diderot, and Sexology in the Enlightenment', in *Essays on the Age of Enlightenment in Honor of Ira O. Wade*, ed. Jean Macary (Geneva and Paris: Droz, 1977).

VIALLANEIX, PAUL, and EHRARD, JEAN (eds.), *Aimer en France 1760–1860 (Actes du colloque international de Clermont-Ferrand)*, 2 vols. (Clermont-Ferrand: Faculté des lettres et sciences humaines de l'Université de Clermont-Ferrand II, 1980).

VIGARELLO, GEORGES, *Le Corps redressé* (Paris: Delarge, 1978).

VIGÉE LE BRUN, ELISABETH LOUISE, *Souvenirs*, ed. Claudine Herrmann, 2 vols. (Paris: Editions des femmes, 1986).

VILA, ANNE C., *Enlightenment and Pathology* (Baltimore: Johns Hopkins University Press, 1998).

VIROLLE, ROLAND, 'Noverre, Garrick, Diderot: pantomime et littérature', in *Motifs et figures* (Paris: Presses Universitaires de France, 1974).

WEEKS, JEFFREY, *Sexuality and Its Discontents* (London and Melbourne: Routledge and Kegan Paul, 1985).

WILLIAMS, ELIZABETH A., *The Physical and the Moral* (Cambridge: Cambridge University Press, 1994).

WILSON, ARTHUR M., *Diderot* (New York: Oxford University Press, 1972).

WILSON, LINDSAY, *Women and Medicine in the French Enlightenment* (Baltimore and London: Johns Hopkins University Press, 1993).

WITTGENSTEIN, LUDWIG, *Bemerkungen über die Philosophie der Psychologie*, ed. G. H. von Wright and Heikki Nyman, 2 vols. (Oxford: Blackwell, 1980).

WITTIG, MONIQUE, *The Lesbian Body*, trans. David Le Vay (London: Peter Owen, 1975).

YOLTON, JOHN, *Locke and French Materialism* (Oxford: Oxford University Press, 1991).

—— (ed.), *Blackwell Companion to the Enlightenment* (Oxford: Blackwell, 1991).

ZANER, RICHARD M., *The Problem of Embodiment* (The Hague: Nijhoff, 1964).

INDEX

abstinence 122, 127, 125
abstraction 1, 10, 12, 72, 108, 109, 177
academicism 77, 104
Académie des sciences 41, 47
Académie royale de chirurgie 117
Académie royale de peinture et de sculpture
    47, 48, 50, 51, 52, 97, 98, 102
acting 92, 97, 96, 102, 111–12, 147, 187
actio 90, 94, 178
action 7, 17, 19, 20, 27, 67, 76, 90, 91, 92,
    106, 108, 182, 185
actor 70, 77, 91, 97, 94, 102, 177, 184
adaptability 55, 61, 171–2
Addison, Joseph 46
Aine, Suzanne d' 20
Albert moderne, l' 144 n. 26
Alembert, Jean Le Rond d' 14 n. 18, 70,
    40, 41, 47, 69
alienation 22, 172–7
ambiguity 15, 80, 97, 100, 104, 111, 152,
    155, 167, 178
amputation 117, 127
Amyot, Jacques 7
anatomy 6, 9, 11, 18, 70, 79–57 *passim*, 61,
    69, 114, 115, 117, 127, 147, 148, 149,
    152, 157, 156, 157, 162, 178, 180, 182,
    187
anthropology 10, 61, 170
Antinous 54–6, 72, 154
appearance 68, 69, 154
appetite 75, 76, 124–5, 128–70
    sexual 26, 110, 129
Aquinas, St Thomas 152
Ariès, Philippe 62 n. 4
Aristotle 8, 152
Arnould, Sophie 104, 157
Aron, Jean-Paul 144 n. 27, 145 n. 70

arousal 5, 6, 17, 26–8, 67, 77, 119, 171,
    174, 158, 168
asceticism 2, 12, 70, 170, 171
attitude 56, 70, 77, 74, 80, 90, 102, 104,
    106, 108, 110, 147, 182, 185
Augustine, St, *City of God* 27
Aumont, Arnulphe d' 176, 152
automaton 12, 70, 74, 77, 89, 97, 96, 109
autonomy 27, 70, 71, 77, 96, 174, 181

Bachaumont, Louis Petis de, *Mémoires secrets*
    41
Baertschi, Bernd 78 n. 12
Barker, Francis 87 n. 2
Batteux, Charles, *Les Beaux-arts réduits à un
    même principe* 74
Baudouin, Pierre-Antoine 79
Beaujon, Nicolas 127
beauty 2, 55, 66, 82, 84, 161, 167, 168,
    177–4, 180
behaviourism 25, 105, 112, 187
Berkeley, George 77 n. 1, 100
Bernardin de Saint-Pierre, Jacques-Henri
    27
    Paul et Virginie 82
Bernis, François-Joachim de Pierre, cardinal
    de 126
Betzki, Ivan 42
Bichat, Marie-François-Xavier 40
Biheron, Marie-Catherine 70, 40–6 *passim*,
    52, 58, 171
biology 2, 5, 6, 19, 26, 77, 126, 170, 171,
    180
bleeding 115
blindness 8–9, 76, 77, 116
body, male and female 7, 11, 46, 148–9,
    152–4

body language 4, 6, 87
body-language 1, 4, 78, 87, 89–112 passim,
     147, 159, 177, 180, 184–5
   see also mind–body relationship
Boerhaave, Herrmann 115
Boileau, Nicolas 44, 46
Bologne, Jean-Claude 87 n. 18
bone 6, 41, 48, 83, 89, 158, 180
Bonnet, Jean-Claude 145 n. 45, n. 46
Bordeu, Théophile 24, 27, 40, 58–9, 118,
     120, 134, 137
Boucher, François 49, 72, 73–4, 79, 163
Bougainville, Louis-Antoine de, Voyage
     autour du monde 153
brain 12, 17, 26, 28, 29, 99, 135, 180
Brantôme, Pierre de Bourdeilles de, Les
     Dames galantes 157
breast 78, 83, 117, 163, 174, 180
Brewer, Daniel 64 n. 45, 176 n. 30
Brookner, Anita 112 n. 3
Brown, Theodore M. 145 n. 55
Buffon, Georges-Louis Leclerc, comte de:
     Histoire des animaux 153
     Histoire naturelle de l'homme 7, 24, 57,
        60–1, 89, 99, 139
Bukdahl, Elsa Marie 63 n. 38
Buonarotti, Michelangelo 45
Burke, Edmund 106

Cabanis, Pierre-Jean-Georges 150
cadaver 39–44 passim, 47, 51
Calvinism 181
cancer 120, 137
Candaux, Jean-Daniel 144 n. 18
Canguilhem, Georges 38 n. 14
Castiglione, Baldassare, Il Cortegiano 68
castration, castrato 150, 152–3, 172
categories, sexual/gender 147–75 passim
Catherine II of Russia 41, 42, 44, 74, 117,
     141, 179
Caylus, Anne-Claude-Philippe, comte de
     98, 100
Challe, Charles Michel-Ange 142
Chardin, Jean-Baptiste-Siméon 125, 126
Chartier, Roger 87 n. 8, n. 10
chastity 18, 26, 67, 172
Chateaubriand, François-René, vicomte de,
     Mémoires d'outre-tombe 111–12

Chereau, A. 146 n. 65
Cheverny, comte de 122
childbearing 123, 152, 161, 165, 167, 171
childbirth 10, 116, 138
Christianity 2, 6, 11, 77, 158, 167
civility 62, 65–87 passim
Clairon, Claire de la Tude, dite la 94, 98,
     104–5, 106, 138
climax 5, 67, 132, 134, 139, 156, 162
clitoris 7, 57, 149, 162
clothing 12, 79, 82–6, 159
code 4, 13, 68, 76, 78, 185
Cohen, Huguette 14 n. 25
Coleridge, Samuel Taylor 82
colic 122, 125
Collège de chirurgie 40
Comédie-Française 96
compositio 106
conception 61, 77, 140, 164, 167, 182
concupiscence 129
Condillac, Etienne Bonnot de 8, 9, 91, 93
     Traité des sensations 16, 93
conduct-book 68, 69, 76, 80, 93
confinement 65, 120, 138
consciousness 17, 18, 25, 75, 133
constraint 11, 17, 33, 65, 86, 128, 136, 179
contagion 132, 134
control 27, 30, 31, 33, 37, 65, 67, 68, 75,
     76, 115, 123, 147, 181, 182
convent 67, 72, 84, 130, 132, 134, 157, 159,
     172
convention 92, 97, 147, 169
convulsion 121, 133, 135–6, 179, 184
Convulsionnaires 135–6
coquette, coquettishness 85, 173, 174
Corneille, Pierre, Horace 90
Correspondance littéraire 27, 43, 84, 95, 179
Coulet, Henri 14 n. 20
coup de théâtre 105
court, courtier 69, 74, 108
courtesan 81, 85, 142, 165
Crébillon, Claude-Prosper-Jolyot de, fils 4
Creed, Barbara 175 n. 4
Crocker, Lester 64 n. 46
Croismare, Marc-Antoine-Nicolas, marquis
     de 159, 174
cure 65, 135
Curtius, Philippe 44

Cyclops 58, 153
Czartoriski, Adam, prince 84

Damilaville, Etienne-Noël 20, 120
dance 73, 91, 95–7, 110, 128, 147
David, Jacques-Louis 80, 90, 98
  Le Serment des Horaces 89–90
decency 5, 6, 7, 77, 79
Deffand, Marie, marquise du 69
deformity 56–8, 83, 107, 180
Delacoux, A. 44
Delon, Michel 63 n. 27, n. 35, 175 n. 22
Démoris, René 14 n. 16
Deneys-Tunney, Anne, *Ecritures du corps* 13,
  38 n. 6, n. 7, 145 n. 53, 175 n. 17
Descartes, René 99, 108, 134, 139
  and the *cogito* 23, 35
  and dualism 1
  and mind-body problem 1, 23–4
  and *res cogitans* 1, 12
  and *res extensa* 1, 12
desire, sexual 5, 8, 11, 18, 26, 129, 130,
  132, 140, 164, 165, 168, 169, 183
detachment 21, 111, 134, 158, 183
determinism 17, 18, 19, 30, 31, 86, 172,
  181
deviation 51, 57, 155
diagnosis 22, 118, 119, 135
diaphragm 6, 35, 137, 170
Dictionnaire de l'Académie 68
Diderot, Angélique *see* Vandeul
Diderot, Anne-Toinette 119, 123, 138
Diderot, Denis:
  as art critic 1, 3
  and behaviourism 25–6, 105, 112, 183
  and bodily depiction 45–56
  and crime 11
  and decorum 4–5, 7, 65–87 *passim*
  and dialogue 26
  and dramatic theory 1
  and excess 122–5
  and feminism 11, 150, 152, 174
  and gender 147–75 *passim*
  and medicine 1, 2, 3, 11, 25, 112,
    114–43 *passim*, 164
  and nature 29, 46, 53, 55, 61, 70, 74, 75,
    76, 104
  and science 6

and the science of man 1, 3, 180
  moral preoccupations of 78–82 *passim*,
    178–9
  visual gifts of 8, 94
  Les Bijoux indiscrets 5, 8, 11, 17–18, 21,
    26, 58–9, 81, 157, 160, 162, 164, 179,
    182
  Ceci n'est pas un conte 3, 18, 26, 120, 148,
    163, 169
  contes 11, 12
  Correspondance 1, 3, 4, 183
  Les Deux Amis de Bourbonne 54
  Eléments de physiologie 1–2, 9, 11, 24, 25,
    27, 28, 34, 51, 52, 57, 60, 61, 86, 90,
    99, 118, 133, 134, 137, 140, 141, 149,
    153, 155, 156, 162, 166, 173, 180, 183
  Encyclopédie (ed.) 3, 4, 7, 14 n. 18, 24,
    30, 40, 42, 61, 65, 68, 69, 70, 75, 83,
    98, 114, 115, 116, 117, 118, 124, 125,
    129, 135, 136, 139, 153, 154, 180
  Entretien d'un père avec ses enfants 120
  Entretiens sur 'Le Fils naturel' 3, 54, 75,
    90, 91, 93, 95, 105, 178, 182
  Essais sur la peinture 48, 53, 56, 72, 97,
    98, 99, 100, 102, 104
  Le Fils naturel 3, 5, 10, 18, 25, 26, 95, 96,
    106, 147, 177, 179
  Jacques le fataliste 4–5, 11, 16, 17, 18, 23,
    26, 30, 81, 84, 117, 120, 129, 164,
    166, 177, 179, 181, 182
  *Lettre apologétique de l'abbé Raynal à M.
    Grimm* 155
  Lettre sur les aveugles 6, 8, 36, 57, 59, 77,
    116, 177, 179
  Lettre sur les sourds et muets 6, 7, 16, 74,
    90, 93–4, 95, 98, 107, 110, 178, 179,
    184
  Madame de La Carlière 3, 163
  Mémoires pour Catherine II 14 n. 30, 41,
    42, 43
  Neveu de Rameau, Le 3, 4, 6, 12, 13, 16,
    18–19, 21, 26, 27, 31–5, 36, 65, 66,
    76, 86, 96, 99, 108–10, 127–9, 132–3,
    142, 143, 147, 163, 165, 171, 178, 179,
    181–3, 184
  Paradoxe sur le comédien, Le 6, 30, 35, 75,
    93, 95, 102, 108, 136, 137, 138, 143,
    147–8, 149, 178, 180

Parents et l'éducation, Les 151
Pensées détachées sur la peinture 49, 56, 91, 97, 106
Pensées philosophiques 66, 69, 135, 181
Pensées sur l'interprétation de la nature 51, 59, 60
Père de famille, Le 95, 96, 111
Plan d'une université 13
Réfutation d'Helvétius 2, 14 n. 27, 20–1, 24, 73, 93, 137, 176
Regrets sur ma vieille robe de chambre 84–5
Religieuse, La 3, 5, 6, 8, 11, 13, 18, 21–2, 25–6, 32, 36, 65, 67, 70, 72, 78, 84, 97, 98, 99, 107, 111, 119, 130–2, 134–5, 136, 139, 143, 152, 156–60, 162, 165, 169, 170, 172, 174, 178, 179, 181, 183
Rêve de d'Alembert, Le 2, 4, 5, 6, 7, 11, 16, 19, 21, 23, 24, 26, 27, 30, 32, 34, 37, 40, 45, 56, 57–8, 60, 61, 86, 119, 120, 126, 135, 137, 141, 143, 149, 151–2, 153, 155, 157, 160, 170, 172, 177, 179, 180, 183
Salons 3, 8, 10, 15, 27, 41, 42, 45, 46, 48–9, 54, 71, 72, 73, 75, 78–9, 80, 82, 84, 85, 91, 92, 97, 98, 99, 100, 101, 102, 103, 125, 133, 142, 154, 157, 163–4, 178, 179, 180
Supplément au Voyage de Bougainville, Le 4, 6, 10, 11, 12, 26, 28, 55, 61, 70, 76–7, 81–2, 84, 148, 153, 160, 161, 164–5, 166–8, 172–3, 182
'Sur les femmes' 6, 11–12, 28, 43, 135, 136, 138, 140, 147, 149, 150, 151, 160, 162, 164, 166, 168, 170, 171, 172, 183
Diderot, Didier 124
Dieckmann, Herbert 62 n. 2, 144 n. 7
diet 24, 123, 124, 126–7, 128–9
digestion 6, 24, 125, 128, 129
Diogenes 27, 110, 141, 143, 165
disease 3, 114, 133, 143, 181, 183, 184
venereal 3, 4, 142
dissection 9, 39–40, 42, 43, 158
distance, aesthetic/psychological 21, 67, 111, 134, 158
Dorveaux, P. 62 n. 12, n. 16
Doyen, Gabriel-François, *Le Miracle des ardents* 48, 133

Doyon, André 38 n. 15
drame 54, 95, 96
drapery 45, 82, 178
dressage 12, 31, 61, 70, 72, 73, 182
dualism 1, 16, 23, 24, 26, 32–5, 37, 86, 127, 177, 183
Dubos, Jean-Baptiste, *Réflexions critiques sur la poésie et sur la peinture* 67, 90, 91, 99
Duchet, Michèle 175 n. 12
Dumesnil, Marie-Françoise Marchant, *dite* Mlle 104–5

Eagleton, Terry 14 n. 29
écorché 46, 158
Edmiston, William F. 37 n. 5
education 4, 29, 62, 70, 73, 150, 151
of women 43, 151, 173
effeminacy 154
Eidous, Marc-Antoine 81, 115
embryo, embryogenesis 58, 60–1
emotion 9, 18, 20, 25, 37, 65, 67, 94, 98, 100, 101, 102, 119, 133–4, 151, 158, 160, 183, 184
empiricism 1, 3, 19, 44, 177, 184
enargeia 108
energy 2, 24
Enlightenment 3, 9, 20, 25, 44, 47, 65, 68, 70, 81, 108, 114, 117, 121, 140, 153
enthusiasm 75, 132, 133
epigenesis 60
Epinay, Louise Tardieu d'Esclavelles de La Live, madame d' 150–1, 152, 171
Erasmus, Desiderius, *De civilitate morum puerilium* 68
erection 18, 28, 184
Ermenonville 83
Escherny, comte d' 74–5
etiquette 74, 82, 182
eugenics 10, 58, 172
eunuch 152
evolution 60, 152
exercise 83–4, 121
expression, facial 3, 80, 98–102 *passim*, 163, 183
expressiveness 3, 4, 11, 66, 72, 86–7, 89–112, 178
externalization 3, 25, 105

Falconet, Etienne 24, 81, 101, 109, 122, 154
Faret, Nicolas, L'Honnête Homme 69, 93
fasting 122, 125, 126, 130, 131
fat, fatness 45, 46, 47, 49, 50, 126–7
feasting 124, 125, 127–8, 130
feeling 66, 91, 97, 110, 119
Fel, Marie 130
femaleness 6, 150, 153
femininity 150, 153, 163, 173, 174
feminism 11, 150, 153, 175
Ferrein, Antoine 43
fever 22, 118, 132, 133, 134
fibre 18, 36, 60, 135
Fink, Beatrice 145 n. 31, n. 32, n. 37, n. 49, n. 50, n. 52
Flandrin, Jean-Louis 145 n. 35
flesh 23, 47, 48, 110, 158, 174, 180
Fontenay, Elisabeth de 145 n. 43, 146 n. 59, n. 60
food 6, 33, 35, 75, 123–31 passim
see also diet
Foucault, Michel 6
  Histoire de la folie à l'âge classique 13, 66, 145 n. 54
  Histoire de la sexualité 14 n. 11
Fouquet, Henri 36, 65
Fragonard, Jean-Honoré 48
  Corésus et Callirhoé 15, 154
France, Peter 87 n. 7
Francis of Sales, St 129
freak 58, 66, 152
Frederick II (the Great) of Prussia 160, 179
free will 16–18, 27, 29, 32, 75, 76, 147
French, R. K. 38 n. 13, n. 14
Fréron, Elie 160
Freud, Sigmund 13, 129, 150
frigidity 28, 164
frustration 132, 143
Furetière, Antoine 29, 68

Galen 139, 141, 143, 149, 152
Galiani, Ferdinando 150
Gardeil, Jean-Baptiste 120, 138, 174, 175
Garrick, David 95, 102, 184
Garrison, F. A. 63 n. 34
Gatti, Dr 100, 117–18
Gelfand, Toby 62 n. 8, n. 9, n. 10

gender 2, 6, 11, 148–75 passim, 180
generation, spontaneous 60
Genette, Gérard 37 n. 5
genitals 5, 12, 17, 43, 179
genius 35, 74–6, 93, 95, 96, 108, 109, 128
Genlis, Stéphanie-Félicité, comtesse de 44
genre painting 52, 103, 106
Geoffrin, Marie-Thérèse 74, 85
gesticulation 75, 91, 103, 105, 108
gesture 3, 13, 75, 80, 91, 92, 93, 99, 102, 103–4, 128, 159, 183
Gillot, Claude 72
Girardin, Stanislas, comte de 83
Goncourt, Edmond and Jules de 78, 79
Goodden, Angelica 87 n. 4, 112 n. 5, n. 8, 113 n. 26, 145 n. 39, n. 40
gourmandise 124, 125, 126
gout 37, 118, 121, 122–3, 127
grace 72, 73, 154
Grandval, Charles-François Racot de 96
Grandval, château de 124
greed 124–5
Greuze, Jean-Baptiste 3, 10, 49, 80, 99–101, 103–4, 105, 106, 157, 178, 182
  L'Accordée de village 101, 103
  Le Fils ingrat 103
  La Jeune Fille qui pleure son oiseau mort 54, 80, 100
  Le Mauvais Fils puni 103, 106
  La Mère bien-aimée 10, 79–80, 97, 163–4
  La Piété filiale 100, 102, 103
  Portrait de Mme Greuze 79, 101
  Septime Sévère 51–2, 53, 99, 103
Grimm, Friedrich Melchior, baron von 41–2, 43, 74, 84–5, 130, 138, 154, 156, 160
Guibert, Jacques-Antoine-Hippolyte, comte de 119
Guiffrey, J. 63 n. 22
gut 31, 35

Hallé, Noël 73, 82, 103
  L'Empereur Trajan partant pour une expédition militaire 103
Haller, Albrecht von 28, 117
  Primae lineae physiologiae 41, 51, 115
  Elementa physiologiae corporis humani 51

Haviland, J. N. 63 n. 22
Hazlitt, William 88 n. 22
health 3, 65, 114–43 passim, 153
hearing 6, 16, 94
heart 29, 39, 116
Helvétius, Claude-Adrien 29
Hercules 54–5, 56, 154
hermaphrodite 15, 42, 150, 153, 155–6
heterosexuality 136, 160, 161, 181
hierarchy, artistic 9, 51–2, 126
hieroglyph 107, 184
Hill, Emita B. 63 n. 40
Hippocrates 115
history painting 47, 51, 106
Hobbes, Thomas 25, 108
Hoffmann, Paul 144 n. 3
Hogarth, William, Analysis of Beauty 72
Holbach, Paul-Henri, baron d' 20, 24, 69,
    74, 118, 124, 154, 160
homosexuality 57, 131, 154–61
Huet, Marie-Hélène 63 n. 40
Hume, David 122
humours 56, 127, 129, 164
hunchback 55, 56, 180
Huysmans, Joris Karl 79
hygiene 1, 2, 10, 65, 70, 114, 115, 119,
    126, 128, 147, 182
hypochondria 114, 121
hypotyposis 108
hysteria 59, 114, 121, 123, 136, 137, 139,
    148, 179, 184

Idea 15
ideal 54, 56
identity 148, 152, 161, 171, 172
illegitimacy 67, 111
illness 114–43 passim, 183
image 15, 101, 106–8, 185
imagination 81, 82, 104, 106, 133, 185
imaginationism 61, 184
impotence 26, 28, 61, 168
impregnation 165–6, 170
indigestion 114, 121, 125, 184
individuality 109, 182
infidelity 20, 139, 165, 168
inhibition 33, 81
inoculation 117
instinct 12, 18, 29, 33, 68, 74, 76, 110, 147

intellect 12, 15, 35
intention 16, 18–19, 33, 147, 159
intercourse 4, 57, 140, 160
intestine 29, 33, 35, 52
involuntariness 17, 18, 27–9, 181
irregularity 53, 56, 66, 155
irritability 28, 29

James, Robert, Dictionary of Medicine and
    Surgery 115, 121, 139
Jaton, Anne-Marie 14 n. 22
Jaucourt, Louis de 30, 36, 65, 68, 69, 83,
    98, 115, 124, 153
Jeanneret, Michel 145 n. 41
Jodin, Marie-Madeleine 102
Johnson, Dorothy 112 n. 2, 113 n. 19, n. 20
Jordanova, Ludmilla 62 n. 20, 175 n.10
Josephs, Herbert 112 n. 4, n. 6, n. 9,
    113 n. 32

Kant, Immanuel 19
Keyser, Dr 142
Kors, Alan Charles 87 n. 9
Kunzle, David 88 n. 25

La Boétie, Etienne 154
Lacan, Jacques 13, 150
La Chaux, Mlle de 120, 138, 148, 163, 165,
    174
Laclos, Pierre Choderlos de, Les Liaisons
    dangereuses 4, 31, 34
Lafon, Henri 145 n. 48, n. 51
La Grenée, Louis-Jean-François 50, 51, 52,
    53, 73
    La Charité romaine 78, 80, 84
Laidlaw, G. N. 63 n. 40
Laissus, Yves 62 n. 6
Lamarck, Jean-Baptiste 57, 60, 129
La Mettrie, Julien de 25, 60
Lamy, Bernard 108
Lander, Kathleen 62 n. 3
Landois, Paul 11, 16, 26, 27, 29, 32
Langres 124
language, problems of 5, 6–7, 9, 81, 91,
    109
Laocoon 45, 52
Laqueur, Thomas 14 n. 10, 63 n. 30, 146
    n.62

La Salle, Jean-Baptiste de, *Règles de la bien-séance et de la civilité chrétienne* 69, 70
La Tour, Maurice Quentin de 47, 75–6
La Trappe 127
Laver, James 88 n. 21
Laverdet, Auguste-Nicolas 63 n. 23
Lawrence, Christopher 144 n. 5
Le Brun, Charles 80, 97, 98, 99, 102, 134
Le Camus, Antoine 118, 123, 165
Le Gendre, Marie-Charlotte (*née* Volland) 118–19, 122, 156, 160
Lebreton, David 62 n. 4
Leibniz, Wilhelm Gottfried 12, 160, 184
Lemire, M. 63 n. 22
Le Prince, Jean-Baptiste 141
Leroy, Alphonse, *Recherches sur les habillements des femmes et des enfants* 83
lesbianism 5, 36, 67, 78, 119, 130–2, 134–5, 136, 139, 143, 149, 156–60, 165, 168, 172, 174, 183, 184
Lespinasse, Julie de 69, 119
Lessing, Gotthold Ephraïm, *Laokoon* 9, 106
Liaigre, Lucien 38 n. 15
libertinism 17, 79
libido 22, 25, 129, 172
life drawing 47, 48, 81
Locke, John 8, 16, 24, 71, 92, 108, 184
Locquin, Jean 63 n. 29
Louis XIV 66, 117
Louis XV 117
love 19, 21, 26, 162
Lovejoy, Arthur O. 87 n. 15
lovemaking 5, 77, 139, 164, 166, 179
Lucretius, *De rerum natura* 57, 59, 60
Luppol, Ivan Kapitanovich 64 n. 46

Macbeth, Lady 94
McCormick, E. Allen 113 n. 28
McCracken, Janet 175 n. 8
machine 12, 34, 143, 169
madness 114, 132, 133, 143
Maire, Catherine-Laurence 146 n. 58
makeup 173, 174
maleness 150, 152, 153
malformation 58
manía 133
manneredness 70, 72, 74, 86, 97, 100
Marat, Jean-Paul, *De l'homme* 1

Marcel (dancing master) 71–2, 85, 89
Marcel, Louis 144 n. 17
Marcus Aurelius 77
Marivaux, Pierre Carlet de Chamblain de 4, 10
Marmontel, Jean-François 36
marriage 10, 42, 130, 139–40, 165, 167, 168
masculinity 150, 153, 157, 173
masochism 22
masturbation 4, 114, 136, 140–3
materialism (philosophical) 1, 2, 9, 12, 16, 23, 24, 26, 37, 86, 126, 143
maternity 78–80, 154, 162, 164, 170, 172, 174
Maupertuis, Pierre-Louis Moreau de 139
Maux, Jeanne-Catherine de 19
May, Georges 145 n. 33
May, Gita 113 n. 28
Mayer, Jean 62 n. 8, 63 n. 36, n. 40
mechanism 17, 25, 26, 30, 34, 86
medicine 3, 4, 36, 65, 114–43 *passim*
    see also Diderot and medicine
melancholy 135, 139, 141
melodrama 3, 48, 67, 104, 132
memory 25, 26, 31
Ménageot, François-Guillaume 98
menopause 121, 137
menstruation 137, 153
Ménuret de Chambaud, Jean-Joseph 139, 140–1, 143
Mercier, Louis-Sébastien:
    L'An 2440 7
    Le Tableau de Paris 41, 69
Merleau-Ponty, Maurice 21
metaphysics 1, 2, 9, 12, 23, 24, 56, 86, 94, 114
Michie, Helena 14 n. 26, 88 n. 24, 175 n. 25
Miller, Lady Anne 145 n. 39
mimesis 45, 46, 92, 184
mimicry 35, 111, 133, 184
mind 20, 35, 92, 185
mind–body relationship 1, 3, 15–37 *passim*, 65, 86, 92, 109, 128, 132, 147, 148, 177, 183
    see also mind
misogyny 170

Mitchell, Juliet 175 n. 6
model 40–6 passim, 47, 178–9
    life– 27, 47, 50, 51, 71, 79, 98
modesty (pudeur) 6, 76–9, 107, 143, 164,
    179
Molière, Jean-Baptiste Poquelin, dit, Le
    Malade imaginaire 39
Molyneux, William 8
monism 19, 24, 26, 32, 65
monster 56–8, 60, 61, 107, 121, 153, 156
Montague, Jennifer 113 n. 13, n. 15
Montaigne, Michel de 4, 7, 36, 71, 92,
    140, 154
Montanari, Massimo 145 n. 35
Montesquieu, Charles de Secondat, baron
    de, Lettres persanes 152
Montgomery Wilson, John 113 n. 14
Montpellier medical school 24
morality 32, 76, 79, 178
Morand, Sauveur François 41, 62 n. 16, 116
mortification, religious 11, 70, 110, 131
movement 2, 3, 9, 10, 36, 73, 90, 91–2, 97,
    101, 105, 106, 108, 111, 147, 180, 183
Munteano, Basil 87 n. 3
muscle 26, 41, 46, 50, 57, 89, 158, 180
music 107, 109, 110, 111, 128, 170, 184
mutability 9, 10, 92

Naigeon, Jacques-André 68
narrative, first- and third-person 21
naturalism 5, 147, 182
nature 46, 61, 76, 155, 172
    see also Diderot and nature
neo-classicism 49, 73, 180
Neptune 107
nerve 6, 19, 26, 29, 58, 121, 152, 158
nervous system 19, 31, 36, 58, 137, 152
Niklaus, Robert 64 n. 46
norm 52, 55, 56, 79, 155
Northcote, James 82
Noverre, Jean-Georges 95–7
nude, nudity 27, 50, 79, 81–2, 178
nutrition 126–9

obstetrics 42, 43, 171, 178
Œdipus complex 86
opera 96, 184
orality 129, 130

'organization' 29, 37, 132, 153, 156, 170
'organological federation' 59
organs 9, 27, 28, 35, 36, 37, 57–8, 59, 60,
    61, 86, 128, 151, 158, 162, 170
    sex 5, 6, 12, 26–7, 28, 29, 42, 43,
        149–50, 164, 165, 166, 170, 182
orgasm 5, 28, 67, 79, 135, 139, 140, 149,
    164, 179
Orléans, Louis-Philippe, duc d' 96
ornamentation 77, 84, 173
Outram, Dorinda 13
ovary 6, 60

Palais-Royal 44, 142
'pantomime' 30, 34, 66, 71, 90, 91, 94, 97,
    108, 109, 128, 147, 181, 184
paralysis 3, 103
parasite 33, 34, 99, 128, 129
Pâris, François de 135
Parish, L. C. 63 n. 22
passion 16–17, 19, 69, 75, 90, 91, 92, 98,
    108, 122, 128, 133, 134, 159, 181, 184
pathogen 3, 133
pathognomy 99, 134
pathology 3, 6, 65, 116, 131, 134, 164
    see also woman and pathology
penetration 4, 149, 166
penis 28, 135, 136, 150
perception 8, 10, 15, 18, 19, 36, 37, 81,
    184
perfectibility 115, 121, 147, 171
performance 8, 35, 91, 94, 96, 97, 102,
    105, 109, 111, 147, 181
periphrasis 5, 6, 7, 179
Perronneau, Jean-Baptiste 72
Petit, Antoine 40–1, 45, 47, 52, 55–6, 57,
    118, 127
Petites-Maisons 66, 133
phenomenology 8, 143
physicalism 2, 19, 177
physician 114, 116–17
physiognomy 13, 80, 90, 97–8
physiology 6, 9, 17, 26, 28, 36, 39, 45, 65,
    114, 133, 147, 148, 180
pictorialism 8, 9
Plato, The Republic 15–16
pleasure 2, 7, 28, 34, 76, 77, 79, 140, 141,
    166, 165, 167, 183

Pliny 152
politeness 5, 7, 20, 62, 70, 86, 89, 179
Pompadour, Joanne-Antoinette, marquise
    de 127
Portal, Antoine 40
Porter, Roy 144 n. 25, n. 26
portrait 10, 27
    see also Diderot and portraiture
'position' 96, 110
'possession' 21, 130, 133, 135, 136, 164, 165
posture 89, 182
potency 129, 163
Poussin, Nicolas 102–3, 105
preformation 59
pregnancy 61, 153–4, 162, 164, 165–6, 170,
    173, 182
Premnia, L. 63 n. 22
Préville, Pierre-Louis Dubus, *dit* 102
Pringle, Sir John 41
procreation 10–11, 28, 61, 79, 140, 173
proportion 51, 52, 53, 54, 55
propriety 2, 7, 66–87 *passim*, 178
prostitute 3, 35, 108, 142, 166, 184
Proust, Jacques 38 n. 16, n. 17, 98, 99,
    113 n. 16
prudishness 81, 178
psychology 3, 10, 25, 65, 162, 170, 174
psycho-physiology 18, 21, 23, 75, 86, 100
psychosomatic conditions 132, 133, 137,
    183
puppet 30, 34, 74, 93, 105
purgation 115
Pyke, E. J. 63 n. 22

Rabelais, François 71, 128
Radcliffe Richards, Janet 175 n. 15
Ramsay, Allan 10
Ramsay, Matthew 144 n. 2
rape 165, 166, 168
realism 182, 184
referentiality 4, 5, 7, 81
reflex 28, 32
regularity 53, 56
relativism 80
remedy 118, 123, 143
representation 9, 13, 15, 96, 178, 180, 184
re-presentation 45
reproduction 5, 27, 129, 149

res cogitans see Descartes
res extensa see Descartes
response, bodily 2, 19, 27, 31, 78, 148
rhetoric 106, 108, 114, 140
Ribémont, Bernard 87 n. 20
Riccoboni, François, *L'Art du théâtre* 93
Riccoboni, Marie-Jeanne 73, 93, 95, 96,
    105, 106
Richardson, Ruth 144 n. 6
Richardson, Samuel 182
Roberts, K. B. 63 n. 22, 88 n. 23
Roche, Daniel 88 n. 27
rococo 48, 79, 97, 180, 184
Roger, Jacques 63 n. 41, 64 n. 44, n. 47
Rogers, Pat 145 n. 38
Roland, Manon 100
Rose, Jacqueline 175 n. 6
Rousseau, G. S. 144 n. 25, n. 26, 146 n. 56
Rousseau, Jean-Jacques 10, 19, 23, 29, 65,
    71, 74 84, 91, 105, 114, 115, 119, 123,
    130, 150, 181
    Les Confessions 14 n. 21, 130
    Emile 70–2, 83, 130, 149
    Essai sur l'origine des langues 105
Rubens, Peter Paul 48, 76
rules 53, 54, 66, 74, 93, 97, 98
Russia 55, 74

Sade, Donatien-Alphonse-François, marquis
    de 4
sadism 11
Saint-Lambert, Jean-François de 75
Saint-Médard 135
St Petersburg 55
Salignac, Mélanie de 36, 77
Sartre, Jean-Paul, *L'Etre et le néant* 21
Saunderson, Nicolas 9, 57–8, 59, 177
Saurin, Bernard-Joseph 162
savage life 4, 10–11, 12, 76, 172
Schiebinger, Londa 63 n. 30, n. 31,
    175 n. 2, n. 5
science of man 1, 3, 180
Scruton, Roger 175 n. 1
secretion 67, 158
secularism 10, 32, 70, 181
Sedaine, Michel-Jean 75, 90
seduction 157, 159, 166, 181
seed 60, 139, 140, 143

'seeing-as' 100
self-denial 12, 123
self-indulgence 115, 122, 123
Seguin, Jean-Pierre 14 n. 8
semen 141, 153
Sénac, Jean-Baptiste, *Traité de la structure du cœur* 116
sensation 25, 92
sensationalism 16, 93–4, 170
senses 8, 15–16, 36, 77, 170, 183
sensibility 3, 6, 9, 18, 23, 28, 29, 33, 35, 37, 65, 75, 86, 92, 109, 115, 121, 126, 131, 134, 136, 137, 152, 181
sensorium commune 28, 29
sensuality 49, 130
sentimentality 3, 119
sex 6, 11, 18, 77, 148, 150, 151, 157, 164, 167, 173, 174, 179
sexism 140, 151, 182
sexology 5, 61, 76, 148
sexuality 5, 17, 135, 152, 156, 162
Shakespeare, William, *Macbeth* 94
sight 6, 8, 16, 21, 77, 94, 107, 116, 121, 185
Simmel, Georg 87 n. 19
skeleton 47, 83
sketch 5, 10, 81, 97, 100, 103, 178
skull 47
smallpox 117–18
smell 16
Smolnyi Monastir 42
sobriety 124, 128
sodomy 155–6
Soemmering, Samuel Thomas von 82–3
solar plexus 137
soul 1, 10, 24, 25, 105
spasm 35, 75, 122, 128, 136, 151
speech 6, 17, 106, 162
sperm 129
Spinoza, Baruch 19, 24
Spitzer, Leo 22, 179
spontaneity 31, 33, 69, 92, 97
Stafford, Barbara Maria 14 n. 19, 37 n. 1, 87 n. 13
Starobinski, Jean 87 n. 7
starvation 31, 33, 48, 126, 128, 129, 130, 181
sterility 77, 173

Sterne, Laurence, *Tristram Shandy* 120
Sticoti, Antonio Fabio 95
stimulation 22, 115, 162
stomach 12, 122, 125, 128
Streeter, E. C. 63 n. 34
Stuart, Alexander 29
suckling 141, 174
Suë, Jean 47
suffering 11, 22, 120
suggestiveness 80, 82, 106, 107, 178
Suleiman, Susan Rubin 175 n. 11
surgeon, surgery 116–17
Sydenham, Thomas 121
symbol 13, 80, 99, 107
symptom 112, 134, 139, 142, 143, 183
syphilis 142

tableau 8, 105, 106, 111, 178
tableau mouvant 105
taboo 12
Tahiti 6, 10, 12, 28, 55, 76, 77, 148, 161, 162, 165, 167, 168, 173, 182
Tarczylo, Théodore 146 n. 63, n. 64, 175 n. 18
Tarin, Pierre 115
taste 16
temperance 123
testicle 6, 20, 60, 152, 165
theatricality 104, 178
Therbusch, Anna 27, 42, 50, 81
thinness 127
Thomas, Antoine-Léonard, *Sur le caractère, les mœurs et l'esprit des femmes* 150–1, 170
Thompson, C. J. S. 63 n. 22
Thuillier, Jacques 113 n. 24
Tilghman, B. R. 113 n. 18
time 9, 10, 105, 106, 107
Tissot, Samuel 4, 114, 123, 129
Essai sur les maladies des gens du monde 114, 123
L'Onanisme 13 n. 4, 114, 140–1
De la santé des gens de lettres 12, 114, 121, 125
Tomlinson, J. D. W. 63 n. 22, 88 n. 23
torture 9, 13, 131, 132, 135, 181
touch 8, 9, 13, 16, 132, 135, 176, 181
Tourneux, Maurice 87 n. 16

Toussaint, François-Vincent 115
    Les Mœurs 6
training 29, 50, 69, 73, 89, 93, 171
transformism 60
Tronchin, Théodore 115, 118, 120, 122, 123
Tussaud, Marie 44
typology 80, 134
Tytler, Graeme 113 n. 17

ugliness 163
unconscious, the 17
unconsciousness 133
undressing 22, 78, 159
utilitarianism 11, 28, 180

vagina 6, 57, 58
Vandenesse, Dr 115
Vandermonde, Charles-Augustin 89
    *Essai sur la manière de perfectionner le genre
    humain* 89
Vandeul, Angélique de (*née* Diderot) 39,
    42–3, 120, 178–9
vanitas 126
Van Loo, Carle 50–1, 73, 82, 107
    Auguste faisant fermer le temple de Janus
    103
    Les Grâces 50–1, 73, 82
    Médée et Jason 104–5
Van Loo, (Louis-)Michel 10, 85, 101, 154
vapours 114, 118, 135, 140, 171
Vartanian, Aram 37 n. 2, 38 n. 8, n. 18,
    109, 112 n. 7, 113 n. 31, 145 n. 42,
    175 n. 23, 176 n. 30
Vaucanson, Jacques 30, 34, 75, 89
'veiling' 4, 7, 157, 173, 178, 179
Verdier, César 41
Vernet, Joseph 92, 165
Viallet 118
Vien, Joseph-Marie 48, 49, 180
    *Marc-Aurèle faisant distribuer au peuple du
    pain* 103
    La Marchande d'amours 49, 73, 80
Vigarello, Georges 89
Vigée Le Brun, Elisabeth Louise 127
Vila, Anne C., *Enlightenment and Pathology*
    13, 38 n. 6, n. 19, 63 n. 43, 87 n. 1, n.
    6, 144 n. 4, n. 16

Vincent, François-André 98
Vinci, Leonardo da 45
virginity, loss of 100
Virolle, Roland 112 n. 10
virtue 17, 29, 79–80
vitalism 24, 92, 177
Volland, Sophie 12, 19, 27, 36, 55, 56, 70,
    74, 77, 92, 117, 119, 121, 122, 124,
    150, 154, 156, 159, 160, 162, 164, 165,
    166, 168, 173, 174, 180, 182
Volland, Mme 117–18
Voltaire, François-Marie Arouet, *dit de* 181
    Tancrède 94
voyeurism 43, 157, 178
vulva 57

Warens, Louise-Eléonore de La Tour du
    Pil, baronne de 130
Watteau, Antoine 72
Weeks, Jeffrey 175 n. 7
weeping 36, 134, 136
Whytt, Robert, *Essay on the Vital and Other
    Involuntary Motions of Animals* 28, 29
Wilkes, John 41
Wilson, Arthur M. 144 n. 19
Wilson, Lindsay 146 n. 57, n. 59
Wittgenstein, Ludwig 100, 113 n. 20
Wittig, Monique, *Le Corps lesbien* 158
woman:
    and decency 78
    and feeling 119
    nature of 11–12, 17–18, 26, 47, 138, 147,
        148, 151, 167, 170, 171, 174
    and pathology 59, 117, 118–19, 121,
        131, 134–8 *passim*, 140, 151, 152
    rights of 182
    and sex 139–40, 162, 164, 166, 173–5
    shape of 47, 55, 154, 161, 162, 163
womb 6, 43, 57, 58, 59, 83, 123, 136, 137,
    148, 150, 151, 171
worldliness 4, 72, 114, 123

Yolton, John 38 n. 9, n. 10

Zaner, Richard 37 n. 4
Zoberman, Pierre 113 n. 29